What Psychology Majors Could (and Should) Be Doing

What Psychology Majors Could (and Should) Be Doing

An Informal Guide to Research Experience and Professional Skills

Paul J. Silvia
Peter F. Delaney
Stuart Marcovitch

American Psychological Association • Washington, DC

First Printing January 2009
Second Printing October 2009

Published by
American Psychological Association
750 First Street, NE
Washington, DC 20002
www.apa.org

To order
APA Order Department
P.O. Box 92984
Washington, DC 20090-2984
Tel: (800) 374-2721; Direct: (202) 336-5510
Fax: (202) 336-5502; TDD/TTY: (202) 336-6123
Online: www.apa.org/books/
E-mail: order@apa.org

In the U.K., Europe, Africa, and the Middle East, copies may be ordered from
American Psychological Association
3 Henrietta Street
Covent Garden, London
WC2E 8LU England

Typeset in Minion and Goudy by Circle Graphics, Inc., Columbia, MD

Printer: United Book Press, Baltimore, MD
Cover Designer: Mercury Publishing Services, Rockville, MD
Technical/Production Editor: Harriet Kaplan

Library of Congress Cataloging-in-Publication Data

Silvia, Paul J., 1976-
    What psychology majors could (and should) be doing : an informal guide to re-search experience and professional skills / Paul J. Silvia, Peter F. Delaney, and Stuart Marcovitch.—1st ed.
        p. cm.
    Includes bibliographical references and index.
    ISBN-13: 978-1-4338-0438-0
    ISBN-10: 1-4338-0438-7
    1. Psychology—Research. I. Delaney, Peter F. II. Marcovitch, Stuart. III. Title.

    BF76.5.S497 2009
    150.72—dc22

                                                                2008042782

British Library Cataloguing-in-Publication Data
A CIP record is available from the British Library.

Printed in the United States of America
First Edition

Contents

Preface

College was fun, but we're glad it's over. Aside from the usual reasons—it's nice to spend our quarters instead of hoarding them for laundry—we graduated during an easier period for psych majors. There are more psychology majors now. More than 88,000 people received an undergraduate degree in psychology in 2008; it's one of the most popular majors in the nation. It's hard to get precise figures, but there are probably more than 250,000 people majoring in psychology—it boggles the mind. But here's a cold fact: There are not enough grad school spots and attractive, degree-related jobs for everyone. To get more out of psychology, and to prepare yourself for life after college, you need to get experience in research; to join clubs and professional organizations; and to build your writing, speaking, and thinking skills. At most schools, the psychology curriculum won't teach you these things—you will need to get out of the classroom and do it yourself. We wrote this book to help get you started.

The book's cover isn't big enough to fit all the names of the people who helped. Linda McCarter,

Emily Leonard, and the valiant-yet-patient crew in the Books department at the American Psychological Association were a class act. (We think the idea for this book was Linda's, in fact, but no one is sure anymore.) Our friends at the University of North Carolina at Greensboro, which has a psychology department with a vibrant tradition in undergraduate research, offered many good tips and suggestions. Finally, many of our undergraduate research assistants and honors students read this book; we thank them for their suggestions and their snarky ridicule.

What Psychology Majors Could **(and Should)** Be Doing

1

Introduction

Most psychology majors will admit that psychology was not what they thought it would be. Confess—before college, you probably thought that psychology had to do with analyzing your dreams, exploring your early childhood, or uncovering deep facets of personality that ought to stay covered. Many students are surprised when they encounter college-level psychology. Real psychology is broad and deep, scientific and statistical. It's more technical and nerdy than Intro Psych students expect. Instead of Jungian archetypes, we have Piagetian stages. Instead of the analysis of dreams, we have the analysis of variance.

The most surprising feature of real psychology is its emphasis on research. Your professors are always yammering about "research this" and "research that." You take courses on statistics and research methods, where you face time-honored topics like main effects versus interactions and within-person designs versus between-person designs. Your friends wish you would stop saying "behavior" and "cognitive" all the time. Once you find yourself answering a question with, "That's a good question—there's probably research on that," then you'll know that psychology has seeped into your bones.

RESEARCH AND YOU—YES, YOU, SITTING IN THE BACK

Who does all this research? Your stereotypes of psychology researchers might not be far off, particularly if you imagine pale, dispirited graduate students working in windowless labs, wincing when they see the sun. But undergraduates form the biggest group working in the trenches of research. In the past 20 years, psychology has seen a transformation of undergraduate research; undergrads are more involved than ever before. There was a time—a more innocent, sepia-toned time—when courses like Statistics and Research Methods were optional. Just about every psychology department now requires students to take these courses, and most departments have created extra opportunities for hands-on research experience. In the past, it was uncommon to see undergraduates attend scientific conferences, let alone present research at them. Undergraduates now make up the biggest block of attendees at many conferences.

Why are undergrads so involved, and why are departments encouraging undergrad research experience? And why did we write this book about it? First, research experience is the best way to get a hands-on, in-the-trenches view of how psychology works. In the typical college experience, students experience research indirectly: They hear about it in their classes and read about it in their textbooks, but they don't do it. Passive, detached learning is fine—many people enjoy sitting through lectures and reading $120 books full of tired stock photographs—but you'll get more out of psychology if you get involved.

Second, research experience is a great way to build *professional skills*, the practical abilities needed to succeed in the world of work. You need these skills. As hard as college is, the postcollege world—derisively known as the *real world*—is far worse. You'll face a world where most people aren't in their early 20s; you'll meet people without instant messaging accounts and people who don't read books; you'll understand what people mean when they complain about The Man and The System. Your years in college are your only chance to build the skills necessary for success in this dreadful real world. For example, most of the jobs you'll want will involve some form of high-stakes public speaking or professional writing: You'll be speaking and writing to your clients, potential clients, managers, and bosses, all of whom will judge your competence based on how well you do. But the typical student fears public speaking and writes like a ponderous monk with a nightshade hangover. Are you prepared? Can you compete against the students with training in speaking and writing?

And third, learning research and professional skills is a way to take initiative for your learning, to go beyond the minimum. Here's what the typical undergraduate experience of psychology looks like: Students go to class most of the time, do most of the reading, and get respectable grades. Going to class, doing the reading, and studying are the bare minimum that you could do. If you attend every class and get excellent grades, then we congratulate you—you are excelling at the bare minimum. You are doing what tens of thousands of psychology majors are doing. (If you sleep through your 2 p.m. classes, this is grim news—you're doing less than the minimum.) Grad schools and employers want people who did more than simply show up to the classroom on time: They want people who took some responsibility for their professional development, who chose to learn more than they had to. You don't want to be the job applicant who gets asked, "What did you do in college? It looks like you just took classes."

WHY SHOULD I GET INVOLVED IN RESEARCH?

All undergraduates in psychology would get a lot out of research experience. Research and professional skills are equally important to the "I'm going to grad school" students and the "the thought of more school makes me throw up in my mouth—I want a job" students. Here's why.

Going to Grad School?

Grad school is hard, but it will teach you to appreciate life's nerdier pleasures: a good cup of coffee, an interesting report on National Public Radio, an evening cuddling with the ferret while watching *Six Feet Under* reruns. You have a lot to look forward to, but first you must get in—grad school is as competitive as you've heard it is. What are you doing to stand out? What will your professors have to say about when they write letters of recommendation? How do you know that you'll like grad school? Do you know which area of psychology you want to study?

Most applicants to graduate programs have some research experience, and some applicants have a lot. You'll be competing against students who have written an honors thesis, worked in a research lab for several years, and presented posters at conferences. These students are your competition. If you have no research experience, you have nearly no chance. Strong research skills can compensate for other weaknesses—such as low GRE scores or a grade point average hobbled by a bleak semester as an Interior Architecture major—and show grad schools that you like research enough to pursue training in it.

Beyond making you more competitive, research experience will show you whether you enjoy research. Graduate school in psychology is mostly research. Grad students who dislike research are like dentists who dislike gums and morticians who dislike decaying bodies: They're out there, but they tend to weep openly at inappropriate times. Working in research for a few semesters and attending a couple of conferences will help you decide. Students usually become more excited about research and graduate training after they get involved, but some students learn that grad school isn't for them: They have better things to weep about.

Not Going to Grad School?

Most psychology undergrads don't go to grad school, and that's a relief. Grad school isn't for everyone, and you can do more than you think with an undergraduate psychology degree. But we have a surprising secret to share: If you don't plan to go to grad school, you need research experience more than the grad-school bound students need it. For them, nearly any research experience will suffice: They merely must show that they tried it, liked it, and performed well enough to get a letter of recommendation from their research supervisor. And they have their many years of graduate school to learn and polish their professional skills. But you, the career-bound, have only your remaining semesters in college to build the skills you'll need for success in the job market and the professional world.

Why is research experience necessary for you? The competition among people with a bachelor's degree in psychology is fierce and relentless. We, your valiant authors, live in central North Carolina—it's an educated place, with more than 10 colleges and universities within a 60-minute drive. How many people do you think graduate with a psychology degree each year? How many then look for a job in the area? Most of them, certainly: Few grab their diploma and then emigrate to Slovenia. Are there enough great jobs for all of them? How about where you live? How many colleges and universities are in the region, and how many people graduate with a psychology degree from your school? Those people are the competition: You'll see them at career fairs and in employers' waiting rooms, nicely dressed and waiting for their job interview.

Psychology is one of the nation's most popular majors: More than 85,000 people got an undergraduate degree in psychology in 2005 (National Center for Education Statistics, 2007). That's a lot of people looking for jobs. What are you doing to compete? What makes you a stronger candidate in the eyes of employers? Employers don't care that you went to class and got good grades. Employers already expect that of you, and they have plenty of applicants who excelled at the bare minimum. They want to hire people who went beyond the minimum, who acquired skills, showed initiative, and interacted with professionals.

Research experience will give you two advantages. First, the mere act of showing initiative will demonstrate to employers that you won't be a bare-minimum employee. Employers would rather hire someone with good grades who chose to get involved over someone who merely got great grades. Second, research experience will help you develop useful, attractive skills. Employers aren't hiring people to read textbooks and take tests. They want people who have experience with public speaking, statistical reasoning, writing, working in teams, and learning new things.

What We'll Talk About

This book is a practical guide for students who want to get involved in the science of psychology. Your time in college is short, and it's never too early to start building useful skills that will prepare you for grad school or for the world of work. No one regrets being too involved in hands-on, practical experience, so let's get started.

The first few chapters show you how to get involved in research and how to get a lot out of it. Chapter 2 describes how to get started in research, including how to find research opportunities and how to find a research mentor. In chapter 3, we'll consider the benefits and challenges—euphemisms for *fun parts* and *painful-but-important parts*—of research experience. Once your feet are wet in the fetid waters of science, you can get more involved in psychology as a lifestyle. Chapter 4 shows you hidden opportunities for learning outside the classroom, such as campus groups and national organizations that allow you to meet like-minded psych majors.

The next few chapters tackle the core skills that you'll need to reach the next level—the next level down and slightly to the left—in your research training. In chapter 5, we discuss the dreaded field of statistics. You are a psych major for a reason—for many students, the relative lack of math is that reason. But you'll need to be strong in statistics if you want to get involved in research. Chapter 6 describes how to find, read, and understand the dry, perplexing research articles that fill psychology's research journals. And chapter 7 shows you how to write one of these dry, perplexing papers. Writing an honors thesis, research paper, or research proposal for the first time is hard; we'll pass along some practical advice on how to do it well.

The final three chapters talk about the seamy world of scientific conferences. Psychologists present their research to each other at conferences. Undergraduates are welcome to attend, network, gossip about their professors, and present research, and you ought to do it. But conferences strike students as foreign: Most students don't know what to expect before they attend their first conference. Chapter 8 thus gives a crash course on conference norms, rules, and etiquette. You may need to present a poster at a conference, so chapter 9 provides some tips on how to make a good poster and how to present it. Perhaps you need to give a research talk; chapter 10 provides some tips on managing public-speaking anxiety, designing a good slide show, and unleashing your talk on your audience.

The Epilogue wraps up the book and sends you on your way into the feral world of psychological science—pack a flashlight and a change of clothes, just in case.

2

Getting Involved in Research

The worst movie genre—worse than romantic comedies—is the inspiring-teacher genre. So far, Hollywood hasn't made a psychology version: A troubled student lurks at the back of a giant lecture hall, and her revolutionary scientific genius attracts the attention of a dedicated, caring professor. The professor invites her to solve crucial theoretical problems, but the student's personal demons drive her to resist the offer. The heroic professor then tracks her down and helps her exorcize her demons. In the process, the student reluctantly agrees to accept a highly paid research assistant position, a corner office, and a letter of recommendation. The student goes on to win the International Society for Hypnotherapy Career Award. A happy ending ensues—with an audience standing and clapping, of course.

But getting started in research is not like a movie—or at least not that kind of movie. First of all, it's probably going to be up to you to find a mentor and persuade him or her to work with you, not the other way around.

Good things come to those who make them happen, not to those who wait. Second, you should lower your expectations about a corner office, for there are few paid research assistantships featuring corner offices. There aren't even many paid research positions that come with a shared cubicle in the moldy sub-basement. A typical university has a lot of great students, and the rare paid positions go to the students who already have research experience.

This chapter will describe how to find a mentor, navigate your way through the interview process, and get started in research. You will soon see that the research process doesn't resemble Hollywood movies, although it does have some similarities with kung fu movies—hence the battle-scarred look of graduate students. Fortunately, as in most kung fu movies, a happy ending awaits the student who persists in the face of many trials.

WHERE DO I SIGN UP?

Research experiences range from implanting electrodes in the heads of transgenic pigeons to creating a laboratory simulation of life on a pirate ship, but they have one thing in common: the *research mentor*. Like a kung fu teacher, a mentor offers advice, provides cryptic answers to questions, and cultivates important skills. A mentor also suggests ancient manuscripts of wisdom—known as journal articles—to read. Though the manuscripts are not usually written in ancient Chinese, they are often equally incomprehensible to the nonnative speaker.

The first step toward gaining research experience is finding one of these mentors. An easy way to get started is to take a research methods course or a psychology lab course. They have some built-in research mentoring in the form of the instructor. These classes teach research skills and often require a research project—sometimes conducted with a group of other students—that you design, conduct, analyze, write about, and present. If you write a paper about research you conduct in research methods or a lab course, save it. You can show a potential mentor that you have the chops to do research.

For a more in-depth research experience, some form of independent study is usually the route to take. Most psychology professors do research and want bright, motivated students like you to staff the lab. Big research universities—a category that includes most of the state universities, private universities with graduate programs, and some liberal arts colleges—expect professors to publish papers regularly. As a result, professors at big schools usually have laboratories populated with teeming hordes of research assistants. Smaller colleges may not have special research space for each faculty member, and the professors may be doing a lot more teaching than at the big research universities. But professors at smaller colleges will often give you more attention—there are fewer students per professor. Either way, independent study gives you experience and usually counts toward your psychology degree.

A good first step is to find out how your school supports undergraduate research. Inquire at your psychology main office, visit your academic advisor, and check the undergraduate catalog about courses that give credit for independent study. Your department will probably hand you a gargantuan sheaf of paper detailing the available courses. It will usually feature courses with names like Directed Research, Directed Reading, Independent Study, or Mentored Research Experience. Unfortunately, you usually can't just sign up by phone or Web as you do for the Seminar in Neo-Freudian Concepts of Self. You'll need the instructor's permission to sign up, so you need to figure out who the instructor will be. So, for the moment, just forget about that big stack of papers and think about how you would choose a research mentor.

How to Choose an Independent Study Mentor

You will need to approach potential research mentors, not the other way around. The idea of talking to professors for a reason other than extra credit may strike some students as verging on madness. After all, professors sometimes give the impression that in their spare time they delight in pulling the wings off birds and torturing chipmunks. Some professors seem so nerdy that merely visiting their office could cause permanent contamination. But once you get to know your professors, you will find that most are less cruel than they pretend; some are even interesting people with surprisingly hip hobbies, like rock climbing, collecting mid-90s rap-rock bootlegs, or building Viking longships in their garage from wooden sticks.

How do you find a good mentor for independent study? One way is to think about your likely career goal. For example, if you're thinking about becoming a cognitive neuroscientist, you probably want to find someone who studies cognition or biological psychology. If you are advanced enough to have a particular area of research in mind already—psychopathology in feral children, expertise in ballooning, or whatever else strikes your fancy—ask around your department about who works on a problem that seems at least loosely related to your intended topic area.

If nobody does the kind of work you're interested in, it's fine to work with someone in an area that you aren't initially excited about. Students often like an area of research after they understand it better. For example, one of our research assistants was originally interested in studying "gay, lesbian, bisexual, and transgendered persons of color who were coping with AIDS," but he ended up quite happily doing experimental research on how people solve puzzles. Research is research, and some of the skills you learn will apply to any future research you conduct.

If you aren't sure what you're interested in or if nobody seems to do that kind of work, you could just drop in on some possible mentors. Think back to which psychology courses tickled your fancy, and visit the instructors of these courses. Or dust off your Intro Psych textbook; each of the chapters is a branch of psychology, and if you liked one of the chapters, you might look for someone who works in that area. Or make a list of the faculty members who seem approachable. Find out when their office hours are, and stop by to ask about whether they are looking for a research assistant. Many psychology departments maintain a list of faculty who offer mentored research experience. Ask the psychology main office if they have such a list. You might find flyers on the walls around the department advertising particular research labs. It's worth checking the bulletin boards in the psychology building to see what's advertised. Psi Chi members—Psi Chi is an honor society for psychology students—may be able to point you in the right direction. Joining your local chapter of Psi Chi or the campus psychology club can net you some leads on who accepts undergraduates into their labs. (For more on Psi Chi, see chap. 4.)

You can search outside of the psychology department, too. An oddity of the modern university is that psychologists often get jobs in other departments. If you can't find what you want in the psychology department, see if there is a counseling program on campus. Other allied disciplines that may have psychologists include communication, marketing, human development, education, public health, exercise and sport science, nursing, family studies, biology, gerontology, linguistics, and medicine. These departments may have different names on your campus, but some of them will have researchers who might serve as mentors.

Your search for research experience could take you to exotic, foreign lands. Study-abroad programs will place you at a partner institution in another country for a semester—longer if you are arrested for international espionage. Check out the foreign institution's Web page to see if you can get research experience with a foreign professor while you're there. Perhaps the Royal Naval Academy of Lesotho has a research-oriented psychology department. If so, you'll need to e-mail the professor in question to indicate that you're interested in helping out for a semester to get research experience. If you decide to go this route, keep in mind the tips for interviews given later in this chapter—you may have a phone interview with the potential mentor.

Another way to find a mentor is to search the Web for a summer research opportunity. The National Science Foundation—a branch of the federal government that converts tax dollars into money that supports the nation's best research—funds a program called Research Experience for Undergraduates (REU). Many universities apply to host an REU, and you can find out who has one by searching at the National Science Foundation Web site. Each REU program takes place at a host college and allows talented undergraduates from all over the country to apply for a summer of research experience with the scientists working there. If you are accepted into a program, you get a stipend—in other words, spending money—and the host school provides free or subsidized housing and food. Usually about 10 students per site are accepted, so you will meet new friends who will be good contacts later on. While at the host school, you work closely with a research mentor and gain the kind of research experience you get from independent study, and you take specialized classes with the other REU participants.

What Happens Once You Find a Possible Mentor?

Once you make first contact with a possible mentor, you will probably be invited for an interview. The interview may be conducted by the professor or by someone working in the lab, such as a lab manager, postdoctoral researcher, or harried graduate student. Regardless of who interviews you, remember that research positions are competitive, and the more friends that you encourage to buy this book, the more competitive they'll become. Just like when you apply for that coveted position as a stock clerk at the Kitten Factory, you need to leave a good impression. The professor is about to invest time training you and wants to know if you're worth the effort. Professors may seem like they spend all day drinking coffee and discussing the latest National Public Radio special report, but most do a fair amount of work on top of the coffee chatter. They have papers to write, grades to calculate, and requests for extra credit to turn down, so they'll want some indication that you're the kind of student worth setting aside those other tasks and their coffee mugs for.

What will they ask during the interview? You'll probably be asked about your grades, the courses you have taken, and your long-term professional interests. The purpose of those questions is obvious: They want to know if you are bright, hard-working, and motivated, or if you are a knuckle-dragging slacker aspiring only to commit welfare fraud. With that in mind, feel free to volunteer information that helps them decide to choose you, even if you're not asked about it. For example, you might want to mention that you are a member of an academic honor society; have experience working with children (if you are applying to work in a developmental psychology lab); or have read the professor's long, boring book on motivation. On the other hand, no matter how proud you are that you are a member of a fraternity or are in training to eat more hot dogs in 60 seconds than Kobayashi, there's no need to bring up information that is irrelevant to your ability to do research.

In addition to the obvious questions designed to find out if you're qualified and interested, you may also be asked some oddball questions. For example, we sometimes ask students if they know any languages other than English. There's no right answer to these questions; just be honest. It may be that they are looking for someone to create Swahili–English word pairs for their latest memory study, and knowing Swahili may be a big plus. On the other hand, don't be flustered if you answer no to most of those questions. It may be great if you know how to solve differential equations, but if you don't, you might still make a fine lab member. Remember throughout that it's important to leave the impression that you are professional, reliable, and motivated.

Top 10 Mistakes in Applying for Research Experience

One thing that provides job security for professors is that a new generation of students arrives each year and proceeds to make the same mistakes as the previous generation. This section will help you to break the cycle by providing 10 tips for avoiding the mistakes that potential mentees—that's you—have made in the past.

Gift Horses' Mouths Are Off-Limits

Even though you should be active in seeking out a research mentor, and a mentor probably won't come to you, maybe you are lucky and a professor picks you as a likely research assistant and approaches you about it. Irish luck worked for Peter, a coauthor of this book, whose first research position came when a class he signed up for was cancelled. By way of apology, the professor offered him a research assistant position in her lab.

If such a gift horse comes your way, you should think long and hard before turning it down. A lot of students put off doing research because it doesn't fit their schedule, because they aren't sure they want to be a part of the psychology major, or because the professor's work involves counting the number of times first-grade thespians say *oh* and *um* while performing the theme song in *My Happy Marshmallow*. If someone has asked you to do research, you are already viewed favorably. Maybe your mentor sees greatness in you that you don't see yet.

Find Ways to Circumvent Administrative Barriers

You would think that administrators would be delighted if students want to do 10 semesters of research for course credit. Unfortunately, universities often put up administrative barriers in the form of rules and regulations that make it hard to take research courses. Although professors can take a hard line about turning in late assignments, many harbor an anti-establishment subversive streak. Even if the course catalog says you have to have taken Comprehensive Introduction to Ponderous Psychological Analysis and Millisecond Timing before doing independent study, instructors sometimes waive the requirements, especially if you seem to know what you're talking about and if the professor wants to work with you.

If your requests for an exception are denied, rules are rules, and you have to follow them, but sometimes there are ways around the rules that do not technically break them. Maybe your university says that you can't get course credit for independent study until you're a junior, but is that a reason why you can't volunteer in the lab "just for the experience"?

Read the Professor's Papers Before Your Meeting

If you think you want to work with someone, get a few of his or her articles and read them. Campus libraries have most journal articles online. Reading up on a professor's work will let you say what you like about it, why you are interested, and what you didn't quite follow; for the perplexed, chapter 6 provides advice about finding and reading articles. You may be the first person ever to read your professor's "Expert Decision Making by Armenian Maritime Lawyers" article, which is worth major brownie points.

An Exact Match of Interests Is Unnecessary

It's ideal if you can work with someone in an area that excites you, but any research experience will help you, and so will a good recommendation from any professor. You might find yourself getting excited about an area that you used to think would never be interesting. More than one student has experienced the thrill of serving as a foot soldier in the bitter war between single high-threshold recognition models and two high-threshold recognition models. We know it sounds like we made that up, but we didn't.

Don't Assume the Most Senior Scientist Is the Best

Though it's helpful if a well-known senior scientist writes a letter of recommendation for you, don't exclude mentors just because they're professorial newbies. Junior scientists can be excellent mentors, and they may be more famous than you think. Even if hired straight out of graduate school, young professors have their own network of friends—the faculty and graduates of the university they got their doctorate from, people they meet at conferences, and people who read their papers.

Don't Mass E-Mail

"Hey all you psychology faculty members! I'm Rod but I go by PAC*MAN + I'm a sophomore psychology major looking for a PREFERABLY PAID research opportunity. E-mail me back ASAP if you want to work with me. Thanks, Rod." Nobody we know ever answers generic e-mails looking for independent study. It's different if someone e-mails one of us personally to ask about a position in our particular lab. Even so, it's far better to introduce yourself in person.

Once You Agree, You're Committed

Once you agree to work with someone, don't suddenly change your mind. Figure out who you'd like to work with, and indicate at the interview that he or she is your top choice. If you're offered a spot in the lab, either accept or reject the offer right away. Once you've accepted, you are committed—even if that tasty spot running experiments on avian visual cognition opens up. Agreeing to join a lab and then opportunistically switching it for another makes you look flighty, and makes it difficult for professors to plan how their lab will be staffed. Believe it or not, all your professors know each other—most of them hang out together, lamenting "kids these days." If you drop one lab, claiming you are preoccupied with caring for your sick hamster, but immediately add another, the faculty will find out, and your reputation will be besmirched. Obviously it's different if you work for a while in a lab and become unhappy with it. If so, it's fine to talk to your mentor about dropping. Most faculty will understand if your interests changed or if it wasn't what you thought it would be.

Get Approval From Both Mentors When Joining Multiple Labs

Most advisors don't mind if you work in multiple labs, but some do. If you'll be visiting off-campus research sites, for example, it may be important to focus on that to the exclusion of other lab research. It may be hard to know whether you'll finish testing children at the local day care center in time to get back to extract milky, acrid-smelling substances from the warty newts in the amphibian behavior lab. If you plan to work in multiple labs, make sure that all of the research mentors are aware of it and are fine with your decision.

Don't Play Hard to Get

Either you want to join the lab or you don't. Don't try to make yourself expensive or say that you will have to consult your cousin Vera about whether you can get a babysitting job instead. It makes you look like you're not serious, and you want to look serious and be serious about research.

Ask Smart Questions

Your meeting with the mentor is a good time to find out whether this will work out for you. Table 2.1 gives

TABLE 2.1. Some Questions for Potential Mentors and Why You're Asking Them

Question	Why You're Asking
How much flexibility will I have to schedule my own hours?	It's up to you to know how to budget your time, but if you work in addition to going to school, fixed hours may be necessary. But some projects—like those involving visiting classrooms and testing kids—require that you be available when the need arises. Will you sometimes need to work more hours, or will it be a fixed number of hours?
What am I expected to produce at the end?	Is there a final test? A paper? A project proposal? Don't be turned off by extra requirements: They'll teach you something. Just be mindful of what you have to do so that it isn't a surprise.
What will I do in the lab?	What's a typical day like? What kind of work does the professor do? Will you be alone or working with others?
Does the professor expect a multisemester commitment up front?	Most don't. Some do. You need to know what you're signing up for.
Is a senior thesis or honors thesis a possibility if I work in the lab for several semesters?	A thesis looks great when you're applying to graduate school or for a job. It shows you can complete a big project. Not every professor, however, is willing to mentor a thesis. You might also find out if any students have actually completed a thesis with this professor: That will give you a clue about the realistic chances of writing one.
Who are the most important authors working on the research topic so I can go read up a bit in advance?	Don't you want to be informed about what the professor's work is about?

a list of some helpful questions that may be useful in making a decision about whether to work in this lab. Although you shouldn't necessarily require that your lab experience be perfect, you should know whether you can realistically complete what is required of you and what the possibilities are for advancing your career.

Grants, Competitions, and Honors

Once you have some research experience, you may start thinking about designing your own project. Because most universities do everything they can to give undergraduates ways of getting involved in research, they often create programs to reward students who continue doing undergraduate research. For example, many psychology departments have an honors program that lets you write a senior thesis or honors thesis.

Ask your department, college, and research mentor about university-wide competitions that support research. Often, searching your school's Web page for "undergraduate research" will reveal competitions and prizes that even your professors don't know about. Many universities support an annual poster session or mini-conference where students present finished research projects and potentially win prizes. If you have done work that might qualify, see if you can find out about the competition and enter it. You might win, and that would look great on your resume. Sometimes, professional conferences also offer prizes for student research, a topic we discuss further in chapter 8.

Many universities offer undergraduate research grants you can apply for. A grant is like a competition in which you write a proposal and send it away for review by a panel of experts. If your proposal is among the best, then you get some money to spend on the research project. If your project on the impact of including the story of Orpheus and Eurydice in persuasive arguments wins, you'll get a small budget to pay for research expenses and possibly some pocket money. If your college has undergraduate research grants, you should definitely apply if you are starting a senior thesis or honors thesis.

Wrapping Up

We started out wishing that getting started in research was like a Hollywood movie, but it's more like a kung fu flick. You start as just one person among many who desires the treasured and secret kung fu lore of research methods. But to achieve that goal you must find a teacher, using all the resources at your disposal. Perhaps you may even travel to a far-off land, like the marketing department, in search of a mentor. Once you find the right mentor, you must convince him or her that you are worthy of training. The best way to do that is to be dedicated, reliable, and persistent. If you are lucky, carrying cauldrons filled with boiling water will not be necessary. And with the proper training, you will soon develop into a research kung fu master in your own right.

3

Rewards and Challenges
of Research Experience

One psychologist recounted the story of her admittedly atypical first undergraduate research experience, which involved running experiments on the effects of fear on memory. Her mentor had the brilliant idea of inducing fear by bringing a live rattlesnake into the room with the research participant. His reasoning was that rattlesnakes are deadly and scary, so therefore the experimental condition, which involved his research assistant wearing a rattlesnake around her neck, would be more frightening than the snake-absent control condition. It's hard to argue with this logic, but it neglects one important fact—the undergraduate student running the study *would have a live rattlesnake draped around her neck*. They did defang the animal and keep it in a cage when it wasn't in use terrorizing freshmen research participants. Still, our heroic research assistant was not thrilled with the idea at first. Apparently neither was the snake: It escaped its cage several times, allowing the research assistant to gain valuable snake-capturing skills. Fortunately, she persisted with the project, ran participants for an entire semester, helped analyze data, and earned herself a great letter of recommendation for graduate school and some outstanding research skills.

So what did our heroine learn from all this? Her specific research topic—fear and learning—provided knowledge that was useful in graduate school. She also gained skills that are frequently part of a research experience, such as learning how to interact with people during experiments, the ethics and ethical review of experiments, research design, analysis of data, and the daily ins and outs of laboratory research—skills that could be brought to any future employer or lab. And she also demonstrated, as part of her research experience, the kind of dedication and initiative that appeals to future employers and graduate mentors. Last but not least, snake hauling provided the student with some great stories to tell on interviews.

Not every research experience is so memorable. Nonetheless, we haven't talked to a single student who worked in a research lab and regretted it. On the contrary, a lot of students discovered a seemingly bottomless and abiding love for scientific discovery. They thrilled at being the first people in the world to catalogue the hierarchical levels of consciousness in motor control by expert Frisbee throwers, became addicted to newer and more arcane statistical procedures for analyzing data, and found themselves ignoring their former favorite periodical—the *Blue Dragongirl* #488 comic—to anxiously await the latest issue of the *Journal of Experimental Psychology: Human Perception and Performance*.

In this chapter, we'll discuss what it's like to do research and why you might love it, even if you never look forward to the latest riveting discoveries on the "Effects of Agency on Movement Interference During Observation of a Moving Dot Stimulus" (Stanley, Gowan, & Miall, 2007). We'll also tell you how to get more out of your research experience and offer some encouraging words on how to stick with it.

GAMES RESEARCH ASSISTANTS PLAY: SUCCESS IN BEGINNING RESEARCH EXPERIENCES

Beginning research experiences don't usually involve snakes or personal danger. They might involve counting how many times a pigeon pecks at a key in an hour or asking hundreds of different people the same 12 questions about motivation. Or they could involve entering responses from a pencil-and-paper survey into a computer. None of these things is itself thrilling or illuminating, but you can still learn a lot. The secret is to imagine that you are a detective who is trying to figure out the purpose of all this work. What are the items on the survey measuring? How will they be analyzed? You can ask these questions of your fellow research assistants and try to figure it out yourself, or you can talk to the graduate students in the lab or ask your mentor directly. However you play detective, you will get much more out of the research experience if you actively try to find out *why* you are doing what you're doing. As with every other aspect of research, you can do the minimum required work, but it's hard to compete with the students who are doing more than the minimum.

We're sure you're wondering what gripping activities await the first-time undergraduate researcher. In this section, we'll list some of the typical things that undergraduates do and explain why those activities might be more important than you think. You can refer back to this section when you are applying for jobs or graduate study or when you're slaving over a personal statement, wondering what to say about what you've learned.

Collaborative Work: Playing Well With Others

Companies complain about college seniors who can't collaborate with others, so students who work in a big lab can list "experience working with teams of people" on their resumes. The most important part of working effectively in a team is remembering to share information that others need to know. For example, if you schedule participants for another experimenter, it's a good idea to let him or her know that participants are coming. If something goes wrong during the experiment—like forgetting that you left your participant up in the lab doing the math filler task 4 hours ago—then you need to let your mentor know that you made an error instead of just filing the data in the locked steel cabinet.

Experiments: An Exercise in Professional Responsibility

In a lot of research labs, you will learn about running experiments. Unless your participants are prairie voles or nonhuman primates—in which case you can talk about whatever you want—you'll need to establish yourself as an authority figure. Be friendly, but project that you are in charge and a person to take seriously. People in charge don't self-disclose about that weekend trip to Downstairs@Club Jungle-Ra-Mazon or about failing History of Postmodern Textiles. Instead, they ask about mundane things, such as how classes are going or what classes are cool to take. If you're dealing with people from the community instead of other students, you may just be curious about their lives. Similarly, you shouldn't mock people about getting the lowest score ever in the experiment. Jokes about participants seemingly having severe medial temporal lesions may be funny to psych majors like you, but probably not to anyone else, and they are inappropriate when directed at research participants. As with any job, behaving professionally and courteously is universally appreciated.

An important part of running experiments is recruiting human participants. Recruiting can be as easy as getting Intro Psych students to sign up online, or it can involve mailing out flyers, calling people at home, or visiting workplaces. Recruiting is not always fun, but it's good work experience, and the people you meet can be interesting. Perhaps you will meet the woman who founded your sorority's annual Save the Platypus dance-a-thon or the 1973 world champion of the ancient Greek martial art Pankration.

Ethics Training: Avoiding Whispered Aspersions About Your Moral Character

Ethics training features prominently in most research experiences, and you can list it on your resume. Every research experience involves ethical questions about proper treatment of human participants or animals. Human safety and human dignity are strictly protected by psychologists—unlike by some other professionals, such as television producers. We admit that professors love reality shows as much as the next person—at least when we aren't taking a stand against consumerism by killing our televisions. Nothing thrills like watching blindfolded narcissists unknowingly ingest African hissing cockroaches to win a million dollars. In the distant past, professors amused themselves with similar experiments, but thanks to the advent of ethics boards, roach is unlikely to be on the menu in your experiments. As part of your research experience, you'll learn why psychology experimenters inform their participants in advance about the research, provide the opportunity to withdraw at any time without penalty, and get their project reviewed by an ethics board. Day-to-day experience applying ethics rules brings home the message behind the dry presentation that shows up in your research methods text.

Moreover, during your research experience, you will find yourself facing ethical dilemmas, such as whether you should terminate an experiment if a participant starts crying (we think yes) or whether you have the right to end an experiment if a participant becomes disruptive to others (again, we think yes). As these situations arise, make your best judgment call and then discuss what happened with your mentor and get guidance for the future.

Grunt Work

Although the glamorous life of running experiments may be yours, you may also be involved in shadowy back-room activities like mailing, scoring data, and entering data into computer programs. One research assistant we talked to was part of a mammoth effort to stuff 1,800 envelopes with forms and return envelopes, seal them, address them, and get them mailed—in 3 days. Students in another lab told us about how they had to transcribe what people were saying out loud as they worked on a problem. Each of these jobs was part of a larger project, and the students attended lab meetings and learned about how their efforts were contributing to the research. If all you did was stuff envelopes and you never learned anything about the research, you would feel exploited. But if the work gives you a chance to find out about the methods and results of the study, then you are gaining something valuable. Don't be afraid to pester your mentor or other students with questions about what the project is about, how you are contributing, or ways to do better.

ADVANCED RESEARCH EXPERIENCE: YOUR OWN STUDIES

Once you move beyond the beginning research experiences, you will probably want to try doing your own research project. A good first step is to find a topic to investigate. Your mentor may provide you with a topic and assign you some reading to get started. If not, you may have to come up with an idea yourself. One approach that often works is to try to extend or modify one of the experiments you've already run in the lab. If you want to do more than that, then a good rule of thumb is to pay attention to what your mentor studies and to find a topic that dovetails with those interests. If your mentor is interested in how children learn to count, your project should probably have something to do with that, too.

We know what you're thinking: "I wanted to study how children learn to interpret Bernese mountain dogs' emotions, but my advisor is a biological psychologist who studies hippocampal lesions in transgenic sheep and goats." A good reason to stick with what your mentor knows is that for an advisor to advise, he or she needs to know something about the topic. Contrary to popular belief, good ideas don't just appear out of thin air, from the heart, or from natural smarts. They come from reading. Before you can stand on the shoulders of giants, you need to know what the giants said about your topic, and that means hitting the library. What's even more difficult is that sometimes there are papers on a topic that you just didn't find. An expert in the area, though, would know all the relevant papers. The more your mentor knows about the topic, the more likely it is that you're doing something interesting and innovative. It's also more likely that your experiment will work because your mentor will know what kinds of things typically go wrong in his or her own area.

Once you've picked a topic, you have to buckle down and do the work to read up on the topic, write, and conduct the studies. It's at this stage that your time management skills will be put to the test. College students have a lot of other activities that draw their attention, including studying for exams, working, dating, and debating whether aliens landed at Roswell in 1947. There are always things that need to be done immediately, so it's easy to let your research time slide by. Unfortunately, your research won't get done if you don't do it.

We've found that it's helpful to set concrete goals every week with your mentor and then to try to meet those goals by setting aside some time each week to work on research (Silvia, 2007). Treat your scheduled research time just like a biochemistry exam: It can't be moved; it can't be changed; and if for some terrible reason you miss it, you had better go take the scheduled make-up. If you are rigid about making a schedule and sticking to it, you will be amazed at how fast your project can go. If you work on it only when you feel like it, you'll be equally amazed at how little you accomplish every week.

Resist the temptation to skip a day. The temptation comes when you look at how much else you have to do and think, "Next week I'll have a lot more time." Research on time estimation shows that we always think that we will have more time in the future than we do now. It also shows that we're almost always wrong about that—every week is busy, and we'll never have more slack time than we have now (Zauberman & Lynch, 2005). Putting off until tomorrow what you need to do today is a recipe for not finishing.

PERSISTENCE AND RESILIENCE

In chapter 2, we point out that professionalism is the key to getting started in research. It's even more important to maintain that level of professionalism throughout the entire experience. At many universities, a student can feel invisible; there may be no consequence for skipping class, for showing up late, or for taking a nap during a 300-person Intro Psych course. In research experience, though, you are not only visible but constantly watched. You need to demonstrate that you can show up consistently, be on time, and do things competently. It's through these professional qualities that you earn the respect of your mentor and a good letter of recommendation for graduate study or work.

Among students who get top grades, there's sometimes a myth that it's enough to be brilliant to become a great scientist. Our experience is that some brilliant people never make it in science. The difference between people who make it and people who don't is the ability to keep showing professionalism when things get boring, difficult, painful, or stressful. By comparison, students who wig out when things get tough are the ones who never amount to much. Employers and graduate schools know that everyone is going to have hard times, and they want to know if you are one of the rare persistent people or just another of the flighty ones.

Scientific work can sometimes be boring. You may find yourself running the same experiment over and over again, and you may start to make mistakes. The majority of research assistants will begin, at the point things start getting dull, to put in the minimum effort, show up a few minutes late sometimes, and do what they're asked but nothing more. You want to be the student who does the opposite. When things get dull, try to find ways to keep them interesting. Figure out why the study is going the way it is. Think of ideas for future studies and discuss them with your mentor. Read articles on the topic. Research on motivation shows that the best and brightest people often find ways to turn boring tasks into fun ones by setting personal challenges, and thus they are able to persist longer (Sansone & Smith, 2000).

Scientific work can be emotionally stressful at times. You may learn that your work wasn't good enough or that your study must be revised and run again. Many studies in science tell you what *doesn't* work and show you a better way to test the idea. Similarly, even after you finish a study, you may discover problems that require that you reinterpret your results or even start over. This can be disheartening, especially if you feel that it's a sign that you personally are failing. But take heart—even the best scientists get their papers rejected, have experiments that blow up in their face, and have to fix things and try again. As with most jobs, there is no easy way to be a success. You have to keep trying, and sometimes you will fail despite your best efforts. Coping with disappointment is hard, but everyone goes through it. If you think your mentor is the type who can soothe the pain, talk to him or her. If not, share with your fellow research assistants. Having friends going through the same experiences can make you feel better and give you the energy to keep going. You can also adopt a friend by visiting your local animal shelter. Bernese mountain dogs are great listeners, and they love you no matter what.

The same goes for other stressful events in your life. Sometimes, everything does go wrong. Maybe you break up with your boyfriend, maybe your grandmother is sick, or maybe you are doing poorly in an important class. At such times, seek out social support from your friends, family, or a therapist. Free or inexpensive counseling is usually available on campus for students in distress, and it can make a big difference.

During the hard times, there's always the temptation to drop your research experience and focus entirely on other things, but use good judgment. Ask your mentor for a few days off if you need to deal with life stress—but not for 2 weeks off if you feel the urge to go skydiving in Aruba. If you cannot continue, consider withdrawing from school entirely and returning when you feel better. Do what needs to be done, but try to resist quitting or using life events as an excuse to slack off. Ultimately, if you can find a way to keep meeting your duties as a student scientist, you will be glad that you didn't quit.

MAKING MISTAKES: WHATEVER, IT HAPPENS

Everybody makes mistakes: We have all shown up for the costume party dressed as a police officer and learned that the toy handcuffs were real. But that's okay—it doesn't mean you're a failure as a human being. There is no need to don monastic robes and go on a mission to the top of a mountain to cleanse your soul. When you make a mistake, just own up to it. Write down what happened and explain it to your mentor. You should be careful and avoid mistakes, but research sometimes goes awry. It's far better to admit it than to pretend it never happened and wind up with useless data. The purpose of science isn't to appear perfect to your mentor; it's more important that the data be accurate. Mentors will eventually appreciate your honesty, even if they need to take a moment to flip out first.

WRAPPING UP

Learning to be a good researcher is hard, just like learning Russian, mastering differential equations, or figuring out whether your yellow corduroy bell-bottoms and

Panama hat are cool or not this year. Fortunately, research is also immensely rewarding. What separates the best student researchers from the mediocre ones isn't how much fun they have during the good parts of research—nobody quits because their work is too awesome to handle. People quit during the boring parts, the disappointing parts, and the emotionally tough parts. If you want to reap the rewards of research experience, stick with it and make the most of your time by asking questions and trying to learn as much as you can. As you learn more, you can begin to think about designing your own projects and leaving your mark on the scientific world.

4

Getting Psyched: The Joys of the Psychology Lifestyle

When people in the 1960s decided to follow a jam band around the country in a VW bus, wearing tie-dyed T-shirts and subverting the system, they were announcing a lifestyle choice. Maybe they originally got into it just because they liked a song or two, but by the end, they had devoted their life to peace and free love. Being a psychologist is also a lifestyle choice. Maybe you originally got into it because you weren't sure what other major to pick, but now you find yourself cracking obscure jokes about the Stroop effect at the frat party, calculating your own d prime in multiplayer online games, or even laughing at the jokes professors tell in class.

It's time to come clean: You're a *serious* psychology major now. The next step? Find other people who will support the choice you've made. And that means getting more involved in the wider world of psychology. It's also time to let your love of psychology creep into other aspects of your life, such as the courses you take

outside your department, your habits, and your apparel.
In this chapter, we'll show how you can get more involved in your beloved major by reaching beyond the
classroom and infusing your life with the artesian waters of psychology. Web links to sites or topics mentioned in this chapter are given in Exhibit 4.1. Before
you know it, you'll be transformed from an everyday
psych major to the type of person who attends Claude L.
Steele talks around the country, wearing a tie-dyed
"Stereotypes Threaten Us All" T-shirt (Steele &
Aronson, 1995).

JOIN CAMPUS AND NATIONAL ORGANIZATIONS

Connecting with psych majors locally and worldwide
begins in your mentored research lab—those other
people in the lab are likely to be excited about psychology, just like you. Beyond that core cadre, some
campus groups assemble psychology students. For example, many universities have a psychology club that meets

regularly. They may bring speakers to talk about psychology careers, introduce you to graduate students, and give you a chance to ask questions about getting in to grad school. And sometimes they serve free pizza.

Many colleges have a chapter of Psi Chi, the national honor society in psychology. To join, you need to be in the top third of your class and have at least a 3.0 grade point average (GPA). Once you're accepted, you get a stylish lapel pin and a subscription to their magazine *Eye on Psi Chi*, which contains articles that can help you make the most out of your psychology experience. Maybe you'll even be one of the people writing for the magazine. If your college doesn't have a Psi Chi chapter, consider starting one—you'll almost certainly be the president, which looks great on your vita or resume.

You can also become a student affiliate of one of the national or international organizations. The big ones are the American Psychological Association (APA) and the Association for Psychological Science (APS). APA is the largest organization for psychologists, and they provide free resources for students on their Web site. Membership is inexpensive, and they give you discounts on books and videos published by APA; send you the *Monitor on Psychology*, a monthly professional magazine about psychology; and throw in a free subscription to the journal *American Psychologist*. Not only will you get some great reading material, but you will also be on their mailing list, which means you'll be informed about opportunities that other students might miss.

APS is a similar organization that's dedicated specifically to the science of psychology. You can join for a small fee and get subscriptions to several journals, including *Psychological Science*, which contains short and interesting articles on many different topics, and one of our favorites, *Current Directions in Psychological Science*, which contains short review papers by top researchers. These journals are meant to be accessible to students, and they can be fun to read. You also get the *APS Observer*, which is similar to the *APA Monitor*. The APS student caucus provides ways of receiving online mentoring, publishes a free newsletter, and gives small grants. APS has a spiffy Web site that contains resources for student scientists, too.

Although those are the two largest organizations, you may also be interested in joining specialized groups that support your kind of research. Many psychology organizations have some kind of student affiliate membership that provides resources to students at a low cost.

PARTICIPATE IN CAMPUS EVENTS

As a student on campus, you may come across flyers advertising talks with titles like "Heisenberg's Uncertainty Principle as a Guiding Force in the Development of Sexual Mores in 20th Century Bermuda." Maybe you never thought that these were open to you, but as it turns out, they are. Watch the walls of your psychology department for flyers advertising a *colloquium* (plural *colloquia*), which is a free scholarly lecture that's open to the public. You can also watch for *job talks*, which happen when people are applying to work at your university and they are going to come and talk about their research. Finally, there are usually *brown bag talks* that focus on a particular topic or research area where faculty and grad students present their latest research. Colloquia and job talks are almost always open to the public and free. Brown bags are usually more intimate settings, so you may want to find out who's in charge and ask if it's okay if you attend. If you go to enough of them, you may be allowed to present some of your research there, too.

Even if you're not enthralled with the topic of a talk, showing up increases your visibility in the department and exposes you to new ideas. You'll also get a chance to see how professional talks work and to observe the good, the bad, and the ugly. Take notes on what works and what doesn't (for more on developing a research talk, see chap. 10). The same skills that are used in giving a professional talk are used when making a sales presentation in the corporate world. And sometimes brown bags and colloquia have free food or free coffee.

You can also check for events at other local colleges, if you are fortunate enough to be in a region with several schools. If you are going to take a trip out of town, you can consider inviting some of your friends from Psi Chi, especially if one of them is willing to drive. You can split the gas costs and have company to boot.

BUILD A LIBRARY

The books in a psychologist's office aren't, as it turns out, just there to look nice—although like eyeglasses and white lab coats, they do make professors look smarter in photos. Professors use their books to check out what has been done in a particular area, give references to students, and find the latest research about a topic. Most of them started collecting books from the time they were an undergraduate student like you.

On a student budget, books seem expensive, but they are worth having. It's never too soon to start building a personal library, starting with a few textbooks. It's tempting, after you finish a course, to sell back the books for the $3.78 that the bookstore pays, but you should keep some of them. If nothing else, the books help you prepare for the GRE. If you find yourself week after week checking out the library's only copy of *Qualitative Theories of Metacontrast Masking in the Autistic Brain*, maybe it's time to bite the bullet and buy your own copy. Check the publisher's Web site and buy direct, order it from your favorite local bookstore, or order online. Or ask your mom to buy it for your birthday— don't worry, she still remembers that time when you were little that she bought you a book about model trains instead of the pink plastic doll house. She'll prob-ably still get that MP3 player you wanted in addition to the book.

Some books are more useful than others. You should certainly have the APA *Publication Manual* (APA, 2001) if you're heading for graduate school. Books on professional skills, like this one, are great to have on hand when you need some advice or a motivational pick-me-up. A good starter list for books on professional issues can be found in the Appendix of this book. Another good kind of book to have is a *handbook*, which is a collection of chapters describing the state of the art in a particular research area. When we see a new handbook in an area we're interested in, we usually buy it and add it to the bookshelf. These are the ones you're going to break out someday when you want an answer to your supervisor's psychology questions or when you want to know about the latest breakthroughs in rational emotive therapy, personality dynamics, or mollusk conditioning.

Go to Conferences

Even if you aren't presenting a paper or poster, you should look for interesting conferences (for more on this, see chap. 8). You can always make a pilgrimage to the APA or APS convention, especially if one of them happens to be nearby. Get some of your fellow psych majors to put on their Psi Chi pins, book a hotel room, and go together. If there are local or regional conferences that you can drive to, they may be even more fun. There are regional psychology associations like the Eastern Psychological Association and Midwestern Psychological Association that host annual meetings. Many states also have a state conference that is within driving distance, so you can use the conference as an excuse for a road trip.

TAKE USEFUL CLASSES IN OTHER DEPARTMENTS

For a lot of students—like that slacker with the gold chains who shows up to class twice a semester—picking courses is as easy as finding out what's required and making sure it doesn't conflict with the other required courses. But picking classes can do more than that for a motivated psychology major: It can be a route to new ideas, a way to pick up new research skills, and a way to become more competitive. Psychology is the study of behavior, so almost anything you take in school can be combined with psychology to produce a research topic. Like sports, art, or music? There's a psychology of expertise that deals with how people become great in each of these areas. Interested in health and wellness? You'll find courses in public health, nursing, education, nutrition, and sport science. Thinking about law school? Take courses in social and cognitive psychology that discuss eyewitness memory, effective police lineups, and decision making. You can't go wrong just taking courses that seem fun and interesting—they enrich you as a person, and you'll never get another chance to take things simply because they sound interesting.

For a more targeted approach, consider finding some courses that can teach resume-building skills that make you more marketable for graduate schools, professional schools, and the job market. For example, psychology students often avoid mathematics. Math courses can provide you with ideas and ways of thinking that you can't learn elsewhere. A course on graph theory may give you new ideas about how to visualize data. You may be surprised to find that advanced mathematics isn't as dreadful as the soul-destroying math classes you took in high school. Along the same lines, statistics courses are a great way to augment your skills, and pharmaceutical companies and grad schools are both impressed if you can analyze how the price of free dinners influences doctors' decisions about prescription drug choices (for some tips on doing well in statistics, see chap. 5).

Another underappreciated option is a course or two in computer science. Learning how to program a computer sounds scary, but a beginner's course will show you that it isn't that difficult. If you can learn the difference between operant conditioning and classical conditioning, you can learn the difference between a for-next loop and a while loop. These days, many psychologists write their own programs to process data, for experiments, or just for fun. If you know how, it will be a big plus when you apply for graduate school. Future employers are also impressed with the nerdier arts, particularly if—unlike some of your less reputable friends from computer science—you are also bathed, well dressed, and socially skilled.

Biology classes are also a big help to psychology students. This is an era of rapid growth in the life sciences. Biology, neuroscience, and genetics are an integral part of modern psychology. If you have a background in the life sciences—or at least know what transcription RNA is—it will make you more marketable as a future psychologist. And needless to say, if you're thinking about going to medical school, a working knowledge of human biology is certainly helpful.

Finally, in some schools there are classes that involve psychology but don't have psychology in the name. For example, a course on consumer behavior is really psychology applied to marketing and business. A course on organizational behavior management is really psychology applied to the workplace. A course on exercise and sport science is probably the psychology of motor skill, and a course on educational research is really about the psychology of learning applied to the classroom. Watch for these hidden gems. They can be interesting and provide a way of getting more psychology-relevant classes than are listed in your department—and thanks to your extensive psychology knowledge, they might also be an easy GPA booster.

Wrapping Up

For the most successful psych students, psychology isn't just a major—it's a lifestyle. Most of the things we have described in this chapter seem optional, and they are. But getting more involved in the psychology lifestyle is a good way to becoming more marketable than other students. Distinguish yourself from the pack by seeking out courses in other areas, going to conferences and lectures, building your library, and joining campus or national organizations.

Soon you will discover a secret—the psychology lifestyle is fun. Professors and grad students like to whine about how they're underpaid and underappreciated, how hard they work, and how disruptive it is to have to travel to Paris annually for a conference in a four-star hotel. Don't believe the gripe: If they hated their job, they would have long ago quit to become marketing consultants or statisticians. The academic life is oddly fun, and as a student, you have a lot of ways to enjoy yourself while building your skills. Lastly, part of the joy of becoming a psychology student is that you get to meet a lot of great people who are on the same path. Don't miss out; go find them.

5

Analyzing People, Analyzing Data: Getting More Out of Statistics

When nonpsychologists—the scientific term for normal people—hear that we are psychologists, they always quip, "Oh, so you're analyzing me; I better watch what I say." We chuckle and allay their concerns; "Psychologists don't really do that," we say. But it's a lie, a dastardly deception—as professors of psychology, we have fearsome mind-reading powers. We shouldn't share this cabalistic secret, but professors can read you like an issue of *The Economist*. The proof? Here's what one of us intuited in a recent statistics class:

> This clock must be slow. I feel like I've been here a lifetime. Who is this guy? Does he actually like this? They didn't do stuff like this in the Intro class—we just talked about babies, brains, and weird people. Psychology isn't supposed to be about math; that's why it's called psychology. Why do they make me take this course? Is that another Greek letter? I must have learned the whole Greek alphabet by now. Hmm, I wonder how they learn stats in Greece? Wouldn't Greek letters just be letters

to them? This is pointless. Even if I actually tried to understand this stuff, how would it help me? How am I ever going to use this in life?

But you needn't have similar fearsome powers to have known this. These are common thoughts in statistics classrooms in psychology departments across the country and around the world—except, perhaps, in Greece. No other subject in the psychology curriculum elicits such fear.

Why do departments require students to take statistics? Here are some standard answers:

- Statistics is needed to analyze data objectively.
- Statistics makes psychology a science.
- You can't understand journal articles without understanding statistics.
- You need to learn computational skills to perform statistical analyses.

Here's a dark secret, a fact more furtive than professorial mind reading: These aren't true. Data analysis is subjective and always open to scrutiny; the scientific method and respect for evidence, not statistics per se, are what make psychology scientific; you can understand articles without mastery of statistics; and software, not your brain, ought to crunch numbers.

Despite these misconceptions, learning statistics is immensely valuable, whether or not you plan to analyze data for the rest of your career. You will learn how to construct an argument—similar to legal argumentation—for why people should be convinced by your findings. Just as a defendant is innocent until proven guilty, your findings are random until proven systematic. Statistical argumentation typically includes a three-pronged approach: (a) presenting data informatively as graphs or tables; (b) determining how likely it is that your data are not random; and (c) figuring out how practical your finding is. Besides developing a sound base for analyzing the results of psychological research, you will learn how to develop and critique an argument. That's a skill that everyone should have and a good reason to take your statistics courses seriously. To help you get more out of your statistics courses, this chapter presents the five commandments of statistical learning. Exhibit 5.1 displays the five principles in a convenient, ready-to-frame format. These five commandments aren't etched in stone tablets, but they'll start you off on the right foot.

THE FIVE COMMANDMENTS OF STATISTICAL LEARNING

First Commandment: Thou Shalt Read the Book, Attend the Class, and Do Many Problems

In many university courses, instructors stray from the textbook and add material that complements the textbook and makes the class more interesting. In fact, they

EXHIBIT 5.1. The Five Commandments

Thou Shalt Read the Book, Attend the Class, and Do Many Problems
Thou Shalt Study With Others
Thou Shalt Not Use Computational Formulae
Employers Shall Covet Statistical Training
Thou Shalt Use Your Statistical Knowledge in Daily Life

probably chose the textbook because of the great job it does explaining basic concepts; they don't want to waste valuable time covering the same topics in class. This does not happen in statistics classes. Rather, the lectures do not add any meaningful content to what is taught in the book. If you understand the textbook, there really is no need to go to lectures. Why is it, then, that statistics lectures merely repeat the textbook? Because the concepts are tricky and need to be explained again and again. Your professor knows this and hopes that if you read the book for the content and attend lectures so you can comprehend the logical process of statistics, you will eventually understand the material.

A problem, however, is that students pick up on this repetition quickly. As a result, many of them either read the book but skip class, come to class but ignore the book, or skip class and procrastinate reading until the night before the test. If you're reasonably intelligent and your goal is to get a passable grade, you might get away with the first two options. But if you are looking for top grades, or if you tend to struggle in classes, you must learn the material over and over again. That means reading the textbook, attending all of the lectures, discussing stats with friends, and organizing stats-themed toga parties, which give new meaning to the statistical concepts of skewness and deviance.

But it doesn't end there. Even with diligent reading and perfect attendance, the best way to master statistical concepts is to read the chapter and do half of the problems before class, use the class time to ask questions, and then solve the rest of the problems after class. If you're still having trouble, talk to your instructor and iron it out. You cannot save your work for the days before the exam; it must be done consistently throughout the semester. It is impossible to attempt too many problems. At a bare minimum, you should do every problem in your book and every supplemental problem your instructor gives you. If you really want to do well, check out online resources for your textbook and buy a study guide. The more problems that you do, the less likely you will be surprised on tests and the more you will remember.

Second Commandment: Thou Shalt Study With Others

Helping others is a good practice in life, and it is essential in statistics. Study groups work, provided that they consist of the right people. For instance, at least one of the members of the group should understand statistics—many study groups are nothing but the blind leading the blind. More important, all the members of the group must be serious about learning, which doesn't necessarily mean that the group itself must be serious. Everyone must try to keep up with the class and attempt problems on their own before and after the group meets.

Three magical things happen in a properly formed study group. First, it turns out that students learn more from a peer than from a professor or a textbook. We don't know why for sure—maybe it's because they "speak the same language" (i.e., English); maybe it's the one-on-one attention that can be provided; maybe we don't want to look foolish in front of our friends. Second, students who can explain concepts to their friends understand the concepts better themselves. Try it. After any class, go home and tell your roommate what you learned. By the end of the conversation you'll have a better understanding of what's going on. You'll also probably have a host of questions to ask your professor or to look up in the textbook. Third, many textbooks do not give you answers for every problem or walk you through the solving of a problem. In a study group, you can attempt all the problems. If you all get the same answer, then you are all probably right. If you get different answers, then you can learn a lot by explaining to each other how you got your answers.

Third Commandment: Thou Shalt Not Use Computational Formulae

If you go on to graduate school, you will take statistics again. And not just one course, but many, many courses. After all, somebody has to make sure that professors are analyzing data correctly. For the graduate student, psychology *is* statistics. But don't let that dissuade you from applying: Statistics is not about understanding math but about understanding research design and learning how to construct a logical argument. Computer software has taken the math out of statistics. In fact, many of you will learn how to use a software package (typically SPSS or SAS) in your undergraduate courses.

But there does seem to be quite a bit of math in statistics. We believe you will be exposed to two types of math: (a) math that will help you understand the concepts—the *conceptual formulas*—and (b) math that serves no educational purpose—the *computational formulas*. Let's illustrate this point with the important yet simple notion of sum of squares. Sum of squares is used to measure how different scores are from each other. Scores that are close together, ranging from 9 to 11, will have a smaller sum of squares than scores that are far apart, ranging from 0 to 20. How do you find the value of the sum of squares? You figure this out by calculating how far each score is from the average score. This is easy. If the average is 10 and the score is 8, then you are 2 units apart. Do this for every score. Note that these differences are going to be small if they are close to the average, but big if they are far from the average. Now take the square of all the differences. This is also easy, especially if you have a calculator. Note again that scores that were originally close to the average have small squared differences, but scores that were far away have large squared differences. Finally, add all the squared differences, and notice again that the sum of all the squared differences will be bigger if the original scores were far from the average than if they were close to the average. Your statistical software can do this for you, but learning these basic steps gives you an intuitive understanding of the concept of sum of squares: Sum of squares is bigger if the numbers are farther away from the average. Conceptual formulas are good.

There is also a computational formula for calculating sum of squares. Computational formulas are shortcuts that specify how to compute the statistic by hand. We think they are evil because they obscure the concepts: They are easy to compute but hard to comprehend. A computer will do the computations for you, so why bother learning it? For example, here is the computational formula for sum of squares: Square all of the original scores and add them. Then subtract the square of the sum of the original scores divided by the number of scores. This formula is easy enough to follow, but what does it have to do with how close the scores are to each other?

When the textbook or your professor presents the option to use a computational formula, avert your eyes; view it through an eclipse box if necessary. Conceptual formulas are better because they help you learn the concepts. In graduate school, statistics is about understanding concepts—which, incidentally, are mostly based on sums of squares. Nobody will be impressed by your ability to use computational formulas.

Fourth Commandment: Employers Shall Covet Statistical Training

Most students take statistics courses because the curriculum coerces them. After surviving the required courses, they plan to avoid statistics for the rest of their college years and working life. What's the motivation, then, to do well? One reason why employers hire psychology graduates is that psychology students were coerced into courses in statistics and research methods. Statistics may not be required for the job, but employers presume that the course must be hard and that the material is specialized. Show them that you did well, and they will put you on the fast track to wealth and fame.

The key is to market the skills you learned in your statistics classes. Have you entered numbers into a spreadsheet? Then you have experience with data management. Have you calculated a *t* value? That's data analysis. Do you know when to use the appropriate statistic? That's a major aspect of research design. Do you understand hypothesis testing? That's abstract reasoning. Have you used statistical software? You have the capacity to learn novel programs. Statistics isn't about math: It's about research, reasoning, and argumentation; it's about taking information and generalizing it to other contexts. Skill in statistics demonstrates an ability to reason logically. Employers know this, either because they took statistics and know its value or because they haven't taken statistics and imagine that it must be hard. When your boss laments a drop in the average profit per sale, you can save the day by warning against outliers and pointing out that the median profit went up.

Fifth Commandment: Thou Shalt Use Your Statistical Knowledge in Daily Life

We don't want to give you the impression that statistics itself is unimportant in the real world. The knowledge you gain from your basic statistics course will serve you well. When you see the results of the latest political poll, sentences like "This poll reflects a margin of error of 3 points" will make sense to you (*confidence intervals*). You can explain why the restaurant that was excellent the first time you went was merely pretty good the second time (*regression to the mean*). You'll know why personal testimonials—drinking urine cured my psoriasis!—are uninformative (*sample size and random sampling*).

You will also become a smarter consumer of information. You're not going to blindly follow advice from ostensible experts without questioning the facts. When Dr. Gauss claims that people are no smarter than ferrets, you can question the validity of the claim. Were enough ferrets and people tested (*power*)? Were the participants a reasonable representation of the population (*random sampling*)? And if Dr. Bayes counters with his research findings that indeed ferrets are smarter, does he report how much smarter (*effect size*)? The world at large has a lot of conflicting advice—for example, try an Internet search on the best way to lose weight—in part because few people understand statistics and research methods.

FEARLESS RESOURCES FOR THE FEARSOME STATS STUDENT

To get more out of your statistics course, you should use books beyond the textbook. Reading the assigned textbook is the bare minimum; reading additional books will cultivate fearsome statistical prowess. You'll benefit from a second book because the required textbook is probably boring: Writers of statistics textbooks are not renowned for their lively, engaging prose. A livelier book will reinforce the major concepts and give you a second perspective on the material. Our Appendix lists some books that we have found helpful; your campus library ought to have some of them, and your shelf of professional books probably has space for one or two of them.

WRAPPING UP

Some psychology majors love statistics; most find statistics uninspiring or frustrating. Many students aspire to mere survival—they want to get through statistics so they can move on to the "real psychology classes." But statistics is central to understanding psychology and to functioning as an informed person in an information-dense society—there are reasons why essentially every psychology department requires classes on stats and methods. Statistics may never be your friend, but it could be your avuncular neighbor. Like organizing your closet, statistics is oddly enjoyable once you get into it, so go forth and multiply, standardize, and regress.

6

Primary Sources: Finding, Reading, and Understanding Journal Articles

In case you happen to live in one of the 12 remaining cattle ranches that have no access to the Internet, the modern replacement for the encyclopedia is a free online resource called Wikipedia. It's like the encyclopedia—that big set of books that contained all of human knowledge in bite-sized alphabetical entries—but instead of being written by experts on each topic, it's collaboratively written by whoever happens to have too much free time. By virtue of its democratic method of contribution, Wikipedia accurately reflects what topics interest people. That's why you can read a 1,400 word entry on analysis of variance (ANOVA), a statistical technique that occupies the first semester in virtually every graduate program in psychology, or the equally well-sourced 11,600 word entry on the Roswell UFO incident.[1]

---

[1]To find something with a word count roughly as long as the Wikipedia entry on ANOVA, see the entry on Treehouse of Horror XIII. Other topics of interest to us include Bernese mountain dogs (600 words) and ninjas (1,300 words).

If you want the latest, greatest ideas in psychology, you need to go straight to primary sources: journal articles and book chapters. Wikipedia may not be a bad place to start your research, but if you stop there, you're going to get nailed. Good research ideas come from reading the work of real scientists, not from reading an Internet article about the psychology of music cobbled together by the White Plains High School glee club after their annual all-night *Fiddler on the Roof* sing-a-thon.

Finding primary sources sounds easy, but there's more to it than you might think. Back in high school, you probably just pulled a few short magazine articles on a topic, read the good parts, and then wrote a paper. Real research requires that you read long, technical papers, learn from them, and then use those papers to find more papers. You stop reading only when you know the area well. Even then, the more that you read, the better your papers will be. This chapter discusses how to find relevant primary sources, how to continue deepening your knowledge about a topic, and how to know what primary sources are useful. It also gives you some tips for reading articles and extracting what you need to know from them, perhaps without reading every single word in the paper.

LIBRARIANS AND LIBRARIES

Just as students have nightmares about the worst of their professors, so too do professors have nightmares about the worst of their students. One recurring professor nightmare goes something like this: A college senior arrives at office hours asking for help on writing a research paper. Naturally, the paper is due the next day. The professor suggests some articles to read and tells the student to go to the library. The student then says, "Wait, we have a library? Where is it? Like, on campus somewhere?"

If this sounds like you, the first thing to do is to find a campus map and figure out where the library is. That's because your first and perhaps most important library search tool is available only at the library—a group of human beings known as *reference librarians*. Reference librarians are those shadowy figures who hang out behind a desk labeled "REFERENCE," looking bored. Occasionally, nervous freshmen whisper something to them, and they smile, lead them off somewhere, and then return alone. As frightening as that sounds, reference librarians secretly lead a life of quiet desperation, hoping against hope that a young student will come and ask them a question besides, "Where is the bathroom?" They are library evangelists, firmly convinced that they can change your life for the better if only you would let them. They know how every database on the library computer system works, what "BF636.S767 2006 c.1" means, and how to find reference sources mere psychologists can only dream of accessing. If you get stuck on using any of the databases we discuss, ask a reference librarian for assistance. Do be polite, though; who knows what happens to those freshmen amid the stacks?

In the days of yore, library searches began at the library. Not so anymore. Usually they now begin with your university's library Web page. Once you find the library page, look around for databases. *Databases* are computer-based tools that contain information. Each page of information is known as a *record*—not to be confused with those black vinyl things that stored music in the dark era of disco. Most databases have a search line in which you type what you're looking for. They will retrieve a bunch of records for you, and you can dig through them, e-mail them to yourself, or print them out. Usually, you can specify what type of information to search for. If you are looking for a particular author, search by author. Most often, you will search by something called a *keyword,* which means that you are looking for records on that topic. If you've ever searched the Internet, you know how this works already.

Your library's catalog is one useful database. When you search the library catalog, you find records that correspond to books. Each book will have all the important details about the book, including the title, author, year and place of publication, and the call number, which tells you where to find the book in the library. Sometimes, searching for books is a good way to get started learning about a topic. If you are interested in signal detection theory, for example, you could search for the keywords *signal detection* and *psychology* in your library catalog; you'll get a list of books that you can go read about signal detection theory. Any of the books about signal detection might work, but some title phrases hint at ease of reading, including *introduction to, a primer,* and *handbook of.*

FINDING JOURNAL ARTICLES WITH PSYCINFO

Usually, books are not going to be the best place to start because they tend to get out of date quickly. For the latest and greatest research, you will want to find peer-reviewed articles, and that means you need to search for journal articles. Journals are like magazines except that they contain articles that report scientific and scholarly activities and have shockingly few photos of celebrity babies. The good things about journals are that they contain papers by people (usually professors) who know a lot about a topic and who managed to write a paper good enough that at least three other experts were convinced that it made sense.

You can find most articles related to psychology using a database called PsycINFO, which is published by the American Psychological Association. PsycINFO works like your library catalog, except that the records it finds are journal articles. A good way to start is to enter a keyword related to your topic and then add *review* as the second keyword. If you can find a paper that reviews the research on a topic, you have a good start. If not, get rid of *review* and look for a paper in a good journal that is relatively recent. We'll say more about how to know what journals are good later. Some journals publish mostly review papers, such as *Psychological Bulletin*, *Psychological Review*, and *Review of General Psychology*. Likewise, the book series *Annual Review of Psychology* publishes lengthy reviews on some topics, and journals like *Psychonomic Bulletin and Review* publish some long reviews. If you can't find a review there, maybe you can find a book chapter that reviews a particular topic. Failing that, most papers contain a brief literature review in their introduction, and they will often cite a review or theory paper.

Each paper has an abstract listed in its record. An abstract is a short summary, usually no more than 150 words, of what the paper is about. Pick a few that are interesting and go retrieve the article. How do you retrieve it? If you're lucky, your library has a button on the record that says something like "retrieve this article electronically"; you can get it just by clicking the button. Sometimes, though, you have to write down the journal name, year, volume, and page number and find the journal in the library. Searching for a specific journal usually involves looking in your library catalog and searching by journal title. Occasionally, there is a separate database of journals. Once you find the journal, if you're lucky, it's available online and you can download the file. If the journal isn't available online, you may have to write down a call number and trek to the library. If you have trouble, a good place to go is to your library's reference librarians. They're the experts on working with databases, and they love to help.

GOING FORWARD AND BACKWARDS IN TIME: CITED REFERENCE SEARCHES

Once you've found a few articles on a topic, it's easier to find more. You can find out who the author of the paper cited and look up the papers from the reference lists that seem most related. This will take you backwards in time to earlier papers. Or you can go forward in time to newer papers by finding out who has been citing this paper. Chances are good that some of the papers that cite the one in your hands are on a related topic.

To go forward in time, you can use the Social Science Citation Index (SSCI), which is another database, to find papers that cited the coolest papers that you read on a topic. The SSCI will let you enter an author's name using a strange format and find all the papers by that person. For example, if you want to know which desperate souls have cited the second author of this book, you would search for *DELANEY PF* with SSCI. It'll come back with a list of papers by him, sorted by year of publication and journal. The journal names are all abbreviated, so they can be hard to figure out. However, within SSCI, you can find the list of journals and figure out which abbreviation goes with which journal. Or you can try to guess and hope for the best.

FREE BUT FLAWED: WEB-BASED TOOLS

Students like free stuff, and so do we. As of this writing, all the tools on http://www.google.com are free to use and are supported by advertising. Everyone knows about Google's Web search engine. It's a fine tool, but it isn't the best way to search the psychological literature. For example, searching for *working memory and attention* yields some strange sites about brain fitness that seem to be selling something—not a likely choice for scholarly thoughts. The Google search engine may uncover unpublished papers that authors have put on their own Web sites, but you're likely to miss more than you find. Other Web search engines have the same issues. They weren't built to index scientific papers; they were built to find what's popular on the Web.

Another free online tool is Google Scholar, which tries to do some of the same things as SSCI and some of the same things as PsycINFO. You can search published papers by keyword to search for a particular topic. You can also find out who cites those articles and access the records related to that. If you're lucky, it may link to the full text of the article you want. An advantage of Google Scholar is that it's free. Unlike PsycINFO, it indexes journal articles from fields other than psychology, so if you are curious whether people in economics are citing a certain paper, you can find out. On the downside, it's far from a complete index of all of the journal articles that have been published. PsycINFO has broader and better coverage of papers published within psychology.

What's the Best Article to Read?

Having established that some articles are better than others, it's good to know which journals are the best in a given area of psychology. In general, better papers get published in better journals, so picking the articles in top journals is a good way to go. But how do you know which journals are good? One way is to ask your mentor, graduate students, or other knowledgeable people about what journals are good and what journals are not so good. Or you can look at the journals published by the major scientific societies—such as the American Psychological Association and the Association for Psychological Science—because their journals are always reputable. But these methods aren't going to find *every* good journal, and they won't work if you are interested in something other than what your mentor studies. You might want to know which journals are good in some obscure area. For example, your parents might have medical issues, and you might want to know which journals are good for endocrinology so that you can read up on a problem they're having.

To find out what journals are good in any area of science, you can visit another database that's probably available through your library—the ISI Web of Science, published by Thomson Scientific. The Web of Science contains a feature called the Journal Citation Reports that will let you specify an area of research and find out which journals are good for that area. When you access Web of Science, you'll see a pull-down menu at the top of the screen. Use it to select "Journal Citation Reports" and "Social Science Edition." You can use the Web of Science to list all the journals in a subject category, or you can search for a particular journal by name. In either case, you'll see several statistics for each journal. The statistic you want is the *impact factor*, which roughly estimates how many times in a year the papers from that journal are cited by other published papers; more is better. A good rule of thumb for experimental psychology journals (other than neuroscience journals) is that an impact rating of 2 or higher is a top journal. An impact rating lower than 1 is probably read by hardly anyone. Just because a paper is published in *The Southeastern Belgian Transactions on Edutainment*, though, doesn't mean it must be a bad paper. Strong papers sometimes wind up in weak journals, but a good rule of thumb is to start with the best journals and work your way down.

EXTRACTION OF INFORMATION WITHOUT TORTURE: HOW TO READ AN ARTICLE

It is widely rumored that in some not-so-savory countries, hapless prisoners are forced to read journal articles. Once you open your first journal, you'll quickly discover why—these papers are hard to read. It can feel like torture. These are not the light, breezy textbooks that were written for you by professors who actually care if the readers understand them. Journal articles are typically written in a dry, confusing, and awkward style. They are also often loaded with bizarre terminology and arcane statistics. Fortunately for us, journal articles that report experiments are also formulaic. Like a romance novel, they follow a standard formula. Once you know that formula, you can extract the information you need with the minimum pain.

Students usually assume that to read an article they should start with the first page and just plow ahead until the end is reached. In contrast, we usually skip right to the end of the introduction—to the part right before the Method. The paragraph or two before the method explains what the authors were trying to find out and how they went about studying it. Try it—pick up a journal article and read that paragraph. You'll know what the paper is about.

Once you know what the researchers wanted to test, write some notes on it for yourself and then jump to the end. The first few paragraphs of the General Discussion section tell you what the authors found, so it's a good part to read next. It tells you what the authors thought the most important parts of their work were. Again, jot some notes because otherwise you may forget. Next, dig into the results. You needn't read them right away, though. Look at the pictures and tables. The authors were so proud of these data that they put them in pretty boxes, free of encircling text. Look at the data to figure out what they found, and then try to understand what those data might mean. You can't get the whole picture of what the study found, but you can get a good idea of what the authors wanted you to learn.

This is a good place to pause and make a decision about reading the rest of the paper. Was it pointless? If so, get another article. If you might learn something, plunge in and read the whole thing, armed with the foreknowledge about what it is about. Admittedly even then, we sometimes only skim the methods. After all, we don't really care if the researchers showed words in a black 18-point sans-serif font using a J++ program for their PC. We just want to know enough about their method that we understand whether they did things right or not.

Wrapping Up

The world of knowledge beyond Wikipedia is vast—explore it. Meet your librarian, use databases like PsycINFO to find articles, and then keep finding new papers using the ones you found. Follow the literature backwards and forward in time, using still more databases. And if you have a lot of free time, you can even go update the Wikipedia page on your topic. After all, you have all of the sources already stacked at home.

7

Writing Research Papers

Scientific writing—like skateboarding, knitting, and the Heimlich maneuver—is harder than it looks. If you've read scientific articles for your classes, you may find this hard to believe. How can something so stuffy and humorless be difficult? Don't tedium and obscurantism come naturally to professors? We understand if you're skeptical, but we know that you'll agree with us the first time you must write a research proposal, research paper, capstone project, or honors thesis.

Scientific writing is not like your everyday writing. First of all, you must write in English, not in a chain of abbreviations and emoticons. We see punctuation and uppercase letters in your future. Second, you must adhere to the style of the American Psychological Association (APA), known as APA style. If you like slavish adherence to rules, you'll like APA style. And third, people reading your scientific paper will judge your intelligence and sophistication on the basis of the quality of your writing. The pressure is on.

In this chapter, we'll describe how to write a solid research paper, one that will impress your professors and research advisors. Our advice is based on two assumptions about you. First, you are probably not a good writer. You may be huffing and sputtering in anger—if you own *The Gay Talese Reader*, we apologize—but we don't intend to be mean. After all, you probably haven't had good training in writing. Do you feel like you got much out of freshman composition, apart from contempt for the MLA and Chicago styles? Have your psychology classes prepared you for scientific writing? Second, you probably have no experience with scientific, psychological writing. Unless you have had an unusually good undergrad course on writing, you need to learn the grim fundamentals.

WHY DO PSYCHOLOGISTS WRITE RESEARCH ARTICLES?

Why write articles at all? Scientific writing is hard and unpleasant—why go through the trouble? Why not publish your research on your blog? The answer is simple. Imagine you're an intern for a lawmaker, and your task is to find scientific research about the effects of kindergarten enrichment programs on academic success. A quick PsycINFO search turns up a relevant review article published in *Psychological Bulletin*; a quick Web search turns up a long blog entry on the topic. Which would you prefer? You know that *Psychological Bulletin* asks experts to scrutinize each submission and requires authors to make changes based on the experts' comments, a process known as *peer review*. Only 30% of the submissions are accepted for publication, so the quality standards are high. And you know that anyone with an ax to grind can post a blog entry—blogs aren't peer-reviewed, edited, or fact-checked. Which paper would you summarize for your boss?

Scientific articles are routinely cited and discussed in government documents, judicial opinions, public policy statements, friend-of-the-court briefs, and books and articles aimed at the general public. People who care about accuracy will ignore work that isn't peer-reviewed and published in a respectable scientific journal. People who go outside the traditional publication venues are dismissed as quacks—if their work was any good, they wouldn't have to self-publish it. If you want evidence, search PsycINFO for the keywords *urine, drinking, cure,* and *cancer;* then search the Web. Where do you think you'll find essays that claim that drinking your urine can cure cancer? Which would you trust when deciding whether to whip up a frothy, golden brew?

APA Style and the Researchers Who Love It

You probably have traumatic memories of "writing styles"—such as MLA, Chicago, Harvard, and Turabian (whatever that is)—from your freshman composition courses. In psychology, we write according to APA style. APA style is an editorial style: It describes how to organize a paper and how to format your headings, references, and statistics. The bible of APA style is the *Publication Manual of the American Psychological Association* (APA, 2001); apocryphal guides are published by other publishers. There are some good books about APA style, but the *Publication Manual* is the authority. Our little book doesn't have room to review APA style—you'll need the *Publication Manual* for that. Does your shelf of professional books have room for a copy?

At first, many students resist APA style—they feel that their writing is hijacked by arbitrary rules about citations, headings, and tables. But eventually you'll develop the scientific version of Stockholm syndrome: You'll come to adore your captors. Researchers, like teenagers, secretly crave rules and structure. The three of us, your valiant authors, love APA style; we spit in the general direction of MLA and its cursed footnotes. If you don't secretly crave structure, preferring instead a willy-nilly farrago of styles, then you'll need to accept your lot in life. APA style is a fact of life in psychology, so you need to learn it. And before long, you'll be entering numbers into your cell phone in APA style.

CHOOSING SOURCES

Academic writing is mostly reading—finding sources relevant to the topic, reading and understanding them, and working them into your paper. You'll write your paper faster if you stick with good sources. Bad sources will waste your time, add little to your paper, or mislead you.

Good Sources

What makes a source good? As we explained earlier, good sources are *peer-reviewed:* Experts evaluate the paper prior to publication, so obvious mistakes and misrepresentations are caught. Nearly all scientific journals in psychology are peer-reviewed. Good sources are also *accessible:* Readers ought to be able to find the source and read it for themselves. If a source is arcane and obscure—like a pamphlet about binge drinking that your roommate made for her public health class—it isn't helpful to your readers. And good sources are *primary sources:* They advance an original idea, theory, experiment, or analysis instead of simply recounting what someone else did and said. The distinction between primary and secondary sources is sometimes mushy. If unsure, you can use the ease-of-processing heuristic: If an article is dry and hard to understand, it's probably a primary source.

Here's a breakdown of the good sources.

- *Peer-reviewed journal articles.* For your research paper, peer-reviewed journal articles are your major sources. Having read chapter 6, you already know how to track down and read journal articles. Most articles are *empirical articles*—they describe new research projects and present original data. Other articles are *review articles*—they present a new theory or a new point of view on past research. Empirical articles offer depth; review articles offer breadth. You'll need to connect your research to past research, so most of the sources in your reference list will be empirical articles.

- *Scholarly books*. Books are another good source: They review and integrate a big body of work. If you're new to an area, a good scholarly book will bring you up to speed on the state of a field. You'll find these books in your campus library, not in your local bookstore—scholarly books are written for specialists, not for a general audience. Books complement peer-reviewed journals; you can't use books as your only sources.
- *Edited books*. Edited books are collections of chapters written by different people. A good edited book will show you different points of view on the same area of psychology. The chapters in the edited book *Self and Identity* (Kashima, Foddy, & Platow, 2002), for example, were written by 11 groups of authors. People don't read edited books cover to cover; you could read only the handful of chapters that connect with your paper.
- *Handbooks*. Handbooks—a kind of edited book—are great resources. The editors of a handbook invite distinguished researchers to write chapters about an area of research. As a group, the chapters describe the major theories and findings in the area. And there's a handbook for everything. Writing a paper about emotional expressions? Look for the *Handbook of Emotions* (Lewis, Haviland-Jones, & Feldman Barrett, 2008) and the *Handbook of Affective Sciences* (Davidson, Scherer, & Goldsmith, 2003). Writing a paper about personality across cultures? Look for the *Handbook of Personality* (Pervin & John, 2001)

and the *Handbook of Cultural Psychology* (Kitayama & Cohen, 2007). Handbooks will give you good reviews and references to good primary sources.

Bad Sources

Here are the malfeasants and the miscreants: These sources range from merely unhelpful to gravely misleading.

■ *Nearly everything on the Internet.* Don't bother with online encyclopedias, blogs, newsgroups, and magazines. Few of these are peer-reviewed, fact-checked, archived, or even well-written. The experts in scientific psychology don't publish their research in online blogs and encyclopedias. Unless you are writing about the Internet—for example, online research methods or online communities—you won't find relevant and helpful sources online. There are exceptions, of course. The government publishes important documents online, and some important journals (such as *PsycCRITIQUES*, a book-review journal published by APA) are available only online. But these exceptions prove the rule—they are professional publications posted by established institutions. It's no surprise, then, that online sources are uncommon in research papers. Grab an issue of any psychology journal and see how many online sources appear in the lists of references: At most, you'll find two or three per issue. Citing Web sites pegs you as a beginner, so avoid them.

- *Textbooks.* Textbooks distill grey research articles into a cheery, colorful books. Textbooks are easy to read, and they're a good way to learn. But they're unhelpful sources for your research paper—textbooks are one or two steps removed from the primary sources. They omit key details, and they're wrong more often than you may expect. But textbooks can point you toward good primary sources: A quick way to find relevant articles is to look at the journal articles and scholarly books that a textbook cites.

- *Newspapers and magazines.* Newspapers and magazines provide current and interesting articles, but they're several steps removed from primary sources. The good ones are fact-checked, so they're unlikely to mislead you, but you should go straight to the source. If a newspaper article cites statistics from a Department of Justice report, you should use the Department of Justice report as your source, not the newspaper.

- *Ephemera.* Librarians refer to random stuff that doesn't get archived, cataloged, or preserved as *ephemera*. Ephemeral writing—pamphlets, internal memos, working papers, conference handouts, and newsletters—vanishes immediately into the ether, so you'll rarely find a use for it.

SECTIONS OF A PAPER

The dark hour is nigh: You have marked up your sources and thumbed through your *Publication Manual*, and now you must write. Research papers are made up of different

EXHIBIT 7.1. The Sections of an Article

Title Page
Abstract
Introduction
Method
Results
Discussion
References
Appendix (optional)
Author note
Footnotes (optional)
Tables (optional)
Figure captions (include only if you have figures)
Figures (optional)

sections: Exhibit 7.1 lists the sections of an article in the correct order. You'll need the *Publication Manual* to learn the dirty details of formatting, layout, and headings—there's a reason why entire books are devoted to APA style—but these tips will push you in the right direction. For the specifics, let the *Publication Manual* be your trusty sherpa.

Introduction

The introduction to your paper is often the hardest part to write. People sometimes call the introduction a *lit review*—short for *literature*, not *litotes* or *liturgical*—but that's inapt. The point of an introduction is to introduce your hypothesis and to make a case for its merit and plausibility—in short, it answers the following questions: (a) Is this idea crazy, and (b) why should we care? Experienced writers talk about *motivating an idea*, an apt phrase. You can motivate your big idea by illustrating why it is interesting, important, and relevant to the science and practice of psychology. There must be some good reason why the idea struck you as valuable. If your idea's only motivation is that "it hasn't been done before," then you're in trouble.

If you can't explain why your topic is interesting and important, then it probably isn't. People often do research projects without a strong motivating purpose. For example, researchers often put more thought into their methods than their hypotheses, particularly researchers in areas known for methodological cleverness. (This is code for "experimental social psychology"; Ring, 1967.) Many ideas are intriguing but unimportant: They seem flashy and shiny, but they don't connect to any of psychology's enduring concerns. And other ideas are merely new. When researchers motivate an idea by saying, "No one has done this before," we should be wary. There may be good reasons why no one has done it before—ridiculousness and triviality are two that come to mind. Find the good reason—the psychological, scholarly, scientific reason—why you conducted your research.

Ideas become interesting, important, and relevant when they are connected to what psychology already knows and cares about. To motivate your idea, you'll need to describe the background of past research, which establishes the scientific context for your work. But you shouldn't review past work for its own sake. When students review merely to review, their introductions become tedious lists of past experiments. Stay focused on what you're proposing, and stick to the literature—both supportive and contrary—that relates to your work. By the end of the introduction, readers should know the general topic of your research, the important studies in the area, your predictions, and the reasons why your predictions are sensible.

Method

What did you do? Your introduction proposed and motivated a research question; your method section describes how you examined your question. A method section ought to include enough detail for another researcher to evaluate what you did, warts and all. Who participated, and how did they end up in the study? Did you manipulate any variables? If so, how did you do it, and why is the manipulation likely to be effective? What did you measure? You ought to connect your procedures, manipulations, and measures to past research. If other studies have used similar methods, say so, and cite those studies. Readers, like rabbits, fear new things: They'll have more confidence in your study if you based your work on the work of others. Don't introduce statistics here, except for simple descriptions of your sample. Save the numbers for the results section.

Results

The results section contains that part that students hate the most—the statistics. Here you will learn the joys of reporting statistics in APA style. This requires a fastidious eye and a *Publication Manual* next to your keyboard. The statistics that you report will depend on your research design, but a few tips will help everyone. First, take advantage of tables and figures. It's hard to describe means and standard deviations in a paragraph of text, but it's easy to put the numbers in a table or depict them in a bar chart. If you have a lot of correlations, it's easier for everyone if you turn the correlation matrix into a table. Present statistical tests—psychology's beloved *t* tests, analyses of variance, and correlation coefficients—in the text, but slough the descriptive statistics into tables.

And second, couch your results in terms of your hypotheses. A common mistake is to jump into the statistics. For example, beginning writers will start a paragraph with something like this:

> A *t* test showed that the two groups were significantly different, $t(37) = 3.01$, $p < .001$, so the hypothesis was supported.

The readers think "Huh? What hypothesis was that again? Which group was higher or lower?" Instead, bring it all back home:

> Did mood affect people's judgments of their quality of life? A *t* test was conducted to test our prediction that happy people, relative to sad people, would rate their quality of life as better. The quality-of-life ratings in the happy condition were significantly higher than the ratings in the sad condition, $t(37) = 3.01$, $p < .001$, so the prediction was supported. Table 1 displays the descriptive statistics.

This description unpacks the finding for the reader. It restates the hypothesis, reminds readers of the independent and dependent variables, clarifies the nature of the difference, and refers to the dirty details in a table.

Discussion

The final section of the text, the discussion, takes a big-picture view of your study. Your results section described your findings in a detailed, statistical way; your discussion should describe your findings in a general, conceptual way. What did you find? Was this was you expected? And what does it mean? What are the implications for other theories, for past research, or for practical applications? Where should future research go next? What future directions seem fruitless or inefficient?

If you are writing an honors thesis or a paper for a course, you could end your paper with a section about the limitations of your research. Published articles often omit limitations—if the research had grave problems, the journal would have rejected the paper—but your professors like to see you appraise the shortcomings of your research. Considering flaws in your research is a good educational exercise: It builds modesty and discernment. But some students go overboard with self-flagellation, turning minor molehills into austere mountains. Don't cut yourself off at the knees: Just mention some limitations. And when talking about your limitations, describe how future research could remedy them—your professor will be impressed.

References

Reference lists are boring to write and boring to read, but you don't want to make sloppy errors. A pristine reference list shows that you're obsessed with rules and hence a good candidate for graduate school. The *Publication Manual* explains how to format your references; any article in an APA journal will provide examples of reference formats, too. Some students worry that they have too many references—to professors, this is a charming fear. References are like yogurt-covered pretzels: You're only in danger if you have more than 100 of them.

The Inglorious End: Footnotes, Tables, Figures

Your manuscript concludes with the ignominious elements: footnotes, should you have any; tables of data; and figures. The *Publication Manual* provides examples of how to format these things. Avoid footnotes—one or two are fine—but embrace tables and figures. As we mentioned earlier, it's better to throw your numbers into a table than to report them in a paragraph, and a good bar chart or line graph can quickly describe what you found.

SOUND, PURPOSE, AND STYLE

All writing conveys a sense of the author's voice—your writing sounds like something, whether you like the sound or not. Beginning writers find it hard to control their sound: They can write only one way, usually a stuffy "I'm trying to sound smart" way. You can think of your sound as a spot on a spectrum. On one pole of the spectrum, we have the sound of Topanga Canyon hippies and wide-eyed high-school kids: "Leon Festinger was like, 'Cognitive dissonance is motivational, actually,' but Daryl Bem was like, 'Actually, it isn't.' And I'm like, 'Dude, who cares? Cognitive dissonance is so Eisenhower-era.'" On the other pole, we have the sound of maritime lawyers specializing in admiralty taxation: "To the extent that various individuals' beliefs reside in conflict, diverse drive-based motivated resolutions may seem feasible given a multitude of individual factors and, of course, their myriad interrelationships."

The first pole sounds too bubbly, like a conversation between perky semiliterates; the second pole sounds too technical, like an excerpt from the tax code. Different writing projects should use different sounds. This book, for example, is more Topanga Canyon than maritime law: It isn't a scholarly book, if you haven't noticed by now. In your research papers, strive for 35% Topanga Canyon and 65% maritime law. You want to sound like a real person writing for other people, like someone who cares about the topic and has something to say. But you also want to respect the complexity of past research, the subtlety of research methods and statistics, and the diversity of your audience. Striking this balance is hard: Most of your professors, for example, are a shocking 95% maritime—they need to kick up their Topanga.

Playing well with others is a big part of a good scientific sound. When judging and criticizing past work, try not to maul anybody. It isn't easy to be critical without sounding like a disgruntled, egocentric curmudgeon. For example, a common mistake in tone is to write something like: "I think this is a bad study. The sample size of 14 was way too small to justify the authors' conclusions, so it is fatally flawed." Your readers will agree with your claim, but they will think that your opinions are intruding into the paper ("I think this is a bad study") and that you're picking on the ignominious researchers ("so it is fatally flawed"). Make your point without descending into opinions and attacks. Try something like, "The results are intriguing, but the study's small sample ($N = 14$) raises questions about their reliability."

When faced with hard writing decisions, remember that the purpose of scientific writing is to tell people about your ideas and your research. It's closer to journalism than to creative writing: Your readers want the facts, and they want to be able to check your sources. What did you do? Why did you do it? Why is it important? You wrote the paper, but the paper isn't about you and your inspiring research journey. The paper shouldn't be about your opinions, beliefs, or feelings, but readers do want to know your findings, interpretations, evaluations, judgments, analyses, arguments, and conclusions.

Your first few research papers will sound stuffy; the next few won't be pretty, either. Sleek writing, like everything else, takes formal training (e.g., reading books about grammar and style), years of practice (e.g., writing every week for several years), and expert mentors (e.g., asking your professors and research advisors for feedback).

Because building this skill takes years, you should start investing time in your writing: Few psychologists write well, so you'll impress professors, employers, and grad schools if you can write with a warm, natural sound. To learn how to write well, buy some books, read them, write a lot, and get feedback. The Appendix lists a few books that made us feel ashamed of our own writing; they can do the same for you.

WRITING FOR PUBLICATION

There's something fake about the writing that you do for your classes: One person tells you to write about something, you write a paper about it, and then that one person reads and grades it. Class writing has a grader, not an audience. Only one person—usually a pale teaching assistant overwhelmed by students' grammar disasters—will read your class work. In the world of writing, then, your course writing is good for practice but for little else: It won't get published, and no one will read it. Oddly, the triviality of class writing means you should take it seriously: It's excellent practice, and you won't write well unless you practice.

The real deal, of course, is writing for publication. If a stranger publishes your work so other strangers can read it, then you're doing real writing. As an undergraduate, you could publish in two kinds of venues. The first option is to write for newsletters and magazines. Many psychology departments have a house-organ newsletter that talks about geeky news: interviews with new professors, book reviews, achievements of current and former students, nuggets of departmental history, and photos set against backdrops of faux-wood paneling. Editors of newsletters are a beleaguered bunch: It isn't a glamorous task, and it's usually hard to find submissions. You should contact the newsletter editor and ask if he or she is looking for content, such as essays, humor, or brief bits of news. Beyond your department, most organizations—such as regional psychology groups and divisions of APA— have a newsletter with an editor desperate for good writing. Psi Chi has a full-color magazine, *Eye on Psi Chi*, that publishes essays by professors, grad students, and undergrads. You can start your own newsletter, too, to describe and publicize what your Psi Chi chapter or psychology club is up to. You can publish humor, stories from recent conference trips, salacious gossip, and plugs for events hosted by your group.

The second option is to publish scientific research in peer-reviewed journals. It's uncommon for undergrads to publish research in important journals. It used to be freakish, however, so the times are changing. The process of publishing research takes a long time. You have to develop an idea, find a way to test it, clear your study through an institutional review board, run the thing, analyze the data, and write a paper about the sucker. In some areas of research, such as cognitive and social psychology, you need several experiments in your paper. In other areas, such as child development, the research stretches over years. Once the journal reviews and accepts your paper, it can take a year or 2 for it to appear in print. As a result, it's unlikely that any research you do as an undergraduate will appear in print before graduation day.

If you have a chance to get involved in working on a scientific paper, snatch it. You'll probably be one of many authors—many hands make light the data collection—but that's okay. The honor is in being involved at all, not in narcissistically clinging to a particular place in the order of authors. Determining authorship is a tricky business. Even a simple research paper could involve several professors, several graduate students, several honors students, and many research assistants. Who should be first author? Who should be last author? Does merely helping with data collection entitle someone to authorship? Should honors students always be first authors? The field has ethical guidelines for making decisions about authorship. In general, there's one golden rule: Researchers should talk about authorship as early as possible. Beyond that, we recommend (a) reading Fine and Kurdek's (1993) classic paper, which describes the dirty details of authorship, and (b) not freaking out over authorship details.

GETTING HELP

Once your paper is underway, you'll agree that scientific writing is harder than it looks, and you'll want some help. Published articles in your area are the best source for help: You can see how experienced authors handled the writing problems that you face. Use articles from the major journals in your area as role models: Those authors did something right if their paper appeared in a prestigious journal. Perhaps you're struggling with your method section—for example, you may be uncertain about how to describe the self-report scales that you used. How did other authors describe their scales? Perhaps you're unsure how long your discussion ought to be. How long are they in your model papers? How many references do your model papers have? How did the authors use headings? What information did they put in tables?

For more help, you can buy some books about academic writing. You're not the only one who finds writing hard: There are enough sufferers to support a big market of "self-help for scientists" books. Your professional library ought to have a couple of books about writing and publishing. In our Appendix, we list a few of the books about writing that will help. Some books address the kinds of papers that undergraduates write for their courses (e.g., Landrum, 2008; Sternberg, 2003); turn to these books if you struggle with basic problems. If your struggles are more complex, turn to the books written for professors (Silvia, 2007; Sternberg, 2000). Those books will explain the nitty-gritty details of writing and submitting an article to a professional journal. If you read them, you'll have the shiniest honors thesis on the block.

And, of course, your research advisor and professors can help. They've been around the academic-writing block a few times—it's a seedy block, so some of them have been mugged—and they can give you detailed, practical advice. The best way to learn writing is to get feedback from experts. Hand your advisor a hard copy of your paper and ask for comments. You'll wince when you get an ink-drenched draft back, but it builds character. If your school has graduate students, you can hit them up for tips and advice. Graduate students are used to working hard for meager pay, so you can thank them for their comments by buying them a cup of coffee, a bar of chocolate, or a toy for their ferret.

WRAPPING UP

Remember the innocent days of elementary school writing? Working on your first research paper will make you wistful for essays about what you did during the summer, for that sepia-toned era when *research* meant looking in an encyclopedia. Scientific writing isn't glamorous, but it will sharpen your thinking about psychology. "Writing is thinking on paper," wrote William Zinsser (1988, p. 11). Struggling through your introduction will help you understand the literature; writing a results section will help you understand statistics. And writing a professional, scholarly paper is a big step from business-as-usual classroom learning, where you read what other people have written about psychology. Before long, your *Publication Manual* will be dog-eared and grimy, and nothing says "I'm a serious student" like a crusty layer of fungus.

8

Attending Academic Conferences:
The Etiquette of Binge Thinking

Some stereotypes have a kernel of truth. Your professors are, by and large, a bunch of nerdy people who like to read books, dress casually, eat ethnic food, and listen to National Public Radio. Just imagine, then, what happens when large groups of college professors gather in one place to talk about psychology. These large, geeky gatherings are called *conferences*. Professors, graduate students, and undergraduates get together to learn about what's new in psychology, to share the latest gossip with old pals, and to eat at tasty ethnic restaurants. It's the most fun you can have while sitting quietly, listening politely, and drinking coffee.

Attending a conference is perhaps the best way to learn outside the classroom: You'll spend a few days with hundreds or thousands of other people interested in psychology, learning about the latest research. You can see research presentations by some of the field's most famous researchers, meet possible employers or graduate advisors, and gossip about your professors with psych majors at other colleges. Two or 3 days of a conference can fry a mere mortal's brain: Binge thinking can make you nauseated. You'll know that the conference was a success if you leave bleary-eyed and sleep deprived, threatening to throttle the next person who says "independent variable."

AN OVERVIEW OF BINGE THINKING

Why do people go to conferences? What can you expect to get out of going? Researchers attend conferences for a few reasons. First, the world of research moves quickly. It can take a couple of years for research to appear in print, so people go to conferences to hear about the latest findings. People give brief talks (usually 15 minutes) about their research and present posters that describe up-to-date findings. Second, conferences provide good opportunities for building professional skills. Most conferences have sessions devoted to topics like getting into graduate school, becoming a better writer, and finding jobs. And finally, conferences are a good reason to get out of town, stay in a hotel, and hang out with old friends.

As a student, you'll get a lot out of going to conferences. You can meet potential graduate advisors face-to-face, get the dirt on potential programs from current graduate students, and get good tips from workshops on graduate school. If you're working on research, you can present your findings at a conference and get feedback from people interested in your topic. And when you apply for graduate school or for real jobs, you will have shown that you can represent yourself as a professional and that you took the trouble to go beyond the minimum.

Students usually find their first conference to be eye-opening: There's something startling about seeing so many students and professors all in one spot. Psychology looks more human and personal. In your classes, you hear your professors talk about famous studies by famous psychologists. At the conference, you can see these psychologists talk about their past work and about what they're up to these days. If you're working on a research project, you'll probably meet other people who are researching the same area, including some of the people whose papers you talk about in your thesis. You'll run into some of the authors of your textbooks, whom you can accost with an accusing "Why? Why?" And you'll meet many psych majors at other colleges. More than anything else, the mass of well-dressed students reveals how tough the competition is for admission to graduate school.

CONFERENCE FACTS

Psychology has dozens of conferences each year; there are two ways to classify them. Some conferences are *geographical:* They're devoted to a part of the country, and they cover all areas of psychology. Other conferences are *topical:* They're devoted to a particular area of psychology, such as child development, clinical psychology, or social psychology, and all the talks and posters will relate to a topical conference's topic.

The biggest geographical conferences are the massive national meetings. Thousands of people will pour into town for the large national conferences, such as the annual conventions of the American Psychological Association and the Association for Psychological Science. Because they cover the full field of psychology, these meetings have something for everyone. Regional conferences, like the national conferences, cover the major areas of psychology. Exhibit 8.1 lists the major regional meetings. These meetings draw a lot of people, and they're popular conferences for undergraduates. The next size down are small local conferences, such as statewide meetings.

Topical conferences cover only one side of psychology; Exhibit 8.2 lists some big ones. Clinical psychologists, for example, flock to the annual convention of the Association for Behavioral and Cognitive Therapies; social psychologists go to the Society for Personality and Social Psychology's annual conference; development psychologists attend the Society for Research in

EXHIBIT 8.1. Regional Conferences and Their Acronyms

Eastern Psychological Association (EPA)
Midwestern Psychological Association (MPA)
New England Psychological Association (NEPA)
Rocky Mountain Psychological Association (RMPA)
Southeastern Psychological Association (SEPA)
Southwestern Psychological Association (SWPA)
Western Psychological Association (WPA)

EXHIBIT 8.2. Examples of Topical Conferences
and Their Acronyms

Cognitive Psychology: Psychonomic Society

Social and Personality Psychology: Society for Personality
and Social Psychology (SPSP)

Clinical Psychology: Association for Behavioral
and Cognitive Therapies (ABCT)

Developmental Psychology: Society for Research
in Child Development (SRCD)

Biological Psychology: Society for Psychophysiological
Research (SPR)

Psychology and the Law: American Psychology–Law
Society (AP-LS)

Emotion Psychology: International Society for Research
on Emotion (ISRE)

Child Development's biennial meeting; and cognitive psychologists hit the annual meeting of the Psychonomic Society. These meetings attract large crowds, and they focus on only their area of psychology. Some smaller topical meetings focus on special subareas of psychology. No topic in psychology is so obscure that it can't attract people to give talks and present posters. If you like the study of cognitive development, you can hit the annual meeting of the Jean Piaget Society. If you like social psychology, you can go to the annual meeting of the Society of Southeastern Social Psychologists, a small but valiant organization.

Conferences are typically held at a big hotel in a big city. At first this seems weird—who travels to hang around a hotel?—but it makes good sense. Most people will travel to the conference, so the city must have an airport. And most of the conference-goers need a place to sleep, and some of the conference talks start early in the morning. It's convenient to roll of out bed, curse the early hour, and stumble downstairs to the conference rooms to see a talk; it's also convenient to hop upstairs for a brief nap during the day. Huge conferences are held in convention centers, which are flanked by hotels and restaurants. Eating out is part of the fun of conferences, so prepare to gorge yourself silly.

WHAT DO PEOPLE DO AT CONFERENCES?

Listen to Talks

The bulk of a scientific conference is made up of talks. Researchers talk about what they've been up to, and the audience drinks coffee and asks questions. If you've ever had a professor castigate the class for sitting in the back of the classroom, you'll feel vindicated at a conference: Professors like to sit in the back, too. In general, you'll see two kinds of talks at a conference: long and short. Long talks—typically more than 45 minutes—are reserved for invited speakers. Conferences will invite famous researchers to give extended talks about their work; these talks attract the biggest crowds. Long talks are given by keynote speakers, the president of the society that hosts the conference, people who won awards, and miscellaneous famous researchers.

Most of the talks are short talks—typically 15 minutes. These talks are organized into clumps, called *sessions* or *symposia*. For example, a conference might clump six talks about depression into a 90-minute session called "New Directions in Depression Research." Each speaker will have 15 minutes to present a talk. Ideally, the speaker will use 12 minutes for the talk and 3 minutes for questions. But as you know from your classes, college professors typically yammer on and on, so sometimes they get cut off. It's funny to see. The short talks are typically given by professors and graduate students. Undergraduates don't often give talks at conferences, but it's becoming more common. We've seen some good talks by undergraduates at regional conferences in the past few years, so it isn't out of the question. If you're facing your first conference talk, chapter 10 will give you some good tips.

To make space for more talks, conferences have several sessions at once. You can pick which one interests you the most. At a regional conference, for example, there might be six sessions—Animal Learning, Social Cognition, Child Development, Clinical Assessment, Workplace Behaviors, and Memory—at the same time. The sessions may overlap with long invited talks, workshops, and poster sessions, too. There's a lot to see, so it helps to plan your day by marking which sessions strike your fancy. The programming can run from 8 a.m. to 6 p.m.—2 or 3 days of that will try your love of psychology, so take naps and coffee breaks.

Visit the Posters

Poster sessions are another format for presenting research. People write a summary of their research and tack it to a big easel. During a poster session, dozens of posters will be displayed in a big room. People stand next to their posters, and you can browse the posters and talk to people about their research. Posters are more interactive than talks: You can have good conversations about what people did and what they plan to do next. Posters are not for reading—don't stand quietly in front of someone's poster, read it, and then move on. The point of poster sessions is to chat. If a poster seems interesting, ask the person presenting it about what he or she did. Simply ask, "What is your study about?" or "What did you guys do?"

Most students cut their teeth at conference presentations by presenting posters, which are less stressful than talks. If there's a poster session in your future, chapter 9 will show you how to prepare and present a good poster.

Attend Workshops and Practical Talks

Not everything at a conference is devoted to research. Except for the tiny ones, most conferences have programming aimed at undergraduates, graduate students, and people seeking jobs. These practical talks are good ways to get advice and to build your skills. For example, it's common to have a session of talks about applying to graduate school. The group of presenters might include someone who recently started graduate school, the director of graduate studies at a local university, and a professor who works with a lot of graduate students. Other common themes are improving your writing, making the transition to graduate school, improving at research, and applying for grants and fellowships. Don't miss the programming aimed at undergraduates—you'll get good advice.

Check Out the Exhibitors and Buy Books

Most conference have *exhibitors*, which are companies that want to sell things to psychologists. Exhibitors pay the conference money so they can set up tables and show their wares. Book publishers like to sell their books at conferences, usually at a conference discount. Some companies plug their research and statistical software; others promote psychological tests. At larger conferences, you'll see employers seeking to hire psychologists. We once saw recruiters from the Central Intelligence Agency at the annual American Psychological Association convention, and we have the mysterious forearm implants to prove it.

The exhibit tables are a fun part of the conference. You can buy books for your professional library at a good discount, and sometimes you can scarf up free stuff, like pens and foam brains: Nothing impresses your friends back home like a foam brain. The exhibit tables are usually near the posters, so you can check out the tables while browsing through the posters.

Network and Hang Out

We've saved the best for last. Meeting people and hanging out is an important part—and probably the most fun part—of the conference experience. We don't mean networking in the slimy "I'm a business student who wants to be a corporate lawyer" way. You'll naturally meet people and make friends, and that's good. For networking, conferences are the place to get the dirt on graduate programs and to make a good impression on people who work there. If you see people whom you'd like to work with in graduate school, by all means go chat with them. If you see some graduate students from that school, ask them if they like it there. If you're working on a research project, you can get some good information from researchers in your area. If you see people who do research in your area, go ahead and ask them if they have some in-press or unpublished papers on the topic that they could e-mail you.

And then there's hanging out, for which you already have extensive training. Don't feel obligated to chat with the field's famous psychologists. That can be intimidating, and that's okay. If you're an undergraduate, it's good to become pals with other undergraduates—you'll be seeing them at that conference for years. You want friends in the same cohort because you'll go through the professional stages at the same time: You'll both apply to graduate programs, attend grad school, struggle with theses and dissertations, and hit the job market. You'll have a lot to talk about each year at the conference. People in your cohort can give you good advice and sympathetic ears, so don't feel guilty if you spend most of the conference hanging around the coffee shop and gossiping about your research advisor: Chalk it up to "building professional relationships."

CONFERENCE NORMS AND ETIQUETTE

You probably don't need much advice about how to behave. After all, you'll be surrounded by hundreds of well-dressed strangers: Sport jackets seem to activate the superego. But for those of us who need some behavior modification, here are some tips.

Attire

You ought to dress nicely: Think "business casual." This is your chance to wear that nice outfit that you never wear to class. You're attending a professional meeting attended by professionals, so you ought to dress and act like a professional. If you plan to go to graduate school, you'll run into a lot of potential graduate advisors at the conference. You don't want to look like a groupie for a slow-core emo-goth band, even if you are one. At the conference, you'll notice that level of education is negatively correlated with formality of attire. Under-graduate students and graduate students often are the most nicely dressed; some of the older male professors wear threadbare sport coats that could have a "Made in East Germany" label.

Conferences wrap up around 5 p.m., and part of the fun of conferences is getting together with a gang of people for food and festivities. Here's your chance to cut loose in a new city. Pack your attire for clubbing, but don't wear it at the conference. There's plenty of time to put on your purple leather vest and spiked wristbands; you don't have to wear them to the last poster session of the day. Once again, represent yourself as a professional.

Manners and Norms

You don't need advice about manners, but you might wonder about some of the norms. One important conference norm is how to ask questions at the research talks. If you have a question, by all means ask it, but wait until the end of the talk. As a rule, speakers will talk uninterrupted and then field questions at the end. And you'll notice, perhaps contrary to your expectations, that people rarely ask hostile, challenging questions at talks and posters. Picking on people is rude, even when they deserve it. If a talk or poster strikes you as lame, you should gossip about it with your friends afterward, not attack the speaker in public. The Golden Rule—I won't maul you in public if you don't maul me—is a good rule.

You might be shy about asking questions in front of a big audience. That's okay: Shyness is why we're psychologists and not real estate agents. After the talks are finished, the audience breaks up—searching for coffee and bathrooms—and the speakers mill around the front, chatting with people. You can ask the speaker your question after the talks. You will also probably see the speaker around the conference, so you can always ask later.

Conference Costs

So how much will the conference cost you? Your costs will come from (a) paying the registration fee; (b) traveling there and back; (c) finding a place to stay; and (d) paying for miscellaneous expenses, such as eating out, getting coffee, and buying books. Registration fees vary, but they're always cheaper for students than for professors. If the conference is within driving distance, you can save a lot of money by car-pooling with other students. If you must fly, be sure to book your tickets early. Hotel fees can be steep, but think of the conference as a nerdy summer camp: It's a tradition to split hotel bills by piling a bunch of people into one room. As for your miscellaneous fees, that's up to your own level of impulsivity and extravagance. The good news is that your college may have money to reimburse some of your costs—some colleges, psychology departments, and Psi Chi chapters have money for student travel, so ask your research advisor and poke around your college's Web site. Conferences are a good professional investment: You'll be glad you spent the time and money to attend.

Wrapping Up

Conferences are a great way to see psychology in action. Learning about research in a classroom or from a textbook is detached and impersonal, but learning about research at a conference is direct, face to face, and personal. You'll make friends in the field, network with professionals, and see the enormity of the field of psychology; you'll live the psychology lifestyle on a bigger geographic scale. And conferences are a lot of fun, which is why so many of them are held each year. If you see any of us, your valiant authors, at a conference, by all means say hi. You can tell us which parts of this book you detested the most—we won't be offended.

9

Presenting a Research Poster:
How to Overcome Optical Obscurantism

This chapter talks about research posters, and the word *research* should raise your mental red flags. One thing scientists do well is take fun things and make them dry, wordy, and full of math. The posters you'll see at conferences won't have pictures of boy bands, pastel landscapes by French impressionists, Dalmatians dressed as firefighters, or muscular men holding newborns. Instead, they will have graphs, charts, references, statistics, and well-dressed presenters explaining what the posters are about. If you prefer bar charts to firefighting dogs, then we see a poster presentation (and years of grad school bliss) in your future.

RESEARCH POSTER FUN FACTS

Posters are one of the most common ways of presenting research. Conferences are jammed with research talks, but there isn't enough time for everyone to give a talk. One purpose of poster sessions is to create more opportunities for people to present their research. Many people prefer presenting posters to giving talks: You'll chat with one or two people at a time, so you can talk with people instead of talking at them. As a student, your first conference presentation will probably be a poster. After cutting your teeth on a few posters, you'll be ready to give research talks.

Posters are collected into groups called *poster sessions*. A poster session is a block of time in which people tack up posters and stand next to them. People can browse through the posters and stop at the ones that intrigue them. At large conferences, there's almost always a poster session going on. Poster sessions can get loud, crowded, and chatty; they last from 1 to 2 hours, so wear comfortable shoes. The posters are tacked to big poster boards. The poster boards are around 4 feet tall and 6 feet wide, and they stand a few feet off the ground. (Small conferences sometimes use trifold boards, which give the poster session a retro science-fair look.) The session could have 50 to 100 posters; large conferences will have monster sessions with several hundred posters. Conferences usually provide the tacks, but grizzled poster veterans always carry their own tacks and tape.

WRITING YOUR POSTER

Your poster should be a snapshot of your research: what you did, why you did it, and what you found. Here are some tips for making your poster. For the time-impaired,

Exhibit 9.1 condenses our advice into a poster cheat sheet. (To avoid embarrassment, be sure to read the conference's poster guidelines before you make your poster—a few conferences require special sizes or formats.) We're sad to tell you that the old-school poster method that you learned as a child is dead. Set down your glitter; bury your glue stick. Don't make a poster made of construction paper, cut-outs, stencils, and wavy borders: You're a student, but you're not an amateur. Presenting a glue-stick poster would be like presenting a baking soda and vinegar volcano.

Huge Sheet or Small Sheets?

For your first poster decision, you must confront a grave and controversial issue: huge sheet or small sheets? You can print a poster as one huge sheet, such as a 24-inch × 36-inch poster or a 36-inch × 48-inch poster. Or you can make a set of 8.5-inch × 11-inch sheets and tack

EXHIBIT 9.1. A Poster Cheat Sheet

Use sans-serif fonts and make your text big.

Have a huge title.

Remember to list your affiliation.

Include each element of a journal article, including references.

When possible, use figures, graphs, and pictures.

Include your e-mail address.

Make a handout that has the poster's basics and your e-mail address.

Practice your pitch.

Don't just stand there—talk with people.

---

them to the poster board. In the old days, when psychologists rode saber-toothed tigers to the conference, small sheets were the only option. Today, you can choose which method you prefer. Huge sheets are more common at conferences, though, so they're worth the trouble to make. You can make huge posters in PowerPoint. Create a single slide, and then adjust the slide's size to the size of your poster, such as 36 inches × 48 inches. To make the poster, add text boxes, images, and graphs to the slide. You can make small-sheet posters in PowerPoint, too. Just make slides, perhaps 8 to 12, that describe what you did.

Huge posters are nice, but they have some disadvantages. Printing a big poster can cost a lot of money, particularly if your poster is in color. It is heartbreaking to make a poster, fork out the cash to print it, and then discover a disastrous error. You will also need to transport your poster in a poster tube, which you will lug to the airport, carry aboard the plane, and take to the hotel. Small-sheet posters are not as fancy, but you can print them yourself and carry them in a file folder. If you opt for a big poster, see if your college runs an on-campus copy shop, which will be cheaper (sometimes 10 times cheaper) than off-campus shops.

Flashy or Standard?

Your second decision is between a flashy poster versus a standard poster. This is the poster version of the eternal dialectic of innovation versus tradition, change versus stability, skeleton T-shirt versus navy-blue blazer. As a college student, you're probably inclined toward flashy posters—they try to grab the audience by using interesting colors, clip art, logos, images, and sizes. We like flashy posters, too, but they take a lot of time to make. Standard posters are like the base model of car—they lack a sunroof and power windows, but they'll get you where you want to go. Standard posters take less time to make, and they're unlikely to alienate the stodgier conference attendees. We have no strong feelings about this decision, but it's probably wise to start with normal posters and work up to weird posters. During your first poster session, you don't want to learn that what struck you as cool and edgy strikes your audience as trivial and juvenile.

Fonts and Layout

Your poster should look nice. First, if you plan to print your poster in color, you can take advantage of PowerPoint slide templates. Pick something cool but understated—don't let your colors and designs overwhelm your text and pictures. If you use colors, pay attention to the contrast between the text and the background. Choose light letters on a dark background or dark letters on a light background; for the sake of the many color-blind men, avoid contrasting red and green. We're sure that apple green and burgundy are a great combination, but use them when painting your bathroom, not when making your poster.

Second, go visual. Take every opportunity to express something with a figure or graph instead of a table or text. Instead of making a table that shows the means for your 2×2 design, make a bar chart that displays the means. Instead of writing about the correlations, make a correlation matrix and present scatterplots for the most important correlations. If you showed pictures to your participants, put some sample pictures on the poster. If your research involved unusual equipment—response pads, animal mazes, or child-sized shock machines—take a picture of the equipment and put it on your poster.

And third, choose a sans-serif font and make your words big. Few people appreciate the difference between serif fonts (e.g., Times New Roman, Garamond, Palatino, Minion) and sans-serif fonts (e.g., Arial, Verdana, Myriad). Serif fonts are good for small type, like the size for newspapers and books, but they look awkward and chunky when shown at huge sizes. Your poster will have big letters, ranging from 20 points up to 300 points, so you should choose sans-serif fonts. Your title should be easy to read from 15 feet away, and your text should be easy to read from 5 feet away, so don't be skimpy with the font sizes.

Title

Your poster needs a cool title. A common mistake is to pick a technical, long, detailed title. Such a title will accurately describe what your poster is about, but that isn't the purpose of the title. At a poster session, people browse through the rows of posters, glancing at the titles and stopping at the posters that catch their fancy. You need a title that—literally at a glance—captures the core of the poster. You can trim titles by chopping wordy phrases like *the effects of*, *the influence of*, and *the inter-relationships between*. Think of major keywords—*memory, depression, attitudes, parenting, learning, happiness*—and assemble them into a good title. And make the title monstrous—it should have the biggest point size in the poster.

Authors and Affiliation

Below the title, put the names of the author or authors. The order of authorship is something that you determine with your research advisor and your collaborators. By convention, the person standing in front of the poster is the first author—standing on your feet for 90 minutes has its rewards—but this isn't a firm rule. The authors' names should be big, but not as big as the title. Below the names, put the authors' affiliations. Your affiliation is your college. If all the authors have the same affiliation, just write it once. If you're into ornamentation, you can put your university's logo on the poster.

Introduction

The introduction to a poster, like the introduction to journal article, sets the stage for the research. What is the study about? What problem, question, or controversy motivated the research? What are your predictions? An introduction shouldn't be too long—wordiness is the curse of a poster—so boil down your introduction to its most important elements. Some people use bulleted lists for their posters. We don't have strong feelings about paragraphs versus bullet points—although bulleted lists have an unsavory "I used to major in business" flavor—but bullets are worthwhile if they force you to keep things spare and simple.

Method

The Method section describes how you tested your hypotheses. What did you do? Who participated? What constructs did you measure, and how did you measure them? Your Method section deserves some detail; viewers will be interested in the nuts and bolts of the research.

Results

What did you find? In your Results section, you describe the outcomes of your study. You needn't include exhaustive statistical detail. Aim for pictures: Can you show your findings with a bar chart or a line chart? Could you depict a correlation with a scatterplot? Use graphs and figures whenever possible, even for simple findings. Someone standing in front of a poster would rather see a bar chart with two bars than text describing two means. If you want to report a lot of numbers—such as descriptive statistics about the sample, or all the effects in a complex study—you can put the numbers in a table. It's easier to extract numbers from a well-made table than from a paragraph of text that describes the numbers. And because you have a copy of the *Publication Manual* in your professional library—that was a hint, we think—you can consult it for guidance on figures and tables.

Discussion

The Discussion section notes important implications of the research. Keep it short: Just hit the few major ideas and findings. After all, you're standing right there, ready and willing to discuss the research.

References

Posters needn't have many references. A poster isn't a manuscript: You aren't publishing the poster for eternity. But a few readers might be curious to know the reference for one of your citations, so include a reference for every paper that you cite. If you're out of room, you can put the references in a smaller font size.

The Handout

When your poster is done, you need to make a handout. People like to have something they can take with them. If you're making a huge-sheet poster, the easiest way to make a handout is to print the poster on normal paper. If your poster used appropriately big letters, the handout will be legible. If you're making a small-sheet poster, you can print several slides on a single page; all the slides ought to fit on one sheet, front and back. People will read your handout during their idle moments, so be sure that your handout is clear and legible. Bring around 20 handouts to the conference. Most of the people who stop by to talk about your poster will want one, and if you have to duck away to the bathroom, you can tack some handouts to the poster board.

PRESENTING YOUR POSTER

The point of presenting a poster is to talk to people. Don't let people stand there and read your poster. Consider this the Poster Paradox: Even though you made a readable poster, you shouldn't let people read it. When people stop at your poster, engage them in conversation. Say, "Would you like to hear about our study?" or "Hi, want some details?" No one will say, "No, thanks. I'd rather awkwardly stand here while you awkwardly stand there, spending 5 minutes reading something that you could describe in 30 seconds." Instead, people will say "Sure, what did you do?"

You might wonder why we're telling you to talk to people. After all, it's obvious that the purpose of presenting a poster is to talk to people about your research. But when you attend your first poster session, you'll see a few people standing silently by their poster while other people stand silently reading it. This is bad. We understand that some people are shy, and awkward moments can happen why a shy presenter and a shy reader collide. But it's more painful to stand stiffly than to say, "So, want to hear about what we did?" And some people think that they're rudely interrupting someone if they say,

"Want to hear about the study?" while the person is reading. To the contrary, people would rather talk with you than read your poster.

Once the conversation has started, deploy your secret weapon: the pitch. You should rehearse two overviews of your poster. One overview should be short and sweet. Can you capture the gist of your poster in three sentences and 15 seconds? Break out this pitch when the person seems pressed for time. The second overview should be longer, capturing the major elements of your poster. This pitch should be around a minute. To develop this pitch, include a bit of information from each part of your poster. Try to answer the questions, "What did I do, why did I do it, and what did I find?" While giving the pitch, you can point to your graphs and figures. People will probably interrupt you, and that's okay—the point of the pitch is to get the conversation rolling.

People will ask you questions at your poster, but they aren't out to stump you, pick on you, or antagonize you. You won't find malfeasants prowling the posters and looking for trouble. As we point out in chapter 8, conference norms encourage playing nice. There are a few questions that come up a lot: You ought to have some answers for them. Expect questions like "What would you do differently?" and "What do you plan to do next?" Those are good questions: You ought to prepare some answers. You may get asked, "So are you thinking about grad school?" or "Is this the kind of thing you're looking to study in grad school?" These are good questions— they're about you and your professional interests. You ought to have good (and honest) answers. Conversations at your poster may drift away from the poster and toward hanging out. That's fine, too: You went to the conference to meet people and make friends.

VIEWING OTHER PEOPLE'S POSTERS

You'll probably hit a few dead spots—periods in which no one is visiting your poster—during the session. A few dead spots are good: You'll need time to catch your breath and sip some coffee. A lull in visitors is an opportunity to meet some people and to talk about research. If no one is at your poster, take the free time to chat with your neighbors. It's more fun to talk than to stand around by yourself. If you're shy, just ask them about their posters: Say, "So, what's your study about?" (You can secretly compare your pitch to their pitches and perhaps pick up some tips.) Ask them about their college, what they want to do for grad school, what they've seen at the conference, or whether they like ferrets. You might find that you have a lot to talk about.

WRAPPING UP

Poster sessions are a venerable method of presenting research—everyone ought to present a poster sometime. They're an informal way of talking about your work and meeting people with similar interests. Presenting a poster isn't rocket science: You can do a great job even on your first poster, so don't worry if you're a newbie. Put some time into writing the poster, get feedback from your advisor, and practice your pitch. With some preparation, you'll be the poster equivalent of a Communist-era Romanian gymnast: People will fear your poster prowess.

To build professional skills, you need to get out of the classroom. Presenting a research poster is about as far from the classroom as you can get. You traveled out of town and taught some strangers—some of whom were professors and graduate students—about a research project. The transformation from student to professional is nearly complete.

10

Presenting a Research Talk:
How to Survive Your 12 Minutes of Fame

We've heard that surveys have found that people fear public speaking more than dying. We doubt it—the surveys probably omitted dreaded events like "banned from owning a cell phone," "attacked by chinstrap penguins," or "forced to reside in central Canada"— but the basic point is true: Most people avoid public speaking. Only the extraverted and the marketing majors enjoy it; for the rest of us, an upcoming speech evokes anxiety and a trip to the pharmacist. But you need to get over it. If you go to grad school, you'll give presentations in class, present research at conferences, give guest lectures, and teach undergraduate courses. If you want to work after college, most of the jobs you'll want will require public speaking. It's better to build skills now than to overcome your fears on the job.

Pubic speaking is a big part of psychological research. If you want people to hear about your work, you need to tell them about it. When you're at a conference, you'll see a lot of dry, stilted research talks. Each talk follows the same format and has the same time limit. This chapter teaches you how to give one of these talks. We'll teach you the nuts and bolts of writing, practicing, and presenting your research talk—learning the dry, stilted part is up to you.

THE 15-MINUTE CONFERENCE TALK

Most talks at psychology conferences follow the same format. This isn't merely because psychologists are a bunch of conforming sheep—we are, of course—but because a standard format makes it easier for people to prepare their talk. The speaker knows what is expected, and the audience knows what to expect. In the standard talk, a speaker has 15 minutes to describe his or her research. Ideally, the talk takes 12 minutes and leaves 3 minutes for the audience's questions. If 12 minutes sounds long, we can assure you that it's shorter than you think. The 15-minute talks are grouped into a session of talks on a related topic. A 90-minute session devoted to "New Research in Social Development," for example, may have six 15-minutes talks in a row. Because one talk follows another, it is disastrous when one speaker takes too much time. If one person goes over the limit, the other speakers must trim their talks to keep things on schedule. Going too long is thus a cardinal sin of conferences, alongside defacing a poster, mauling people with mean-spirited questions, and pickpocketing someone's jacket flask.

Let's take a brief interlude to beat a point into the ground: Don't talk too long. No one ever criticized a talk for being the proper length. If you have 15 minutes, don't use more than 15 minutes. You'll see speakers yammering on and on, but that doesn't make it okay. The audience gets restless, the moderator gets agitated, and the other speakers get angry because the garrulous speaker cut into their time. Going over your time limit is more mortifying than the audience learning that you hid your good-luck ferret in your jacket during the talk. If you do nothing else right, keep the talk under 15 minutes. Once more, with feeling: Don't talk too long.

Each session has a moderator, a person who introduces the speakers, helps them set up their slides, ensures that the equipment works, and keeps track of the time. The speakers show up early so they can load their slides onto the computer. Each person then presents his or her talk, according to the order shown in the conference program. The moderator sits in the front and times each talk. Most moderators hold up small signs to the speaker that say things like "5 Minutes Left," "2 Minutes Left," and "The End." If there is time for questions, the moderator will invite a couple of questions and then introduce the next speaker. After the session, a few people may ask you some questions about your talk.

WRITING YOUR TALK

Some Nuts and Bolts

Some students just need to be different, and they do so by avoiding The Man's software and using arcane weirdware that they found in some dusty corner of the Internet. If you prefer Joe's Slideshows to Microsoft PowerPoint, good for you. But your talk will be presented on a stranger's computer, probably a laptop PC that runs Windows. That machine will have PowerPoint, but it probably won't have anything else, so you ought to use PowerPoint for your slides. For the same reason, use normal fonts that other computers will have. Stick with the basic Windows sans-serif fonts (e.g., Arial, Helvetica, Verdana), unless you enjoy presenting slides of ASCII characters to an audience of strangers. Get your wool on and join the flock: This is a psychology conference, after all.

Slide Design

If you have read our advice for making posters in chapter 9, you know what we're going to say: Keep your slides simple. The slides needn't have enough information to stand alone; this isn't a manuscript that people will read. The slides help people understand what you're saying—they support your talk, not the other way around. You are the main attraction. Sparse, open slides are better than cramped, packed slides. Bulleted lists are better than complete sentences of text; both are better than paragraphs, which are an abomination against all that is crisp and concise. As with posters, you should use sans-serif fonts at a large point size. People sitting in the back of the room ought to be able to read the smallest text on your slides.

To make cool slides, you can use PowerPoint's design templates. If you don't like the templates, you can go old-school: black text on a white background. There's nothing wrong with black and white: It's simple, high-contrast, and easy to read. Don't be seduced by complex animations or startling slide transitions. They seem like a good idea when you're alone in your room, tinkering with your slides, but they look foolish at the conference. Stick with the simple animations and transitions. Psychology isn't a flashy science, and psychologists aren't flashy people. Save the high-octane slide shows for your talks at interior architecture conferences.

For this chapter, we developed an example of a research talk (see Figure 10.1). The data are fictional—and the hypothesis is ridiculous—but the format and layout are respectable. To show that there is no shame in black and white slides, our slides use black text on a white background. And to make a case for sparseness, we made open, empty slides. These are the barest slides you'll see, so feel free to be more detailed in your presentation. We used Verdana, a sans-serif font that computers running Windows will have. Our presentation has six slides for a 12-minute talk—that gives us 2 minutes per slide. For your slide show, give yourself at least a minute per slide.

The First Slide

The slide show starts with the first slide, which is often on the screen while your talk is introduced. The first

FIGURE 10.1. Slide show.

Does Caffeine Reduce Public
Speaking Anxiety?

Paul Silvia, Peter Delaney,
& Stuart Marcovitch

Department of Psychology
University of North Carolina at Greensboro

Midwestern Psychological Association, 2009
p_silvia@uncg.edu

Public Speaking Anxiety

- Most common phobia (Sturm & Drang, 2007)

- Commonly treated with cognitive–
  behavioral methods
  - Exposure
  - Positive visualization
  - Systematic desensitization

- Practitioners would benefit from simple,
  easy to administer treatments

Caffeine & Public Speaking

- Caffeine may be a practical, effective tool
  for reducing public speaking anxiety

- Easily available (Starbucks, 2004)

- Calming; sedative effect on peripheral
  nervous system (Bogus, 1998)

- Today's study: Does caffeine reduce
  public speaking anxiety?

FIGURE 10.1. Slide show. *(continued)*

Method

- *N* = 80 college students

- IV: Caffeine (high vs. low)
  - Participants ingested 3 cappuccinos
    (high caffeine) or 3 peppermint teas
    (low caffeine)

- DV: Self-reported anxiety during an
  impromptu speech
  - Used a 1–7 scale

Results

- Caffeine increased self-reported anxiety
- $t(78) = 8.5$, $p < .001$

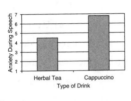

Conclusions

- Contrary to predictions, caffeine boosted
  feelings of anxiety

- Exposure (not coffee) is probably the
  best way to reduce public speaking
  anxiety (Silvia, Delaney, & Marcovitch, 2009)

137

slide from our fictional slide show has the title of the talk, the authors, the authors' institutions, the name of the conference, and the presenter's contact information. It's hard to make a mistake with your first slide, so don't obsess about it. During the talk, say your name and the name of the presentation, like, "Hi, I'm Paul Silvia, and today I'll be talking about whether caffeine reduces public-speaking anxiety." Then move to the introduction.

Introduction

Like the introduction to an article, the introduction to a research talk describes the context for your research. What is the study about? What background does the audience need to understand the research? Crafting a concise introduction is harder than it sounds, but try to keep it short. People can ask questions if they'd like more detail. Our introduction has two slides. Note that we used brief phrases and complete sentences. We cited research sparingly; to reduce clutter, we made the citations smaller. The first slide introduces the notion of public speaking anxiety. Here we would talk about how public speaking anxiety is the most common phobia and give a few statistics that we memorized. We would then briefly hit the major ways of treating it: exposure, positive visualization, and systematic desensitization. After describing these, we would point out that it would be nice to have a brief, inexpensive, and effective treatment.

We then move to the next slide, which introduces our research question. We would introduce our hypothesis—caffeine reduces anxiety—and describe theories and research that led us to our predictions. For this slide, we would point out that caffeine has a sedative effect on most people, so it ought to dampen anxious feelings. Because it is easily available, caffeine looks promising as a means of helping people who are about to give a speech.

Method

The Method section describes the participants and the research design. Strip the Method down to the basics. Who participated? What were the independent and dependent variables? How did you measure what you measured? What was the procedure? For our slide, we would briefly describe the sample of college students who volunteered to participate. We manipulated the amount of caffeine people ingested before giving a speech (our independent variable, or IV): People drank either cappuccino or herbal tea. After telling people that they would have to give a 10-minute speech to a small audience in the next room, we measured their self-reported feelings of anxiety (our dependent variable, or DV).

Results

For your results slides, present your most important findings. Your audience wants to know what you found, so slow down and spend some time on your results. As with posters, you want to present your findings visually. For our slide, we made a bar chart that shows the mean level of anxiety in each condition. Our fictional experiment has only two conditions; we could have simply listed the means on the slide, but visual depictions are more compelling. While speaking, you should unpack figures for your audience. The listeners appreciate it when the speaker orients them to a graph. For our simple figure, we would first point out that our x-axis shows the IV (amount of caffeine) and that the y-axis shows the DV (self-reported anxiety). We would then point out that anxiety was higher in the cappuccino condition than in the herbal tea condition, a significant finding that contradicted our predictions. For the curious, we also listed the outcome of a t test.

Discussion

The end is near—you're at the discussion section. Keep your discussion short. The audience has already heard about what you did and why you did it, so they don't need a summary of what you said 6 minutes ago. Instead, simply highlight the major findings and the major conclusions or implications. For our slide, we restated the experiment's result and pointed out a conclusion that we would draw from the experiment. Research talks don't have reference sections, so you needn't make a slide with the references for the studies that you cited. If an audience member cared to know a reference, he or she would ask you about it at the end of the session of talks.

Questions

After your discussion slide, it's time for questions. End your talk by saying something simple and gracious, such as "Thank you," or "Could I answer some questions?" People will clap and then ask questions. It's hard to predict what people will ask, but don't worry about getting pegged with evil questions—this isn't a cross-examination. Answer the questions politely and briefly; when the moderator gestures that it's time for the next talk, you can sit down, take a deep breath, and covertly give a treat to your good-luck ferret.

FEELING NERVOUS YET?

Public-speaking anxiety is no joke, particularly for the kinds of students who attend conferences. As a student, it's natural to feel nervous when presenting your research to a group of peers, grad students, and professors. How can you manage your anxiety? You probably had to take a communication class in college, in which you talked about effective public speaking. Most of the tips about managing anxiety that you got—positive visualization, positive self-talk—are fine, but only one thing really works. You probably don't want to hear this, but *exposure* is the most effective treatment for public speaking anxiety. If you fear giving talks, then the cure is to give talks—decades of effective behavior therapy has spoken. Over time, you will feel less nervous; eventually, you may enjoy public speaking.

So how can you gain exposure to public speaking? Typically, people avoid it. Avoidance feels better, but it prevents us from getting exposed to what we fear. Your best bet is to practice your conference talk in front of an audience. You can start with an audience of your Beanie Babies and teddy bears. Once you can survive their glassy-eyed stares, move to an audience of your friends. Have your pals, roommates, and relatives watch your talk. They may have little to say about the content, but that's okay—they're there for the exposure, not to grill you about your statistics. Give your talk to other students working in your research lab and to your research advisor. Practice will make you confident; exposure will make you calm.

Practice talks will yield feedback about your slides and your delivery. Are the slides too cramped? Are you speaking too quickly? When practicing your talk, be sure to time yourself. For a realistic conference experience, you can have a friend in the audience hold up time markers. Ask them to hold a up a "5 Minutes" sign at the 10-minute mark, a "2 minutes" sign at the 13-minute mark, and a "Stop Now, For the Love of Humanity!" sign at the 15-minute mark. Remember, the only things to fear are (a) fear itself and (b) going over the time limit.

Public-speaking gurus recommend that you video-tape yourself. This is good advice. Have a friend in the audience use her cell phone's video feature; after your talk, check it out. People are often startled at what they see. Taping yourself reveals all your quirks and peccadillos, like shifting your weight, looking above your audience, or facing the screen instead of the room. But the best thing about taping is that it shows you that you don't look as nervous as you feel. You will be surprised. Most people feel nervous but appear relatively calm. Anxiety tends to make you look formal and stilted, not quaking and stammering. Trust us—research on public speaking anxiety shows that people overestimate how anxious they appear (Rapee & Lim, 1992).

The only way to reduce your anxiety is to practice your talk in front of an audience. Other tricks that you'll hear can't hurt, but there's no substitute for dress rehearsals. If the thought of giving your talk in front of your pals or your research group makes you anxious, then imagine how you'll feel when you face a large room of strangers. Practice, practice, practice. As a small tip, we suggest not trying to memorize your talk, although memorizing your first two sentences isn't a bad idea. Memory is a frail creature, particularly when you're nervous. Develop some notes or use your slides as prompts. And don't make comments about your nervousness: Just get up there, do your best, sit down, and feel proud.

It helps to know that your audience isn't as scary, hostile, or attentive as you expect it to be. One of adulthood's sad truths is that people don't pay as much attention to us as we think. Yes, people are sitting there, watching your talk, but they aren't devoting 100% of their brains to it, and they aren't trying to tear it apart. Here, instead, are what people will probably think about your talk:

- Huh, that was a good talk.
- That person was an undergrad? Wow. I would have peed my pants if I had to give a talk as an undergraduate.

- I'm glad this person was more serious than the last speaker; that guy's stupid jokes were irritating.
- Blast it all, where's the coffee? I don't want to hurt someone, but I will if that's what it takes to get some caffeine in this cursed town.
- That grad student did a good job.

The last comment deserves a note: Unless you identify yourself as an undergraduate, your listeners will assume that you're a 1st-year graduate student. And why shatter their assumptions?

After your talk, do something nice for yourself. You'll feel some negative reinforcement—the end of your anxious feelings—but positive reinforcement is more fun. Go out for a massage, buy a nice lunch, or adopt a ferret from the animal shelter. Then do it all again at another conference. Exposure is the only cure for public-speaking anxiety, so it will take a few presentations to work the willies out of your system. Conference talks, like everything else, become easier with practice and experience.

PRESENTING YOUR TALK

Early in the conference, scout the room where you will give your talk. You'll feel more comfortable knowing where the room is. On the day of your talk, show up 15 minutes early so you can load your slides on the computer. Because you're fearful, you wisely saved your slides in many places: on your USB hard drive, in your e-mail account, and on a friend's USB drive. Load the slides, check to see that everything looks okay, and then say hi and chat with the moderator and other presenters. For the talk itself, get up there and unleash the sucker. After all your practice, you'll be a public-speaking machine.

Most people advance their slides by pressing a button on the keyboard or by clicking the mouse. Those methods are fine—far be it from us to criticize the old-school ways—but you can be the cool kid in your session if you use a wireless clicker. Technically called *wireless presenters* or *presentation remotes*, these are remote controls for the slides. You plug a small device into the computer's USB port, and you hold a small remote in your hand. The remote can move the slides back and forth; some have laser pointers, which are helpful for singling out audience members who forgot to shut down their cell phones.

LISTENING WELL

Not giving a talk? Listening to research talks has its own etiquette. First, turn off the cell phone. *Off* means inert: no ringing, no vibrating, no flashing lights. If your phone rings, vibrates, or flashes during the talk, everyone will turn to look at you and you will feel embarrassed. Another reason to shut off the phone is to avoid the temptation to check your messages, send a text message to your pal, or plug in a few phone numbers you collected during the conference. You're in a professional talk, surrounded by other professional psychologists; covertly checking messages pegs you as a student in a large lecture hall, not as a professional in a conference. (If you see professors covertly checking messages during a talk, you can scoff at their amateurish ways.) Second, don't interrupt a talk to ask a question. There will be time for questions after the talk. If not—some speakers take too much time, after all—there will be time after the session.

Beyond basic etiquette, you should take the opportunity to learn something. Even talks remotely related to your interests are a chance to learn something new. You never know where inspiration will come from: You might see a new kind of research design, a new statistical trick, or a new concept that enhances your research. Think critically about the research, with an eye toward what is good about it. It takes discernment to appreciate the value of a study. Critical thinking is not ridiculing everything—it's appraising research in light of other work and other theories.

WRAPPING UP

Many people think that public speaking is something you are born to do or born not to do. If true, most of us were born not to do it. You will give presentations for the rest of your working life, so now is the time to learn how to do it. Like everything else, expertise in public speaking comes from practice. If you learn some guidelines, practice them, and get feedback, you'll become a good public speaker. You won't love it, but you'll do it well.

Nothing makes you feel less like a student than giving a talk, inviting questions, and seeing a professor raise her hand to ask you about something. If you have presented a research talk at a conference, there is nothing more we can teach you. As in the classic kung fu movies, now the student has become the master. Well done.

Epilogue

According to statistics, the psychologists' friend, you will probably graduate. Graduation day may be far away—those semesters wasted as an apparel-marketing major will haunt you to your grave—but the odds are in your favor. Graduation day is a happy time. Distant relatives will send you their congratulations (translation: expect cash gifts), your family will come into town for the ceremony (translation: expect free meals at fancy restaurants), and dozens of people will ask you, "So, what are you doing next?" (translation: expect a murderous impulse). What's not to like?

But life after graduation is a wistful time, too. Many students find that they miss college. That's right—many students miss college, and they should. The college lifestyle involves meeting people, learning new things, and exploring the shapes that your future might take. The real-world lifestyle, in contrast, involves setting your alarm clock, filing tax forms, and performing scheduled maintenance on your clothes dryer. You'll look back on college with a new perspective, and you might wish that you had done things differently.

Many former students have told us that they didn't get as much out of college as they had hoped. Some students piled on the credits to graduate early only to find that they lacked the practical skills to compete for jobs. Other students dutifully attended class and got great grades only to find themselves losing job offers to people with weaker grades but more hands-on experience. And many students decided that they wanted to go to graduate school after all only to find too late that they needed research experience to be competitive.

But no students have told us that they regret being too involved, that they spent too much time in the trenches of psychology, that they learned too many useful skills. Whether you plan to go to grad school or to start a career, your undergraduate years are your last chance to prepare for life after college. College is like infancy—it's shorter and more expensive than you think, so get as much out of it as you can.

Your college or university defines your psychology degree by listing minimum requirements: To graduate, you need a minimum number of credit hours, a minimum number of classes of different sorts, and a minimum grade point average. That's it. You may not have thought of the degree requirements as the minimum requirements, but that's what they represent. Your school doesn't require you to get involved, to build a library, to go to conferences, to join professional societies, or to take advantage of opportunities for hands-on research. Building research and professional skills requires taking responsibility for your professional development and leaving the classroom for the trenches of psychology. Your university, department, and professors won't make you do it. It's up to you, so get started—your graduation-day self will thank you for its answer to, "So, what are you doing next?"

Appendix: Good Books for Your Professional Library

It's never too late to start building your professional library. Here are some books that we have found helpful. Nearly all of them are available as paperbacks, so you can build a big library without taking a job as an au pair.

LIFE AFTER COLLEGE: GRADUATE SCHOOL AND WORK

American Psychological Association. (2007). *Getting in: A step-by-step plan for gaining admission to graduate school in psychology* (2nd ed.). Washington, DC: Author.

Palladino Schultheiss, D. E. (2008). *Psychology as a major: Is it right for me and what can I do with my degree?* Washington, DC: American Psychological Association.

STATISTICS AND RESEARCH METHODS

Abelson, R. P. (1995). *Statistics as principled argument.* Hillsdale, NJ: Erlbaum.

Lockhart, R. S. (1997). *Introduction to statistics and data analysis for the behavioral sciences.* New York: Freeman.

Nolan, S. A., & Heinzen, T. E. (2008). *Statistics for the behavioral sciences*. New York: Worth.

Salkind, N. J. (2008). *Statistics for people who (think they) hate statistics* (3rd ed.). Thousand Oaks, CA: Sage.

ACADEMIC WRITING

American Psychological Association. (2001). *Publication manual of the American Psychological Association* (5th ed.). Washington, DC: Author.

Baker, S. (1969). *The practical stylist* (2nd ed.). New York: Crowell.

Hale, C. (1999). *Sin and syntax: How to craft wickedly effective prose*. New York: Broadway.

Silvia, P. J. (2007). *How to write a lot: A practical guide to productive academic writing*. Washington, DC: American Psychological Association.

Sternberg, R. J. (Ed.). (2000). *Guide to publishing in psychology journals*. Cambridge, England: Cambridge University Press.

Sternberg, R. J. (2003). *The psychologist's companion: A guide to scientific writing for students and researchers* (3rd ed.). Cambridge, England: Cambridge University Press.

Zinsser, W. (2006). *On writing well* (30th anniversary ed.). New York: HarperCollins.

PUBLIC SPEAKING

Kosslyn, S. M. (2007). *Clear and to the point: Eight psychological principles for compelling PowerPoint presentations*. New York: Oxford University Press.

Reynolds, G. (2008). *Presentation Zen: Simple ideas on presentation design and delivery*. Berkeley, CA: New Riders.

References

American Psychological Association. (2001). *Publication manual of the American Psychological Association* (5th ed.). Washington, DC: Author.

Davidson, R. J., Scherer, K. R., & Goldsmith, H. H. (Eds.). (2003). *Handbook of affective sciences*. New York: Oxford University Press.

Fine, M. A., & Kurdek, L. A. (1993). Reflections on determining authorship credit and authorship order on faculty–student collaborations. *American Psychologist, 48,* 1141–1147.

Kashima, Y., Foddy, M., & Platow, M. J. (Eds.). (2002). *Self and identity: Personal, social, and symbolic*. Mahwah, NJ: Erlbaum.

Kitayama, S., & Cohen, D. (Eds.). (2007). *Handbook of cultural psychology*. New York: Guilford Press.

Landrum, R. E. (2008). *Undergraduate writing in psychology: Learning to tell the scientific story*. Washington, DC: American Psychological Association.

Lewis, M., Haviland-Jones, J. M., & Feldman Barrett, L. (Eds.). (2008). *Handbook of emotions* (3rd ed.). New York: Guilford Press.

National Center for Education Statistics. (2007). *Digest of education statistics, 2006* (NCES 2007-17). Washington, DC: U.S. Department of Education.

Pervin, L. A., & John, O. P. (Eds.). (2001). *Handbook of personality* (2nd ed.). New York: Guilford Press.

Rapee, R. M., & Lim, L. (1992). Discrepancy between self and observer ratings of performance in social phobics. *Journal of Abnormal Psychology, 101,* 728–731.

Ring, K. (1967). Experimental social psychology: Some sober questions about some frivolous values. *Journal of Experimental Social Psychology, 3,* 113–123.

Sansone, C., & Smith, J. L. (2000). Interest and self-regulation: The relation between having to and wanting to. In C. Sansone & J. M. Harackiewicz (Eds.), *Intrinsic and extrinsic motivation* (pp. 341–372). San Diego, CA: Academic Press.

Silvia, P. J. (2007). *How to write a lot: A practical guide to productive academic writing.* Washington, DC: American Psychological Association.

Stanley, J., Gowen, E., & Miall, R. C. (2007). Effects of agency on movement interference during observation of a moving dot stimulus. *Journal of Experimental Psychology: Human Perception and Performance, 33,* 915–926.

Steele, C. M., & Aronson, J. (1995). Stereotype threat and the intellectual test performance of African-Americans. *Journal of Personality and Social Psychology, 69,* 797–811.

Sternberg, R. J. (Ed.). (2000). *Guide to publishing in psychology journals.* Cambridge, England: Cambridge University Press.

Sternberg, R. J. (2003). *The psychologist's companion: A guide to scientific writing for students and researchers* (3rd ed.). Cambridge, England: Cambridge University Press.

Zauberman, G., & Lynch, J. G., Jr. (2005). Resource slack and propensity to discount delayed investments of time versus money. *Journal of Experimental Psychology: General, 134,* 23–37.

Zinsser, W. (1988). *Writing to learn.* New York: Quill.

Index

165

About the Authors

Paul J. Silvia, PhD, is a social psychologist at the University of North Carolina at Greensboro. He has served as the director of the department's honors program, and he teaches undergraduate courses on academic writing and professional skills. His other books include *How to Write a Lot: A Practical Guide to Productive Academic Writing* (2007) and *Exploring the Psychology of Interest* (2006).

Peter F. Delaney, PhD, is a cognitive psychologist at the University of North Carolina at Greensboro. He has won several teaching awards and taught thousands of students, and he conducts laboratory research on human memory and problem solving. He also speaks Armenian.

Stuart Marcovitch, PhD, studies cognitive development at the University of North Carolina at Greensboro. He is the faculty advisor for Psi Chi—the national honors society for psychology—and is involved with continuously improving the undergraduate curriculum. If asked, he will lecture tirelessly on why batting averages are not technically statistics.

Yellowstone,
Land of Wonders

Promenade in North America's
National Park

JULES LECLERCQ

Translated and edited by Janet Chapple
and Suzanne Cane

Foreword by Lee H. Whittlesey

University of Nebraska Press
Lincoln & London

Originally published in French as *La Terre des Merveilles:
Promenade au parc national de l'Amérique du Nord*.

The English translation of chapters 7, 8, 9, 10, 11, and 14 previously
appeared in *The GOSA Transactions: The Journal of the Geyser
Observations and Study Association* 11 (2010): 83–102.

Library of Congress Cataloging-in-Publication Data
Leclercq, Jules Joseph, 1848–1928.
[Terre des merveilles. English]
Yellowstone, land of wonders: promenade in North America's
national park / Jules Leclercq; translated and edited by Janet
Chapple and Suzanne Cane; foreword by Lee H. Whittlesey.
pages cm
"Originally published in French as La terre des merveilles:
promenade au parc national de l'Am?rique du Nord"—Title page
verso.
Includes bibliographical references and index.
ISBN 978-0-8032-4477-1 (cloth: alkaline paper) 1. Yellowstone
National Park—Description and travel. 2. Leclercq, Jules Joseph,
1848–1928—Travel—Yellowstone National Park. I. Chapple, Janet.
II. Cane, Suzanne. III. Title.
F722.L3413 2013
917.87'5204—dc23   2012045125

Set in Iowan by Laura Wellington.

Contents

Illustrations

Photographs and Figures

Maps

About the jacket: The painting *Yellowstone Falls (Lower Falls of the Yellowstone River)* by Germany-born American artist Albert Bierstadt (1830–1902) was painted soon after Bierstadt's visit to Yellowstone in 1881. In 1874 two of Bierstadt's landscape paintings were installed in the chamber of the U.S. House of Representatives. The image is used courtesy of the Buffalo Bill Historical Center, Cody, W Y.

Foreword

Lee H. Whittlesey

It is a pleasure to write a few words about Janet Chapple and Suzanne Cane's translation *Yellowstone, Land of Wonders: Promenade in North America's National Park*. Seeing this important historical book finally translated in full from its original French has meaning for me as a professional historian, especially because of my close interest in and affinity for Yellowstone National Park.

More than thirty years ago—in or about 1977—I encountered Jules Leclercq's 1886 *La Terre des Merveilles* languishing on the shelves of the rare book room in Yellowstone National Park's research library at Mammoth Hot Springs. I eagerly plucked it from the shelf for a look and was instantly caught up in its beautiful woodcut drawings and mysterious phrases. Because I had a thorough Latin background, I could read enough French to know that Leclercq's book contained important material from his early trip to this place about which I had so much interest. I knew that it might even contain clues to the origins of Yellowstone's place-names, which I was fervently researching as the topic of my first book.

Unable to read the complete text, I set the book aside for future reference. My chance came two years later, when I met Chris MacIntosh, a fellow Yellowstone employee who hailed from England. She had an excellent understanding of French and a passion for Yellowstone, so I showed her the book and was pleased to learn that she was interested in translating some of it. From late 1978 to 1983, I sent chapters of the book to Chris, and beginning in February 1979 I received her translations by return mail. My copies are still filed in the envelopes she sent to me with their postmarked dates from those years.

As I read her translations I was transported back in time to 1883, the year Jules Leclercq came to Yellowstone, rented horses, and set out "on his own hook" (as they said in those days) to camp his way through the new park. By that time I had learned that 1883 was Yellowstone's "grand opening" year, the year that the Northern Pacific Railroad's rails reached the park and opened it to large-scale tourism. It seemed that Leclercq's book was even more important than I had earlier known. His description of the tents at Norris supplied one of the few actual accountings of this short-lived tourist lunch station (with its Chinese cook) that lasted for only three summers. I realized that his portrayal of the newly built first hotel at Mammoth and his sighting of President Arthur's horseback expedition — and even his report of Arthur's fake abduction by kidnappers — were important. And I soon found that his observations of eruptions of Giantess and Beehive Geysers were detailed enough for me to include them verbatim in my own book *Wonderland Nomenclature*.

Many years later, when Montana State University student Elizabeth Watry was searching for a class project in French, I suggested that she use one of Leclercq's chapters. Her translation further extended my interest in his work.

But alas! Neither Chris nor Elizabeth translated Jules Leclercq's entire work. I thus was excited in 2008 when I learned from my friend Janet Chapple that she and Suzanne Cane were planning a complete translation of Leclercq's book. I followed their progress closely, noting that they quickly produced a corrected spelling of Leclercq's name and a biography of him. I thrilled in his actual meeting of former president Ulysses S. Grant and railroad president Henry Villard on the station platform at Livingston, Montana, and I reveled in his encounter with the local character "Yankee Jim" George.

But Janet and Suzanne's complete translation has revealed much more to us than merely the Yellowstone descriptions of which I am personally so fond. The fact that Leclercq was well educated in an era when many were not makes his observations and his narrative all the more fascinating. We now experience western geography with him — Chicago, Illinois; Eau Claire, Wisconsin; Saint Paul, Minnesota; and the vast open country of Dakota and Montana Territories. Arriving at "Livingstone," so often misspelled then, Leclercq rode south into Paradise Valley first by train, then transferred to a "classic Concord coach," which he described as "an old barouche in the style of Louis XV that one finds from one end of the Rocky Mountains to the other." He then hired a park coach just south of the second canyon, opining that its "jolts made us bounce like peas on a drum," and he soon experienced the "horrifying cannonade" of a prairie thunderstorm. And his fellow travelers on his first coach were so colorful that I cannot resist sharing a glimpse of them here: "My companions looked like authentic Far West bandits, solidly built men with thick, bushy beards, feet thrust into enormous, muddy boots, and heads crowned with immense felt hats. They wore cartridge belts and a whole arsenal of revolvers. The women, brown as chestnuts and dressed in red wool, soaked up whisky like the men, who always took care to help themselves first."

This sounds to us like nothing less than the American West of our imaginations. And Jules Leclercq actually saw it, for this was ten years prior to Frederick Jackson Turner's declaration that the American frontier was "settled up" and thus supposedly wild no more. The establishment of Yellowstone, of course, predated that event by over twenty years, and Leclercq was present for its grand opening. He soon abandoned his coach for the adventures of horseback riding, and that put him in even closer touch with the newly revealed "Wonders of the Yellowstone."

So settle back, open this book, and enjoy the journey. It is easy to pretend that you are there.

Acknowledgments

The translators want to express gratitude to Chris MacIntosh, who translated parts of *La Terre des Merveilles* at the request of Yellowstone Park historian Lee H. Whittlesey many years ago when they were both park employees. Whittlesey kindly gave Janet Chapple copies of MacIntosh's translation of the preface and chapters 1, 3–10, and 12. With her generous permission we have incorporated some of her work into ours. More recently, Elizabeth A. Watry translated chapter 14 for Whittlesey, and she graciously permitted us to compare and use some of her work in our version of that chapter.

We also thank Elizabeth Jung for her careful examination of the translation and her invaluable suggestions for improving and clarifying the English text; Lee H. Whittlesey for his review of the manuscript and constructive advice about expanding the notes; Beth Chapple for early copyediting of the manuscript and for creating the index; Linton A. Brown for creating the English version of Leclercq's Yellowstone National Park map; Janet Dean for assistance with questions about nineteenth-century American English; Evelyne Rossi for help with accurate translations of some French expressions; Aurore Tenenbaum for explaining a French legal term; Paul Schullery and Robert Root for their careful evaluation of the manuscript; Peter Schulman for his meticulous reading and constructive recommendations for enhancing the translation; and Ann Poulos of the Providence Public Library for her genius in researching some sources. Our thanks are also due to librarians at Brown University, the Rhode Island School of Design, the Yellowstone Heritage and Research Center, the Chicago and Oakland Public Libraries, and the Bibliothèque nationale de France for their able assistance and to copyeditor Joy Margheim and our editors at the University of Nebraska Press, Matthew Bokovoy, Elisabeth Chretien, and Ann Baker, for patiently guiding us through publication.

Our very warm thanks go to our husbands, Bruno Giletti and David Cane, both scientists, for valuable advice on numerous issues and unwavering moral support during this project.

Translators' Introduction

Jules Joseph Leclercq (1848–1928) visited Yellowstone National Park only eleven years after its establishment in 1872. Three years later he published the engrossing account *La Terre des Merveilles: Promenade au Parc National de l'Amérique du Nord* (The Land of Wonders: Promenade in North America's National Park), translated here as *Yellowstone, Land of Wonders*. A man of universal erudition, Leclercq was a careful observer and an experienced travel writer. He was the first to describe the natural beauty of Yellowstone National Park in French, and although it was published more than a century ago, his book has never before been completely translated into English.

Leclercq's observations were made when so few people had visited Yellowstone that seeing geysers erupt was a great novelty and a cause for wonder and astonishment. Protective walkways and barriers did not yet separate visitors from the hydrothermal features, although by the time of his 1883 visit the hand of man was already evident in the geyser basins, not only in the several buildings and trails found here and there but also in the vandalism that marred many thermal features, as he discussed in chapter 9.

Leclercq's style of writing was representative of travel literature of the nineteenth and early twentieth centuries: this Yellowstone account fell somewhere between the very detailed and technical approaches found in writings by government geologists, biologists, and army officers—men such as Ferdinand V. Hayden, William H. Holmes, Captain William Ludlow, and Arnold Hague—and the many tourist accounts that told of washing clothes in hot springs, watching geysers spout, and traveling with companions.

A broadly educated man with a sound understanding of science, Leclercq read extensively about his many destinations and recorded his impressions while traveling, as when he wrote that Beehive Geyser erupted "just as I was taking notes in the tent, writing in my lap by the light of a candle." With impressive scholarship, he combined knowledge he acquired through reading with information he garnered through his own experiences and observations during only ten days of horseback travel in Yellowstone. Sometimes he paraphrased or even directly translated passages from his English readings. He produced an informative and accurate narrative based on the best knowledge of the late nineteenth century, often in language both poetic and personal.

Leclercq made references to classical literature and comparisons to items with which he knew his readers to be familiar, such as European landmarks, and he related amusing anecdotes from his own experience. He conveyed his impressions frankly, without pretense or affectation, and his own disposition was revealed in his writings: he was curious, enthusiastic, fair-minded, and undeterred by fatigue or danger.[1] Often including what he felt, smelled, and heard, as well as what he saw, Leclercq chose his words to give readers a sense of actually being there—and his word pictures are delightful.

Take, for example, the beginning of Leclercq's description of Grand Prismatic Spring: "Mute with amazement and astonishment, we gazed upon this expanse of steaming, sapphire-colored water so surpassingly transparent that the thousand fantastical forms on the festooned walls could be distinguished under the crystal liquid. The aqueous layers take on a more and more intense blue color as the eye penetrates deeper into the abyss. Several meters from the edge one loses sight of the bottom of the basin, and the dark color of the water indicates unfathomable depths that are concealed from view."

It was by sheer chance that Leclercq found himself in Yellowstone during the red-letter summer of 1883. He had been on his way overland from New York to Mexico, but arriving in St. Louis in August, he encountered heat so oppressive that he decided to postpone his visit to the tropics and instead visit the mountains. In his book about Mexico he wrote, "At St. Louis I opened a long parenthesis in my itinerary: I went to the Rocky Mountains with the goal of exploring the geysers of Yellowstone, which I wanted to compare to those that I had just admired in Iceland."[2] Leclercq gave himself only ten days in the park, yet he covered an impressive amount of territory on horseback and saw most of the outstanding features.

The summer of 1883 was a record season for Yellowstone visits, chiefly because the Northern Pacific branch rail line had just been extended nearly to the park. Many visitors were notables. As historian Hiram M. Chittenden wrote in a footnote in his 1895 history of Yellowstone, "The list of arrivals for that year includes the President of the United States and a member of his cabinet; the Chief-Justice and an Associate Justice of the United States Supreme Court; the General, Lieutenant-General, and a large number of other distinguished officers of the army; six United States Senators; one Territorial Governor; a prominent railroad president; the Ministers from Great Britain and Germany; the President of the Admiralty Division of the High Court of Justice, England; three members of Parliament; and a considerable number of other eminent personages, both from this country and abroad."[3]

The U.S. president mentioned by Chittenden was Chester A. Arthur, the first of several presidents to visit Yellowstone. He and his large entourage arrived at Mammoth Hot Springs after traversing the park from the south, just as Leclercq was setting out from Mammoth for his horseback tour. Arnold Hague and Walter Weed of the U.S. Geological Survey, as well as German geologist G. M. Von Rath, were all in the park that summer. So were members of the Hatch excursion, celebrating the opening of some park facilities, and the Villard excursion, organized to celebrate the Northern Pacific Railroad's completion of its branch line from Livingston to Cinnabar, Montana Territory, three miles north of the North Entrance.

Although Jules Leclercq was born, lived, worked, and died in Brussels, he traveled the world and, through his writings, opened new horizons for his readers. Having earned doctorates in law as well as political science and administration, he practiced law and fulfilled often arduous duties as a judge in small claims court. His passions, however, were traveling and writing. Known during his lifetime as "The Traveler," he chronicled his frequent expeditions, spending his two months of summer vacation in one or more countries of Europe,

Africa, Asia, South America, and North America. He traveled as far as New Zealand and various remote islands, both polar and tropical. He wrote copiously during a travel-writing career that spanned nearly half a century, and two of his books won prizes from the French Academy. He authored twenty-four volumes of prose, five collections of poetry, translations of Icelandic sagas, and numerous articles for serious journals and popular magazines. The same year that he visited Yellowstone his book about Iceland, *La Terre de Glace* (The Land of Ice), was published. In *La Terre des Merveilles* he compared the thermal features of Yellowstone to those he saw in Iceland.

Ten years after visiting Yellowstone, Leclercq traveled to the British African colony then called the Cape Colony (the present Republic of South Africa). He was entertained at dinner by Prime Minister Cecil Rhodes, who asked his guest to bear a request to Belgium's King Leopold II.[4] Rhodes wanted to link the British Cape Colony in the south with British-occupied Egypt in the north by a railway that would have to pass through Congo territory controlled by the Belgian king. Leclercq carried a verbal request for authorization to his king and transmitted to Rhodes the king's response, which ignored the question of a railway and instead proposed a trans-African telegraph line. According to Henri Rolin, Rhodes did not deign even to acknowledge receipt of the king's letter. Much later both the railway and the telegraph line were partially built, but neither passed through the Congo.

Leclercq was awarded many honors: he was elected to the Belgian Royal Academy of Science, Letters, and Fine Arts; he was a founder, president, and vice president of the Royal Geographical Society of Belgium, where he delivered twenty-eight lectures over the course of thirty-four years; and he was a member of the Geographical Society of Paris. In 1898, after addressing delegates at the Geographical Society of Lisbon, he reported in detail to King Leopold about Portugal's king, Don Carlos, and his court.

In his many travel books, Leclercq did not usually assess governments or heads of state, nor did he express reactions to the suffering of the people he encountered. In a biographical article about Jules Leclercq, Henri Rolin asks, "Was he superficial? He can in no way be criticized on this account. The number of countries he traveled through, the brevity of his sojourns, and the lack of specific research objectives made it impossible for him to make detailed studies."[5]

Leclercq's career as a travel writer ended abruptly in 1914, when he was sixty-five years old, with the outbreak of World War I. Caught en route to the Congo, he returned immediately to Belgium. He wrote, "One realizes with advancing age that there are three seasons in life: the first, when one hopes to travel; the second, when one travels; and the third, when one remembers one's travels."[6] In his own third season Leclercq embraced a new passion: poetry. He published three collections of poems about impressions from his travels, transforming from narrative to poetry some of the images engraved on his mind that still charmed or astonished him: polar and tropical landscapes, mountain silhouettes, monuments to past glories, sunsets from a former time. His poems received warm praise for their evocative imagery and beautiful form. In fact, he realized that "accounts of travel age faster than their authors," but he thought perhaps his verse would survive him better.[7] Curiously, and perhaps because French was the dominant world language in his time, none of the works of this extraordinary man—judge, traveler, writer, poet, translator, and intermediary for a king—has been translated into English, until the present volume.

Translation and Editorial Method

Jules Leclercq arrived at Mammoth Springs at night on August 29, 1883, and left the park on September 8. Although he wrote that he met U.S. president Chester A. Arthur's party at Mammoth Springs on August 30 (chapter 6), the *Livingston Enterprise* places President Arthur's arrival there on August 31, so Leclercq had to be mistaken about the date.

Upon leaving the park (chapter 3), Leclercq went directly to Livingston, Montana Territory,[1] where he met dignitaries arriving to celebrate the joining of the transcontinental Northern Pacific Railroad tracks, a ceremony that occurred on September 8. On the English version of the Yellowstone National Park map at the back of this book, we have entered the correct dates at points where Leclercq stayed each night.[2]

While Leclercq generally wrote respectfully of the people he encountered, he sometimes used terms current in his day that might be considered offensive today, such as "Redskins" for Native Americans or "Celestials" for Chinese. In some instances the translators have chosen to keep such terms, since they contribute to maintaining a nineteenth-century flavor and sensibility in this English version.

Occasionally the author's punctuation and spelling of names are modified, and occasionally his long sentences and paragraphs are broken up for ease in reading and understanding. We have deliberately preserved some nineteenth-century spellings and capitalization, such as "sulphur," "bowlder," and "National Park." In the French original Leclercq used italics for terms that seemed to him typically American (such as *shacks* and *sleeping car*). We have substituted quotation marks for his italics in many such cases in this American translation but left words foreign to both French and English (such as Latin words) in italics. He also used both metric and U.S. units of measurement. We have translated each occurrence directly, providing equivalents only where Leclercq himself did, except in the case of degrees centigrade, which we have converted to Fahrenheit, and hectares, converted to acres.

The few notes written by Jules Leclercq are included with our notes but are identified with his italicized initials at the beginning of the note: *JL.*

We have added many explanatory notes that clarify or supplement the text for twenty-first-century readers. Our primary source for notes about place-names was the pioneering work of Yellowstone Park historian Lee H. Whittlesey, who traced the provenance of Yellowstone Park names in two invaluable works, *Wonderland Nomenclature* and *Yellowstone Place Names*. Likewise, *The Yellowstone Story*, by the park's late historian Aubrey L. Haines, was our indispensable reference for questions pertaining to park history. Information not directly relating to Yellowstone Park came from many standard sources.

Page numbers for the sources of quotations are given in the notes, while the complete references are listed either in Leclercq's "Works to Consult" or in the translators' bibliography, both at the back of the book.

Leclercq paraphrased or translated some passages directly from his English-language sources. When possible, we have used the original English text, as indicated in the notes. The writing style in these passages is therefore that of the original authors rather than that of Leclercq.

A Note on the Illustrators

The wood engravings in *Yellowstone, Land of Wonders* were cut in the nineteenth century by French artists copying images from photographs, paintings, or drawings made by men who had visited Yellowstone National Park. In those days a multistep process was required in order to print photographs in books. An original image was first copied by an artist and then carefully and laboriously cut into wood by an engraver. Sometimes a photograph was transferred directly to the block of wood before cutting began.

Although no credit was given to the American painters or photographers who created the original images, the French artists and engravers usually signed their work. Since paintings, drawings, and photographs were not covered by copyright at that time, the same engravings often appeared in several publications.

Many of the images in Leclercq's book were cropped at the bottom where the signatures would have appeared, but an article about the new national park in the 1874 French periodical *Le Tour du Monde* (Round the world) includes many of the same images, uncropped and containing recognizable signatures.

The list of illustrations below includes the American photographer or artist, when known, followed by the French artist and/or engraver. Earlier appearances of the illustrations are also listed; full citations for these works appear in the bibliographies. Brief information about the artists for which information is available follows the image list.

1. Jules Leclercq. Appeared in Société Royale Belge de Géographie, *La fondation de la Société*, 39.
2. The Giant. Auguste Victor Deroy.
3. Dr. Hayden, United States geologist. Henri Thiriat. Appeared in Williams, *Pacific Tourist*, 30, after an albumen print in the National Portrait Gallery.
4. The Badlands. No information available.
5. Cinnabar Mountain. William H. Jackson photo, 1871; Th. Taylor.
6. Mammoth Springs. Jackson photo, 1872; Édouard Riou, Charles Laplante. Image in Leclercq book is reversed.
7. The Liberty Cap. Jackson photo, 1872; Taylor, Laplante. Reversed.
8. Terraces at Mammoth Springs. Riou, Henri Théophile Hildibrand. Appeared in Hayden, Doane, and Langford, "Le parc national," 327.
9. A bath at Mammoth Springs. Riou, Hildibrand. Appeared in Hayden, Doane, and Langford, "Le parc national," 328.
10. The Lone Star Geyser. Jackson photo, 1878; Deroy.
11. The Minute Man. Riou, Laplante. Appeared in Hayden, Doane, and Langford, "Le parc national," 314.
12. Cone built up by hot spring deposits. Taylor, Charles Barbant. Appeared in Hayden, Doane, and Langford, "Le parc national," 304.
13. Crater of Old Faithful. Jackson photo, 1872; Riou, Hildibrand.
14. Eruption of Old Faithful. Riou, Laplante. Appeared in Hayden, Doane, and Langford, "Le parc national," 309.
15. Eruption of the Beehive. Taylor, Barbant.
16. Crater of the Beehive. Jackson photo, 1872; Riou, Barbant. Reversed.
17. The Giantess. Thomas Moran; Deroy. Appeared in Langford, "Wonders of the Yellowstone," June 1871, 127.
18. Crater of the Grand Geyser. Jackson photo, 1872; Riou, Hildibrand.
19. The Devil's Well and the Castle. Jackson photo, 1871; Riou, Hildibrand.
20. The Grotto. Jackson photo, 1872; Riou, Barbant.
21. The Fan. Moran, Riou. Appeared in Langford, "Wonders of the Yellowstone," June 1871, 113.
22. The Comet. Deroy.
23. Panorama of the Firehole Valley. Moran drawing; Riou. Appeared in Langford, "Wonders of the Yellowstone," June 1871, 121, as "Bird's-Eye View of the Geyser Basin."

24. Geyserite deposits at the Castle. Deroy.
25. Diagram of a geyser. Langlois. Appeared in Peale, "Report of A. C. Peale, M.D.," in Hayden, *Sixth Annual Report*, opposite page 421.
26. Appearance of a geyser after eruption. Deroy. Probably Splendid Geyser.
27. Excelsior Geyser. Deroy.
28. The large, boiling spring. Riou.
29. The Mud Caldron. Jackson photo, "Mud Puffs, or Hot Mud Spring, in Lower Firehole Basin," 1872; Barbant. Probably Fountain Paint Pot.
30. Indian chief. Riou, Barbant. Appeared in Hayden, Doane, and Langford, "Le parc national," 350.
31. The Yellowstone Lake. Jackson photo, 1871; Hildibrand.
32. Mud spring crater. Jackson stereo view, "Mud Puffs in Lower Geyser Basin," 1872; Riou, Barbant.
33. Rocky Mountain bear cubs. Théophile Louis Deyrolle, Laplante. Appeared in Hayden, Doane, and Langford, "Le parc national," 330.
34. Cougar. No information available.
35. After the hunt. Joshua Crissman photo, 1872; Deyrolle, Laplante. Reversed.
36. Rocky Mountain moose. Deyrolle. Appeared in Hayden, Doane, and Langford, "Le parc national," 302.
37. Rocky Mountain deer. Deyrolle, Alfred-Louis Sargent. Appeared in Hayden, Doane, and Langford, "Le parc national," 352.
38. Sulphur Mountain. Deroy.
39. Upper Falls of the Yellowstone. Jackson photo, 1871–; Taylor.
40. Lower Falls of the Yellowstone. Jackson photo, 1871; Taylor.
41. The Grand Cañon. Jackson photo, 1878; Taylor.
42. Eagles' nest in the Grand Cañon. Deroy.
43. Tower Fall. Jackson photo, 1871; Taylor, Laplante.
44. Basalt Walls of the Grand Cañon. Deroy. Appeared in Hayden, *Twelfth Annual Report*, opposite page 46.

Contributing Artists

American Artists

JOSHUA CRISSMAN (1833–1922). Photographer living in Bozeman, Montana Territory, during the early 1870s. Photographed in Yellowstone four summers, two of them alongside W. H. Jackson. Sold his photographs and stereo views only locally and to other photographers. Some were later attributed to Jackson.

WILLIAM HENRY JACKSON (1843–1942). Photographer for Hayden expeditions, 1870–78. Took many of the earliest views of Yellowstone and other western subjects. His pictures appeared in numerous publications throughout the late 1800s.

THOMAS MORAN (1837–1926). Painter influenced by his brother Edward and by other Philadelphia artists and also by the works of English painter J. M. W. Turner. Visited Yellowstone with the 1871 Hayden expedition, earlier than his rival Albert Bierstadt. Produced numerous Yellowstone paintings from his sketches but drew the panorama in figure 23 before seeing Upper Geyser Basin.

French Artists and Engravers

CHARLES BARBANT (1844–1922). Illustrator and wood engraver, son and student of wood engraver Nicolas Barbant. Exhibited at Salon de Paris. Produced work for many publications, including Jules Verne's novels.

AUGUSTE VICTOR DEROY (1823–1906). Painter and lithographer. Son and student of Isodore Laurent Deroy. Exhibited his work at Salon des Artistes Français, 1863–89.

THÉOPHILE LOUIS DEYROLLE (1844–1923). Painter of portraits and genre scenes. Studied in Paris but lived in Finistère (France) and developed oyster parks in addition to painting. Won awards at Salon de Paris.

HENRI THÉOPHILE HILDIBRAND (1824–97). Wood engraver. Made engravings for many artists, including for the celebrated Gustave Doré. Exhibited at Salon de Paris. Produced engravings for Dante's *Purgatorio* and Jules Verne's novels. Worked for many publishers, including Librairie Hachette, publisher of *La Terre des Merveilles* and other Leclercq books.

LANGLOIS. No information available.

CHARLES LAPLANTE (1861–1903). Wood engraver and illustrator. Worked with Gustave Doré. Produced illustrations for Jules Verne's novels. Worked for Librairie Hachette and exhibited at Salon de Paris.

ÉDOUARD RIOU (1833–1900). Prolific painter, illustrator, and engraver. Drew genre and hunting scenes, landscapes, and scenes in Italy, Egypt, and Russia. Exhibited at the Salon de Paris, published in periodicals, and provided sketches for the novels of Jules Verne, Alexandre Dumas, Guy de Maupassant, and Victor Hugo.

ALFRED-LOUIS SARGENT (1828–?). Wood engraver of landscapes. Exhibited at Salon de Paris. Brother of Louis Sargent (1830–?), also a French engraver in Paris.

TH. TAYLOR. No information available.

HENRI THIRIAT (dates unknown). Wood engraver of portraits and other pictures for illustrated periodicals. Exhibited at the Salon de Paris; awarded bronze medal in 1877.

Yellowstone, Land of Wonders

Promenade in North America's National Park

by JULES LECLERCQ

President of the Royal Belgian Geographical Society
Member of the Geographical Society of Paris

Work containing forty-two engravings,
two drawings, and three maps

Originally published by
Librairie Hachette et Cie.,
Paris 79, Boulevard Saint-Germain
1886

To
Professor R. B. Anderson
United States Minister to Copenhagen
and to his family

Affectionate remembrance of their cordial
welcome in Wisconsin

Cortenbergh, November 1885

1. Jules Leclercq.

PREFACE

The wonders of the Yellowstone have been known for so few years that they have scarcely ever been described except by Americans. Some few articles scattered among travel and geography collections and in periodicals make up the whole body of French literature relating to this strange part of the globe. The *Tour du Monde* has played the largest part in making it known in France by means of an excellent summary of the travels of the American explorers Hayden, Doane, and Langford.[1] Mr. Paul le Hardy, who accompanied Captain Jones's expedition in 1873 serving as topographer, wrote a short but important account of the Yellowstone.[2] At about the same time, the eminent geologist Mr. de la Vallée-Poussin addressed the subject of this area in a remarkable study of the works of his American colleagues.[3] More recently Messrs. Gauilleur and Seguin published in geographical collections[4] accounts whose only shortcoming is that they are too short. One of these predicts that someday entire books will be written on the Yellowstone; perhaps it is because of this prophecy that I wrote this.

In the United States the Yellowstone has already been the object of numerous and important publications. Explorations organized by the government have given rise to some very well-written reports. The reader who wishes to study the subject in more detail might have recourse to these official works,[5] on which army engineers, naturalists, and astronomers have collaborated. They are scientific monuments that honor the American government as well as the men whose talents and courage made them possible.

The first account that revealed the wonders of the Yellowstone was that of Mr. Langford, published in the American periodical *Scribner's Monthly*. It caused a sensation even in the scientific world.

Since that time, each year has seen new travel accounts appear in America.

That a region known for only a few years has already been the object of so many works and attracts the attention of Americans more than ever—here is a phenomenon that gives a foretaste of just how extraordinary this region is.

CHAPTER I

The Land of Wonders

The Land of Wonders.—Situation, boundaries and area.—Continental divide of the American continent.—High altitudes.—Rigors of the climate.—Comparison with Iceland.—Volcanic phenomena.—Beauty of the countryside.

In 1871 the American geologist Hayden revealed the existence of one of the most phenomenal regions on earth. It was named the "Land of Wonders."

A law of the U.S. Congress has established this part of the American territory as a public park, placed under the surveillance of the state and intended for the enjoyment and edification of the nation. No part of this reserved domain may be settled, given away, or sold, and no one may live there without governmental authorization.

The boundaries set by legal power do not correspond to natural divisions. They circumscribe a zone extending approximately from the 110th to the 111th degree of longitude west of the Washington meridian and from the 44th to the 45th degree of north latitude.[1] It is a rectangle drawn parallel to the meridian, with that geometric regularity that Americans are fond of; it measures 88 kilometers from east to west and 105 kilometers from north to south. Its area of more than nine thousand square kilometers is thus almost equal in extent to one-third of the territory of Belgium. It lies at the junction of one state and two territories that are not yet established as states. The largest portion of the rectangle occupies the northwest section of Wyoming; the rest consists of a strip of southern Montana and a strip of eastern Idaho.

Nature has kept the Land of Wonders hidden in the heart of the Rocky Mountains, in the highest part of that gigantic chain. A formidable rampart of peaks and glaciers defends it. Within this enclosure slumbers large Yellowstone Lake, one of the highest expanses of water in the world. Here, too, fall the snows that feed the brooks that will become giant rivers. Here are born the Missouri and its tributaries, which flow to the Gulf of Mexico; the Snake River, which joins the Columbia and the Pacific Ocean; and the Green River, which rushes to the Colorado and the Gulf of California. It is one of the most remarkable divides on the American continent, a *divortium aquarum* of the first order.

The official designation as "National Park" is not quite precise; it is not so much a park as a group of valleys arranged as so many distinct little parks, each isolated from the next and situated on both sides of the Rocky Mountain chain. These valleys are located at altitudes that are nowhere less than eighteen hundred meters; several of them reach two thousand to twenty-five hundred meters above sea level. The height of the mountain peaks overhanging the valleys varies between three thousand and thirty-seven hundred meters.

These great altitudes make the climate of this region one of the most rigorous in America; even after scorching midsummer days, it freezes almost every night. It is not unusual to see the thermometer fluctuate from +30° to -10° [Celsius; 86°F–14°F] within twenty-four hours. This region is therefore not suitable for cultivation.

Here, as in Iceland, nature shows herself as rebellious to man. Why should this region not be baptized New Iceland, as it has not yet received a definitive name? Are not its scenery and geology constantly reminiscent of the great island in the north? Like Iceland, this is a land of enchantments and marvels, a land where it seems that nature wished to use all her powers and display all her splendors. Like Iceland, this region abounds in volcanic phenomena and offers the astonishing spectacle of those intermittent fountains that shoot columns of boiling water into the air, called by the Icelandic name of *gey-*

2. The Giant.

sers. One would perhaps search in vain through the entire ter-restrial globe for a collection of valleys and basins where the existence of subterranean fires manifests itself so obviously, so close to the surface, and on such a vast scale. There are more than ten thousand eruptive vents, and as yet this country has not been fully explored.

Besides its geologic interest, this part of the Rocky Moun-tains also contains some of the most beautiful scenery in North America. Nature has here gathered together all her alpine beau-ties, verdant valleys, forests, cañons, lakes, waterfalls, rushing streams, and, as sublime frames for these enchanting tableaux, haughty mountains whose eternal diadems of snow sparkle un-der the pure and luminous sky of these high elevations.

I had seen Iceland in 1881; two years later the fortunes of travel brought me to the Land of Wonders. In the month of July 1883 I disembarked at New York. I intended to go overland to Mexico to avoid the yellow fever, which was then reigning with fearsome intensity in Veracruz.[2] The railroad took me to the banks of the Mississippi in two days. In St. Louis I encoun-tered a veritable furnace; the heat was so oppressive that, los-ing all my energy, I let myself be persuaded to postpone until the month of September the continuation of my trip toward the torrid region of Texas and the Rio Grande.

The Rocky Mountains, which I had not revisited for sev-en years, offered themselves to my imagination like an en-ticing mirage. I was only two thousand kilometers from them — bah! — that was only one stride in a country where one thinks nothing of distance. An unwavering idea found ac-commodation in my mind: I conceived a tempting plan: in the Land of Wonders I would seek refuge from the implacable heat of the Union sun.

The Land of Wonders occupies a corner of the Rocky Moun-tains that I was not able to explore in my rapid 1876 excursion.[3] In consulting the map, I felt myself drawn by some unknown magnetic attraction toward this enchanted land and I could not tear my eyes away. The spirit of travel seethed in my brain at the recollection of all I had heard about it.

Against this fascination the will is powerless, and, although an excursion to the northwest United States would divert me by more than one thousand leagues[4] from my Mexican route, instead of taking the road to Rio Bravo del Norte, I took the one to Yellowstone.

CHAPTER II

The First Explorations

Causes of isolation of the National Park. —The explorers Lewis and Clark.[1] —The trappers Colter[2] and Potts. —The Blackfeet. —Captain Bonneville. —The trapper Jim Bridger and his tales. —The trapper Ross. —Legends about the Land of Wonders. —DeLacy.[3] —Wayant. —George Huston. —Cook and Folsom. —Expedition of General Washburn. —Adventures of Mr. Everts. —Doctor Hayden. —Origins of the National Park.

The history of the National Park is very modern. Surrounded by a wide belt of steep mountains, this marvelous region has long remained unknown to man. It is impenetrable from the east and southeast because of natural barriers and glaciers that protect the upper course of the Yellowstone [River] from this side. Only from the west is there easy access to the Park, and that is why an expedition leaving from the west was destined to discover this mysterious region. But the discovery could not have occurred before the intrepid pioneers of the Far West had penetrated the solitudes of the Rocky Mountains.

It is true that by 1805 two American explorers, Lewis and Clark, had ventured into this wilderness; they passed within a few leagues of the geyser basin, but it seems they did not even glimpse its marvels. Even if they knew of the existence of the "Great Lake" marked on their map, it is most doubtful that they saw it with their own eyes; they probably only knew of it from reports by the Indians.

The first allusions to the fountains of boiling water are found in the reports of a trapper by the name of Colter. This man had accompanied Lewis and Clark on their three-year expedition across the American continent. Once the expedition was over,

Colter undertook to return to the region of the sources of the Missouri with the trapper Potts.[4] During a battle they fought against the Blackfeet Indians in the vicinity, Potts was killed and Colter taken prisoner. The hardy trapper managed to escape at a run from the hands of his persecutors; one of them caught him, but Colter grabbed his spear and pierced him in the chest with it. After atrocious privations, the fugitive arrived completely naked at a trappers' post on the Bighorn.[5] Then he spent several years among the Bannock tribe, with whom he was friendly and who made incursions even into the region that has since become the National Park. He was without doubt the first white man who saw the expanse of Yellowstone Lake spread out before him and who, mute with astonishment, contemplated the wonders of the geyser basin. When he appeared briefly in St. Louis in the state of Missouri in 1810, he gave strange accounts of boiling pitch, lands on fire, and fountains of hot water. Naturally, no one attached any credibility to these stories; they knew that trappers generally have an imagination that tends toward exaggeration, and "Colter's Hell" was long thought to be a fairy tale.

Other trappers and other hunters, among whom we find the French names Pierre, Fontenelle, and Portneuf, ventured into this wilderness, but they did not penetrate the Park, for none of them mentions the country described by Colter.

In 1832 a bloody encounter occurred at the foot of the Teton Mountains between a band of trappers and the Blackfeet, but although from the top of these mountains one can see all of the Land of Wonders, none of these adventurers even suspected its existence.[6]

At about the same time, Captain Bonneville[7] visited these regions. He explored the remarkable group of snowy peaks in the Wind River mountain range and, from the summit of one, contemplated a panorama that enthralled him. If he glimpsed the Land of Wonders from afar, he must not have reached it, for neither the account of his journey nor the map that he published mentions the lakes and geysers.

The first person to confirm Colter's accounts is the renowned trapper Jim Bridger,[8] whose name is famous in the Rocky Mountains and who is probably still alive today. He entered the Park through Two Ocean Pass[9] in 1844. When he returned, he related that he had seen a river whose glacial waters at its beginning changed farther along into boiling water, due to rapid friction. He also spoke of mountains of glass and other strange things. He was scoffed at just as Colter had been laughed at, and yet his accounts were perfectly truthful in spite of the absurdity of his explanations. The river he referred to was the Firehole, whose cold waters heat up in many spots where its bed is riddled with those subterranean vents of boiling water that the Americans call "fire holes."[10] In the same way, a trapper could easily take the obsidian rock masses for mountains of glass.

Without doubt, what Colter and Bridger were the first to report, other white men who perished by Indian arrows saw before them, for, without even considering old tales that mention the journeys of Spanish and Mexican adventurers, it is certain that Canadians from Hudson Bay went into these distant regions to hunt for pelts and furs long before anything was written about this country.

This is proven by the 1878 discoveries of Colonel Norris.[11] Near the Grand Cañon[12] he found a blockhouse containing marten traps of a type formerly used by trappers from Hudson Bay.[13] In the vicinity of the Upper Yellowstone Falls, on the western bank, was a stake bearing this inscription: "J.O.R. Aug. 29, 1819." The inscription is ascribed to the famous trapper Ross of the Hudson Bay Company, who was killed many years ago by the Blackfeet.[14]

It was the trappers' accounts that gave rise to the strange legends long circulating in the Far West concerning this mysterious country. They told of petrified forests containing magnificent palaces and temples with soaring spires, with pearl-ornamented doors, and with massive walls and sumptuous courtyards; they spoke of mansions and stately manor houses. All the inhabitants had been petrified as punishment for monstrous crimes and were still standing in place, fierce sentinels forbidding any approach to this wilderness. They said there were sparkling diamonds and inexhaustible gold mines to be found. But there were also plains on fire, smoking furnaces, boiling caldrons, and fountains spurting with a thunderous noise. Therefore the Redskins did not dare approach these places, which they believed to be inhabited by evil spirits.[15]

These fables had a core of truth. In the gorges of the Yellowstone the basalt rocks often take on the form of ruined palaces and fortresses; vestiges of petrified forests are found in many parts of the National Park; what were the palaces of pearls if not the craters of geysers, their walls encrusted with nipples of white concretions? Was not the infernal domain of fire the basin of the Firehole, riddled with geysers and springs of boiling water?

In fact, everyone knew there had to be marvels there, even though they did not know the nature of them. When gold fever attracted a huge wave of immigration to Montana, many wished to experience this mysterious country.

In 1863 the W. DeLacy expedition departed from Montana [Territory] proposing to explore the upper course of the Snake River, with the goal of discovering deposits of gold. But since their explorations yielded only meager results, the expedition was disbanded and it dispersed in different directions. Captain DeLacy, with some of his followers, went up the Snake and Lewis Rivers and discovered Lewis Lake and Shoshone Lake and the geysers in the lower basin [Lower Geyser Basin] and on the Shoshone. The geographical result of this expedition was a map of Montana drawn by DeLacy and published under the auspices of the territorial authorities in 1864–65.

In the spring of 1864 H. W. Wayant[16] departed from Silver City with a caravan of forty men and a considerable number of packhorses to travel up the east bank of the Yellowstone. He explored Emigrant Mountain, East Fork River [the early name for the Lamar River], and Soda Butte. Part of his expedition reached Index Peak and one of the sources of the Columbia River.

In the same year George Huston commanded an expedition to the Firehole River, which he ascended as far as the great geyser basin. But when Huston and his company witnessed the terrifying eruptions of Giant and the other geysers, and when they thought they would be suffocated by the sulphurous vapors, they imagined they had reached the threshold of the regions subject to infernal powers, and in their terror, they decamped as quickly as possible.

Until this time the adventurers who traveled these regions were attracted only by the prospect of lucre. Some came to hunt fur-bearing animals, others to discover gold. In 1869 two inspectors, Cook and Folsom,[17] made the first real journey of exploration through the Land of Wonders. They ascended the Yellowstone, crossed the river near the great waterfalls, continued the ascent as far as the lake, going around its west bank, crossed the geyser basins, and returned by the Madison (Firehole) River. The account they wrote of their journey in the *Lakeside Monthly* of Chicago attracted the attention of the public. It was without doubt the first authentic description of the hot springs region. The veil of darkness hovering over this terra incognita was now lifted and the way was open. From this time on, one exploration followed another from year to year.

The next summer, in 1870, the first official expedition was organized. It was composed of notable personages from Montana, under the supervision of General Washburn,[18] who was then inspector general of that territory. The expedition was accompanied by a small escort out of Fort Ellis under the command of Lt. G. C. Doane.[19] They ascended the Yellowstone as far as the lake, which they circled completely, and visited all the noteworthy points except the sources of the Gardner River.[20]

While they were exploring the shores of the lake, one of the members of the expedition, Mr. Everts,[21] strayed from his companions and became lost. And to make matters worse, his horse escaped, carrying off his blankets and firearms. His companions searched for him for several days, making signals, lighting fires, and firing shotguns; finally, thinking that Everts had turned back, and also finding themselves at the end of their provisions, they set out en route, hoping to come upon him. Before departing they had left some provisions at the campsite, which the unfortunate lost soul did not find. Everts wandered for thirty-seven days in the wilderness, without shelter or food other than the roots he boiled in the hot springs and some fish he managed to catch with a nail. He saw much game but could not capture any for lack of arms. One day he was almost torn to pieces by a mountain lion and escaped only by climbing a tree. The beast prowled around the tree for a long time, beating the ground with its tail and making the forest resound with its terrifying roars. During a snowstorm Everts had no bed other than the hot crust of a thermal spring, no shelter other than some pine branches with which he covered himself for lack of the blankets carried off by his horse. More than once he was on the point of abandoning himself to despair, but the memory of his loved ones left at home gave him an almost supernatural strength. When at last he was found by his friends on a mountain near Mammoth Springs, he had temporarily lost his reason and was little more than a skeleton. However, he returned to health and later published a dramatic account of his adventures.[22]

In the following year, 1871, the American geologist Dr. Hayden[23] undertook his memorable scientific expedition, accompanied by an entire corps of scientists. The results of this journey were published in the well-known reports of the Geological Service [Survey].[24]

This expedition made a great impact in America and even in Europe. Hayden was the one who really revealed the Land of Wonders, and to him is due the honor not only of making this portion of the American continent known to the world but also of having conceived a beautiful and noble idea.[25]

The enthusiasm that took hold of him and his companions was clouded by the fear of seeing this exquisite country soon invaded by a legion of industrialists only waiting for the following spring to take possession of all these marvels in order to sell rare mineralogical specimens, fence off the geysers, establish ticket booths at the waterfalls, and remove from visitors their rights of entry. Hayden was particularly distressed by the prospect of the invaders vandalizing the incomparable

3. Dr. Hayden, United States geologist.

monuments, whose construction had necessitated thousands of years. Well then! It would be necessary to prevent speculation from profaning this marvel of nature as it had already sullied Niagara Falls.

Hayden therefore envisaged putting the newly discovered region under the protection and surveillance of the state; he contacted the government and proposed to establish this portion of the territory of the Union as a recreational public Park, access to which would be forbidden to those chasing after dollars. It would be expressly reserved for the pleasure of the people of America and those of the entire world. The National Park would be converted forever into a domain of the state; it would be inalienable, shielded from all private exploitation.

In support of the project, Hayden noted that this region was entirely unsuitable for agriculture and for raising livestock because of the high altitude of the valleys and the harshness of the climate and that one could hardly expect to find mines in an entirely volcanic region. There was therefore no impediment to protecting it from colonization.

The two chambers of Congress of the United States speedily adopted the proposition. A bill was introduced on December 18, 1871, and passed into law on March 1, 1872.[26]

Hayden considers this act a tribute paid to science by the American Congress; in the name of the American nation and of scientists the world over, he affirms his gratitude to the legislators for this generous donation.

Such is the origin of the Yellowstone National Park. The Geological and Geographical Service [Survey] has especially studied this region of late.[27] Almost every year scientific expeditions have been organized under the auspices of the Department of the Interior. Of all these expeditions, the most important and the most fruitful is that of 1878; it was the object of a voluminous publication, the most complete to have appeared. It contains the report of Mr. Holmes on the geology of the Yellowstone, that of Mr. Peale on the hot springs, and that of Mr. Gannett on the topography of the region.[28]

Thanks to these fine works, the jewel of the American continent is no longer the terra incognita that constituted a blank space on maps before 1871. Americans are hasty. I believed them capable of accomplishing miracles, but I hardly foresaw that by today one would be able to go from New York to that enchanting land more or less as one goes from Paris to the Alps. When I traversed the Park two years ago, it had not yet been invaded by tourists on their honeymoons; since then the access has become so easy that people go there from all over the United States.

Mr. Hayden writes me from Philadelphia on October 27, 1885, that this year more than ten thousand people explored the Park in the months of July, August, and September.[29] Last summer Mrs. Hayden herself visited the marvelous region that her husband had the glory of conquering fourteen years ago.

CHAPTER III

From the Mississippi to the Yellowstone

Departure from St. Louis. — The Mississippi bridge. — Chicago. — Madison. — Eau Claire. — "Welcome." — Appearance of the town and its population. — Egalitarian principles. — Mechanized sawmills. — Saint Paul. — The Mississippi. — The Metropolitan Hotel. — Mr. Lamborn. — The Northern Pacific Railroad. — The Pacific Express. — Dalrymple Farm. — The stations. — The Dakota prairies. — The Sioux. — The Badlands. — Little Missouri. — Montana. — The Yellowstone. — The Rocky Mountains. — Livingston.[1] — The inauguration of the Northern Pacific. — General Grant.

I left St. Louis by the night train, happy to exchange the mosquitoes of the Southern Hotel for the cool of a "sleeping car."

In wonderfully bright moonlight, the train crossed the famous iron bridge thrown across the venerable Mississippi by American engineers. I was thinking about Atala and Chactas,[2] when the train conductor abruptly dragged me from my contemplation to exact a toll of twenty-five cents for the bridge crossing. I recalled the mundane customs officer who came in the same manner to wrest me from my reveries on the suspension bridge at Niagara.[3]

The next morning I was in Chicago, the queen of the lakes. I had hoped to find a little coolness in a city situated on the banks of Lake Michigan. Well, indeed! the rare passers-by who dared to risk going out into the streets muttered to themselves through their teeth, soliloquizing, "It is very warm today." Now, for a Chicagoan to make such a remark, the heat must be taking precedence over all his other preoccupations. Was it not just my luck! After seven years, I found myself here once again in a temperature that I had not known in the most scorching regions of the hot lands of Mexico. By whatever misfortune, this time, just as on my first visit, this abnormal heat burst on the scene just at the moment of my arrival—according to what the inhabitants say—and they assured me that until then the temperature had been exceptionally cool. Nothing surprised me so much as the monstrous appetite of Americans, who, even in such temperatures, ate with the voraciousness of Eskimos; and this did not prevent them from soaking up like dry sponges all sorts of elaborate drinks.

Chicago, which had filled me with amazement on my first visit [in 1876], this time seemed the most excessively tedious city in the United States; it can appeal only to businessmen. I stayed but twenty-four hours.

How much I prefer the pretty little town of Madison to the large metropolis of Illinois. There, in the capital of Wisconsin, I spent two charming days at the home of my friend Anderson,[4] the learned American Scandinavian scholar whom President Cleveland has recently appointed to the post of United States minister in Copenhagen. In this quiet interior I found myself again in Norway, since Mrs. Anderson is Norwegian, and her lovely house is called Asgard, the residence of the Scandinavian gods. And indeed, the abode of Odin[5] was probably not more beautiful nor more agreeable than that charming valley of Madison. The university buildings are admirably situated on the crest of a hill overlooking several romantic-looking lakes. These lakes, which have kept their names with a strong Indian flavor, put me in mind of the tales of Fenimore Cooper.[6] In the Capitol, where the state legislature sits, they keep a stuffed eagle that followed the Wisconsin regiment in the War of Secession; the inhabitants are very proud of it.

After passing through the immense forests of Wisconsin on the train, I stopped for two additional days at Eau Claire, whose name, today distorted by Anglo-Saxon lips, recalls the original colonization of this country by the French.

Mr. Anderson did the honors, showing me around the place. I was fêted and spoiled by members of the press, industry, and the judiciary. The local newspapers published laudatory articles about me with the headline "Welcome." They did not spare me visitation to a single factory or building site; they took me to tea with all the "self-made men," a term that in America means men who have amassed many dollars; they initiated me into the secrets of "poker," a game dear to Americans. They explained to me that this town of Eau Claire, which a few years ago did not exist and of which I had never heard the name, and whose streets are lit by electricity, has today become the second-largest city in Wisconsin.

It is one of those young settlements of the Far West that become established in several months' time. The streets are unpaved, and the one-story houses, built entirely of wood, periodically burn down, only to spring up immediately from their ashes. An entire section of the town had recently been again destroyed by flames.

These western cities have a rough population, imbued with democratic and egalitarian ideas. Whether I was taken to meet a lawyer or a butcher, a dentist or a magistrate, there was always the same profusion of handshakes and the inevitable greeting of welcome: "I am glad to meet you, sir!" The justice of the peace, who took me about in his carriage, never spoke to his driver without honoring him with the title of "Mister." After all, one changes profession so often in the West that the judge and driver might have exchanged roles from one day to the next.

Eau Claire owes its prosperity to its "lumber mills," mechanized sawmills that are perhaps the largest in the entire world. I cannot think of Eau Claire today without hearing the infernal din of its lumberyards; my ears still ring with the deafening squeal of the saws. I seem to feel the earth tremble under my feet, and it seems as if my face is burning as I stand before the furnaces where the sawdust used for fuel is devoured. I can still see the men hewn in the image of Hercules[7] — Norwegians for the most part, shod with immense boots and wearing enormous hats — manipulating gigantic tree trunks that arrive of their own accord at the lumberyard. They are floated down on the river and in less than five minutes leave the mill completely cut up.

One of these mills, that of the Eau Claire Lumber Company, saws up half a million feet of wood in twenty-four hours with the help of 230 workers, half of whom work at night by electric light. The price of labor is sixty-seven cents (three francs, thirty-five centimes) per thousand feet. The equipment is the last word in progress. The saws are moved by a six-hundred-horsepower flywheel. I saw circular saws making 120 revolutions per minute, horizontal saws striking 300 blows in a like time. I saw machines armed with thirty-six parallel saws. In a few seconds they reduced to thin planks the giants of centuries-old forests that cover the banks of the Chippewa and the Eau Claire Rivers, tributaries of the Mississippi. Most of these forests are owned by the powerful company. The president, Mr. Thorp, has accumulated a $2 million fortune in the lumber business. During his tour of Europe he spent six months in Brussels, with which he is infatuated, as are all Americans. He brought back from Italy a number of art objects with which he has decorated his country house. What a delightful residence! From its position at the top of the hill, it commands a pleasant view of the Chippewa River winding its way between graceful hills.

I had to tear myself away from the charms of Eau Claire, where Mr. Anderson wanted to keep me for an entire week. When I tried to pay my hotel bill, I learned that it had already been paid. American hospitality has often left me in a state of embarrassment.

Several hours' train ride took me to Saint Paul. This political and commercial capital of the state of Minnesota is situated on the left bank of the Mississippi, at the point where the river becomes navigable. A little above the town there are rapids that "flatboats" cannot navigate.

Saint Paul is thus the real starting point of navigation on the Mississippi, since from there steamers can go south downstream to the Gulf of Mexico without encountering the least obstacle. From Saint Paul to the mouth of the river is a journey of 3,350 kilometers. What other river in the world creates a more beautiful natural thoroughfare and waters a more vast agricultural region! The Mississippi and its tributaries transport to market the products of one of the most fertile lands of the globe, a land that could comfortably sustain all the countries of central Europe. This region forms the large central valley of the American continent, comprising Minnesota, Wisconsin, Illinois, Iowa, Indiana, Ohio, Kentucky, Tennessee, Missouri, Kansas, Arkansas, Mississippi, and Louisiana. In North America everything is carved in gigantic proportions: valleys are limitless plains, rivers are seas, and streams are rivers.

It has been two centuries since Father Hennepin[8] discovered the region of the Mississippi where Saint Paul now stands, but only yesterday the Indian was still in possession of it. The present site of the town was bought in 1839 for the negligible sum of thirty dollars. In 1840 a French Canadian by the name of Vital Guérin built a "loghouse" on the spot where the theater stands today. The oldest settler in the area, this man still lived in Saint Paul in 1870. It was in 1840 that Father Galtier,[9] a French missionary, built a wooden church that he dedicated to Saint Paul, and this name has remained for the capital of Minnesota. In 1849 Saint Paul had only thirty houses; in 1870 there were more than twenty thousand inhabitants; in 1883 this number had doubled.

Today Saint Paul has become the great commercial center of the Northwest. It is a charming town; I know of none more picturesque in the United States. It does not have the appalling uniformity of other American cities, because it is built on extremely hilly terrain. On one side the town is confined by the Mississippi, on the other by limestone rocks that dominate the river. It extends over three ascending levels of terrain arranged as an amphitheater, and the appearance of the whole is enchantingly beautiful. Charming country houses are scattered on the heights.

I enjoyed walking on a high terrace in the neighborhood of the Metropolitan Hotel, which overlooks the Mississippi valley, and the sight is really magical, especially in the evening by moonlight. It is true that the Father of the Waters [the Mississippi] is not so imposing here as he is at Saint Louis after he has received tribute from the Missouri, the Illinois, and from a hundred other watercourses, any of which, in our little European countries, would be honored with the name of river. Here it is only a small rushing stream, whose shallow waters flow among a thousand islets, but it has not been yellowed by contact with the muddy silt that its numberless tributaries carry along. Its waters flow clear and unclouded among pleasant hills, whose contours have nothing uneven or rugged about them but are covered with lush forests. It is a landscape of classic beauty reminiscent of certain portions of the upper Danube.

It was only at Saint Paul that the Mississippi captivated me. Elsewhere its dirty waters flowing between low banks across limitless plains have nothing enchanting about them. The Meschacebe poeticized by Chateaubriand has a supreme monotony and a majestic gloominess.[10]

I admired the bold style of the Mississippi River bridge at Saint Paul. The roadway lies in an inclined plane 530 meters long that descends from the heights of the city toward the low banks of West Saint Paul. The largest steamers pass underneath.

In spite of having just sprung to life, Saint Paul already has hotels as grandiose and as sumptuous as those of New York or Chicago. The Metropolitan Hotel, where I stayed, is one of the most handsome in the United States. Hotels in this country burn frequently, so the Metropolitan has introduced measures whose widespread adoption cannot be too highly recommended. In my room I found the following notice posted: "Exit in case of fire. — Upon leaving this room, turn left. Thirty feet away you will find a red light indicating a staircase." Fixed to the wall next to the window is a ring wound with a long escape rope. On every floor are found fire extinguishers ready to be used at the first alert. These measures were taken after catastrophes in Saint Louis and Milwaukee, where hundreds of people perished in a single night.[11]

I only stayed in Saint Paul the time necessary to prepare for my journey to the Rocky Mountains. I went to the offices of the First National Bank, where, upon seeing my letter of credit, they stuffed my pockets with American bills. I then went to a colossal, brand-new building of red brick, where they have set up the offices of the new transcontinental line of the Northern Pacific, whose point of departure is Saint Paul.

The "general manager" of the Northern Pacific, Mr. Lamborn,[12] learning that I wanted to compare the geysers of the Rocky Mountains to those of Iceland, declared that the former were infinitely superior, although he had never visited the latter. He proclaimed me to be an intelligent man and immediately became very kind to me.

"Go see Wonderland," he said to me, "the land of enchantments, the most astounding region of the globe! Go rekindle your enthusiasm before the most beautiful, most sublime, most astonishing, and most incomparable sights on our planet, and then go tell in Europe what you have seen!" Here the general manager stopped to catch his breath; he again assured me of his good feeling and launched into another prolonged discourse prompted by his national pride. He paraded before my eyes, with profuse admiring commentary, the magnificent collection of scenes of the Land of Wonders taken by the Northern Pacific's staff photographer.[13] In the end he obliged me to accept a free ticket worth one hundred dollars, good for passage from Saint Paul to Helena, that place in the wilderness of Montana, two thousand kilometers west, which was then the terminus of the Northern Pacific. Decidedly, this kind gentleman pleased me more than I can say.

The Northern Pacific Railroad is the shortest and most rapid route for anyone who wants to reach the Land of Wonders. The stretch of railroad from Saint Paul to Livingston, which had just been completed, worked out just right for me. A year earlier it would have been a long and tedious trip through immense wilderness. In 1882 the part of the Rocky Mountains on which nature has lavished all her surprises was still almost inaccessible. Only men of an adventurous and determined character could bring themselves to cover on horseback or by "stagecoach" those hundreds of leagues that one traversed by rail in 1883.

The town of Livingston, born that same year and not yet entered on any map, was the departure point for a little narrow-gauge branch line that climbed the upper valley of the Yellow-stone and ended almost on the threshold of the mysterious region.

On the most glorious morning that had ever followed an ap-palling night of storms, I took the Pacific Express, which over two and one-half days would transport me to Livingston across the vast states of Minnesota, Dakota, and Montana.

The train was composed of brand-new, reassuringly solid, and irreproachably comfortable cars. The smoking car, with its straw-bottomed seats, was deliciously cool. At mealtimes, one went to the dining car to eat especially good things while devour-ing the miles. A Negro cook who enjoyed a tidy salary of seven-ty-five dollars a month proved himself equal to his job. When night came one could savor the delights of the "sleeping car."

During the day my traveling companions killed time by read-ing. Most of them devoted long hours to reading every line of voluminous newspapers. Whether particularly beautiful scenery was in our view or the setting sun had just displayed its splen-dors, these practical Yankees invariably turned their backs on the scene.

After each station the conductor made his rounds. The im-portance of this personage is generally expressed by a large gold chain swinging from his waistcoat. The "news-agent" like-wise made his rounds, distributing in the "cars" leaflets enti-tled "Homes for the Homeless" and full of enticing promises to immigrants. These leaflets contain advertisements in verse and prose, proclaiming that the two hundred million acres being offered to settlers by the Northern Pacific Company, at prices varying from $2.60 to $4.00 an acre, are "the best in the world."

The case of Mr. Dalrymple could persuade many pioneers to settle in this region.[14] People everywhere mentioned the name of this enterprising man, who established the famous settle-ment known by the name of Dalrymple Farm near the Red River of the North in Dakota. Today it has become one of the Northern Pacific's largest stations. I had the good fortune to be introduced to him and to travel with him from Saint Paul to Fargo. As he himself laughingly told me, he does not look at all like a major landowner. One would more likely take him for a country doctor than for a farmer who this year (1883) grew thirty thousand acres of wheat and who each year adds an average of five thousand acres to those already under cultivation. Two hundred reaping machines were in operation per day, and in the last harvest the farm produced enough to load seventy-five wagons every day. And every day two trains transported Dalrymple Farm's grain to Duluth on Lake Superior; every day a steamer transported it from Duluth to Buffalo via Lakes Superior, Huron, and Erie. To the current profits must be added the increased value that the lands of this region are accruing from day to day. In 1875 the territory known as Dalrymple Farm was purchased for forty cents an acre, paid in shares of the Northern Pacific, a price that was at that time well below par. Mr. Dalrymple told me that today the same lands are worth between twenty-five and twenty-six dollars the acre. I cannot guarantee the accuracy of these figures, but if they are correct, the increase in value of these lands over a period of eight years can have yielded quite a nice profit. The territory of Dalrymple Farm, or rather, the three territories owned by the capitalists whom Mr. Dalrymple represents, comprise no fewer than seventy-five thousand acres. One may conclude from the figures cited that the property, which cost $30,000, is today worth a minimum of $1.5 million. Now that is hardly an ordinary growth of capital over a period of eight years.

But the time has passed when such a deal could be repeated. One can hardly hope that the value of the agricultural lands in this region will much surpass their present value. Whether they will stay at their present value naturally depends upon the ability of the soil to withstand continuous cultivation.

From Saint Paul to Livingston, a distance of 1,657 kilometers, there are no fewer than 133 stations. In the state of Minnesota, which only yesterday was the farthest limit of civilization in the Northwest, these stations serve fledgling towns that have sprouted up like mushrooms along the railroad, clusters of wooden houses built on the prairie or in the middle of a forest. But when one enters Dakota [Territory] the stations are reduced to solitary log houses, or even simple tents isolated in these wilderness regions. The thousands of tin cans strewn on the ground about them bear witness to the sorry diet of the poor exiles who live in them. The eye wanders over vast horizons, dreary and harsh. There is not the slightest sign of cultivation as far as the eye can see; plains unroll with the monotony of an ocean and extend north to the immense territories of Manitoba, Winnipeg, and British Columbia.

Prairie succeeds prairie, occasionally interspersed with lakes or marshlands. Over a distance of more than two hundred leagues one can search in vain for a tree or a shrub. The grass of these "rolling plains" is roasted by a sun more pitiless than that of the tropics. At the hottest hour of the day the thermometer indicates the very high temperature of 53°C [127.4°F]. Fires break out on the prairie almost daily, as shown by the vast blackened spaces to be seen here and there. From time to time a log house comes into view, completely isolated from the world and lived in by a cattleman. Ravens and hawks whirl about in the air.

Occasionally one encounters a wagon train plodding across the prairie, being drawn slowly by horses, a striking contrast between past and present. This past is not long ago, and the Mormons in their biblical exodus[15] had no other means of transportation than these archaic covered wagons.

Something else that recalls the vanished past are the conical tents [tepees] of the Sioux Indians, which here and there come into view in the immensity of the plain. A traveler told me that in 1864, under the orders of General Sully,[16] he fought on horseback against the Indians on these very plains that today are crossed by the railroad and that in ten years will be, he told me, "all settled." Before long the Sioux tents will have vanished in their turn.

I can hardly describe the astonishment I felt when, after having crossed hundreds of miles of a supremely monotonous country, I suddenly saw towers, pyramids, shafts of columns, domes, steeples, and pinnacles rising up on all sides; as far as the eye could see I perceived only weird and grotesque forms. A person might wonder if he were the victim of a hallucination, as the architecture, created by one of nature's most bizarre caprices, seems so extraordinary and improbable. Adding to the unexpectedness of the tableau are the marvelous colors in which these enormous conglomerate masses are clothed; in this place you can see almost the whole range of rainbow colors.

But it is especially at sunset that the scene takes on a magical aspect. Then one would declare it the ruins of an ancient cyclopean city, and the apparition of a procession of phantoms wandering in this somber desolation would cause not the least surprise.

This is the strange country that the Indians referred to by the name of Badlands.[17] They believed it to be cursed by the Great Spirit and only ventured there fearfully; they encountered great difficulty crossing it on horseback and succeeded only by taking a roundabout route, following narrow tracks that skirted the bases of these curious eminences.

The Badlands occupy a territory 320 kilometers long by 80 kilometers wide, situated some 800 meters above sea level. The strangeness of the scenery, the eccentricity of the geological formations, the great number of fossils, and the extraordinary abundance of game attract scientists, tourists, and hunters to this country every year.

One supposes that in past times the region of the Badlands was perfectly flat; it formed a high plateau resting on a bed of lignite covered with strata of clay. At one time the lignite caught fire and the clay burned; when the combustible material was exhausted, the surface of the ground was left deeply disrupted. All parts of the terrain that had not been consumed by the fire maintained their original level, while the weakened parts collapsed.[18] Thus were fashioned these bizarre monuments, whose infinitely diverse forms stagger the imagination.

This geological phenomenon is recent, for the underground fire that produced it is still active in many places. Near the Little Missouri station I noticed fumaroles steaming here and there and emitting a strong odor of sulphur. They come from an immense mine of burning lignite coal found in proximity to the station. The Northern Pacific Company exploits these

4. The Badlands.

valuable deposits on a vast scale. The locality, inhabited by about fifty settlers, is pleasantly situated on the banks of the Little Missouri, in a valley formed by a fold of the Badlands; the surroundings provide excellent pasturage, and Little Missouri seems destined to become one of the future cities of Dakota. Among the residents is a French gentleman, the Marquis de Morès,[19] who works a large farm. When he arrived in the country, a gang of bandits resolved to do away with their new rival. The marquis killed one of them with a revolver, and since then none has dared confront him. In this new country, where the police force is not yet organized, the revolver is the best means of gaining respect.

The train took several hours to cross the ravines and chasms of the Badlands. Upon emerging from this region one comes into the valley of the Yellowstone, where the countryside changes. We entered it in wonderful, bright moonlight. The rectilinear silhouettes of the mountains, taking on the form of castles and fortifications, stood out with an incredible sharpness in the clear air. We were in the state of Montana, which owes its name to its mountainous appearance. Bounded on the north by British possessions, it is crossed from one end to the other by the great chain of the Rockies. Due to the high altitude, the air is extraordinarily pure and dry. American city dwellers go there to restore their strength. There is nothing better than a stay in Montana for constitutions weakened by anemia and by the fever of incessant work.

From Glendive to Livingston, a distance of 550 kilometers, the Northern Pacific runs along the Yellowstone. Scarcely known only a few years ago, this river has today become the most famous one in North America. Its name means "Pierre Jaune." In this part of its course there is nothing to indicate the marvels of its upper course; its shallow waters flow through a wide valley and seem to rest from all the efforts they made to force a passage through gorges resounding with the thunder of its waterfalls. Coming out of a lake situated in the heart of the Rocky Mountains, at 2,358 meters above sea level, it descends nearly 2,000 meters to swell the Missouri five hundred leagues from its source.

Two days after leaving Saint Paul I at last saw the first snowy summits of the Rocky Mountains, like clouds floating in space. When the sun was at its zenith, the "Pullman car" that had been my home for fifty-two hours set me down at Livingston, at the foot of the Belt Mountains, about halfway between the Great Lakes and the Pacific coast.

Livingston is admirably situated in the Yellowstone valley, at the spot where the river exits the mountains that rise in southern Montana and makes an abrupt right angle to turn east. At the time of my visit this town was nothing but a collection of wooden shacks and simple tents, but there were already high-class restaurants, bars, hotels, "stores," and even a daily newspaper. The population seemed to me excessively mixed: pure Yankees were a tiny minority; there were Germans, Irish, Danes, Norwegians, Russians, Negroes, and quite a few Chinese. In the restaurants and hotels the cooks were all "Celestials," afflicted with interminable black pigtails.[20] I came upon one of them writing a letter. He began by grinding his China ink, then dipped in his brush and, holding it vertically, he set about drawing his characters from right to left. His work was as slow as it was painstaking.

Livingston, which in September 1882 had only fifty inhabitants, in August 1883 had twenty-six hundred. When I was there in September, upon the return from my excursion to the Land of Wonders, the population had again increased notably.[21] The station was decked out with bunting, and triumphal arches had been erected on the occasion of the "marriage" of the Northern Pacific line.[22] This ceremony consisted of the solemn placement of a golden spike at the meeting place of the two sections of the line, which have their departure points at the two extremities of the American continent. The company president, Mr. Villard, had invited all the notables of Europe and America to the ceremony.[23]

Chance had brought me to Livingston on the very day when the guests' trains arrived, and since the service of the ordinary trains was completely disrupted, this circumstance set my schedule back a day. The guests numbered 350. They were brought in by three trains in succession, and the whole population of Livingston turned out to greet them. I have never seen such a wealth of parlor cars, dining cars, and sleeping cars. Each train was made up of ten festive cars pulled by three locomotives.[24]

While I was strolling along the station platform, I was quite surprised to be accosted by a gentleman who shook my hand in a frenzied manner. I vaguely remembered having met him before, but since that meeting had taken place four hundred leagues from there, it is understandable that I had some difficulty in collecting my thoughts. That gentleman was Mr. Lamborn, the general manager of the Northern Pacific. He introduced me to Mr. Villard and to the principal invitees. Among them I found General Grant chewing on his eternal cigar and distributing countless handshakes all about him. I had met him at his cottage in Long Branch on the Atlantic seacoast only a short time before;[25] now I was greeting him at the foot of the Rocky Mountains. It only remained for me to present my respects to him a few days later on the shores of the Pacific. From the Atlantic to the Pacific—pooh!—for the American, it is just a casual stroll.

CHAPTER IV

The Upper Yellowstone

The Upper Yellowstone railroad. — A catastrophe. — The "Concord coach." — Traveling companions. — The Gate of the Mountain. — Paradise Valley. — The "shacks." — A pioneer. — The Second Cañon. — The Yellowstone in the Ice Age. — Cinnabar Mountain. — The Devil's Slide. — A danger spot. — Dreadful storm. — The National Hotel.

A narrow-gauge branch line ninety-two kilometers long diverges from the main transcontinental railroad line at Livingston and ascends the upper valley of the Yellowstone River, ending in the south several leagues from the National Park.[1] This line was as yet operational for only half the distance; it would be inaugurated only in early September on the occasion of President Arthur's trip.

The track had been constructed in the typical American style, with such haste that no one had bothered to secure the ties; they had simply been laid on the ground with incredible carelessness, and I can verify that the mere weight of a human body was enough to cause both rails and ties to wobble. Then there were fast curves, terrifying gradients, and rock ledges overhanging frightful precipices. President Arthur just missed being the victim of a catastrophe that occurred in the first days of operation: after a violent storm had caused the ground to subside, a train fell into the Yellowstone River. On my return, I passed the scene the day after the disaster; it was a most heartrending sight. The locomotive was submerged in the river upside down, its smokestack mired in the mud and its wheels in the air. The baggage car had suffered the same fate as the engine; as for the passenger car, it was hanging above the precipice, on the verge of completing the parabolic trajectory it had begun. It seemed that a providential hand had held it back from the brink of the abyss. Thanks to this lucky circumstance, only one death had to be lamented, that of the engineer.[2]

I was transported toward the regions of the Upper Yellowstone first by train and then by the classic "Concord coach."[3] This is an old barouche in the style of Louis XV that one finds from one end of the Rocky Mountains to the other and that I would later encounter again in Mexico, since the legendary Mexican stagecoach is an import from the United States. Solid leather straps replace metal springs, which would never withstand the mountain roads. The Concord coach does sometimes overturn, despite its reputation for stability.

The interior of these rattletraps conforms to type. My companions looked like authentic Far West bandits, solidly built men with thick, bushy beards, feet thrust into enormous, muddy boots, and heads crowned with immense felt hats. They wore cartridge belts and a whole arsenal of revolvers. The women, brown as chestnuts and dressed in red wool, soaked up whisky like the men, who always took care to help themselves first.

The scenery along this route is splendid. At first one wonders how it would be possible to cross the high, snowy mountains rising across the way as a formidable barrier, but scarcely had we left the plain when we entered the lower cañon of the Yellowstone, where the river has carved itself a path through peaks a thousand meters high.

This gorge, called "Gate of the Mountain,"[4] is a magnificent entryway, worthy of the marvelous country to which it gives access. It is scarcely wide enough for the track that runs alongside the river and overhangs it in many spots; the crystalline rock walls rise vertically to dizzying heights. The mountain has been literally sawed in two by the waters.

In prehistoric times and during the Ice Age, the Yellowstone flowed at a much greater elevation. It was then a destructive torrent escaping from the bosom of an immense glacier entirely covering the upper part of the valley. The continual abrasion of the ice and erosion of the waters eventually carved out the gorge existing today.

By inexpressible contrast, the end of the cañon opens onto sunny Paradise Valley, so aptly named. Imagine a remarkably fertile plain three or four leagues wide, dominated by high, snowy peaks, whose pointed and jagged crests are silhouetted against the deep blue sky like the gigantic jaws of a shark. The mountains gradually drop off toward the plain in a series of terraces, and the floor of the valley is an almost perfectly level surface formed of decomposed lavas, over which the Yellowstone has deposited a layer of alluvium covered with a fertile carpet of greenery. The terraces have been formed by successive recessions of the river, which has carved out different beds for itself in different geological epochs. It is easy to see that this valley was once an immense lake basin covered by a sheet of water fed by the Yellowstone; but even before that, it must have been covered by a sea of ice, as evidenced by the moraines with their furrowed sides and by the enormous bowlders dotting the plain at the very spots where the glacier left them when it receded. These bowlders are of a crystalline rock[5] completely different from the surrounding volcanic rock; they bear the unmistakable imprint of the action of ice.

The lower terrace, forming the most sloping portion of the valley, is of unparalleled fertility. The Yellowstone winds through a luxurious growth of pines and aspens, its cold, clear waters flowing over a stony bed where trout abound. As wide and deep as the Seine in Paris, it flows with the speed of an arrow, fed by innumerable icy mountain streams rushing down from high in the snow-capped mountains. The declivity of the river facilitates irrigation of the land; therefore the harvests in this Paradise Valley are superb.

The farms scattered here and there appear to be prosperous, if not elegant. They are crude log houses, known as "shacks" in this country. Built of rough-hewn tree trunks, they do not at all have the picturesque appearance of Swiss chalets, but their solidity can withstand the terrible storms that break out almost daily in summer. Some of these dwellings are veritable fortresses flanked by turrets and pierced by loopholes, because in the past "frontiermen" [sic] were in constant fear of attacks by Indians.

One of these frontiermen, James George by name, is known by the nickname "Yankee Jim." He is a perfectly typical, hardy American pioneer. For twenty-five years he has lived in these wilderness lands, leading the life of a miner and trapper. He knows places frequented by bison, bear, elk, deer, antelope, beaver, and marten; he is the consummate mountain man. Gold fever, which in 1859 lured many adventurers to the Rocky Mountains, induced him to abandon his home in Pennsylvania and cross the plains in an oxcart. Like all miners, he has encountered both good and bad fortune: he has on occasion paid $110 for a bag of flour and $3 for a pound of salt. Many times he has fought the Redskins; in the Nez Perce War of 1877 General Sturgis[6] employed him as an Indian tracker. It was Yankee Jim who first explored the gold veins in Emigrant Mountain, a majestic mountain whose peak pierces space at 3,236 meters above sea level and at more than 1,800 meters above the valley. Gold is abundant in the crevices of its flanks. At the foot of the mountain lies a little mining village called Chico. The placers[7] there were being exploited well before the Indians gave up their rights to these lands.

Yankee Jim's house is located near the Second Cañon, which one enters when leaving Paradise Valley. It was also Yankee Jim who built the wagon trail going through this gorge, and it was not an easy job: in many places he had to dig out the rocks. He spent $25,000, and therefore travelers, horses, and mules pay without complaint the "two bits" he demands from them.[8] Two bits, or two small amounts, is an example of the Yankee idiom. Anyone who has traveled in the Far West knows that the smallest coin in use in the country is a twenty-five-cent piece, equivalent to a quarter of a dollar. The word "bit" refers to this lowly coin. One can exchange a bit for a cigar, a "cocktail," or a "schnapp"[9] of whisky.

The Second Cañon of the Yellowstone [Yankee Jim Canyon] is even wilder than the first. For a distance of five kilometers, the raging torrent swirls, echoing with raucous booming along the bottom of the narrow fissure it has carved through the overhanging metamorphic rock; in many places the channel is not more than thirty meters wide. The magnificent blue-green waters of the Yellowstone break up in a snowy spume against the mossy blocks of gneiss and granite that have tumbled down from the mountain to the bottom of the river.

Here again, the geological history of this region is clearly written in the rocks, which were polished and striated by the scraping of ice; the marks are as clear and fresh as though the glacier had only recently retreated. The eminent English geologist Archibald Geikie, who recently explored this region, expresses the opinion that the Yellowstone glacier was of a quite considerable volume to fill all the space between the two walls of the gorge;[10] that is to say, it must have been three hundred meters thick. But what proves that the thickness was even greater is the blocks of gneiss and granite deposited by the ice on the slopes of volcanic mountains five hundred meters above the present level of the river. The learned traveler believes the glacier not only occupied the main valley but also extended over the nearby hills and invaded the adjacent valleys.

That there were glaciers in these mountains in the past is something one would conjecture at first glance, but that they would have had such gigantic dimensions is something the imagination would not have dared to conceive without such eloquent proof.[11]

One of the most astounding rocks in the vicinity was baptized by the early explorers with the name cinnabar because they attributed the red color of its striations to the presence of mercury sulphide; but what they took for cinnabar was actually iron. Volcanic forces so disrupted the mountain's structure that the strata stand on end. Composed of alternating layers of clay, limestone, granite, and feldspar, these rocks bestow a very strange look on the general appearance of the mountain. On the south side, two gigantic walls drop from the summit to the base, running parallel to each other fifty meters apart. They are dikes of trachyte rock that rise to more than sixty me-

5. Cinnabar Mountain [Devil's Slide].

ters above their base, just as even, just as vertical as if a mason had employed a square.

According to Hayden, these igneous masses were projected during an age when the strata already occupied their current position. If this is so, the power that cast them up is terrifying to imagine.[12]

In the gap between the two walls, the slope of the mountain has been so thoroughly washed and swept by the elements that from a distance one would think it to be one of those slides that delight children. But the incline is too dizzying for the thought of venturing onto it to occur to anyone but the devil; thus it is known in the vicinity by the name of Devil's Slide. The clayey soil that composes it is fiery red, which renders perfectly plausible the hypothesis that His Satanic Majesty must have passed this way.

The Concord coach deposited us at the foot of Cinnabar Mountain. Only fourteen kilometers remained from there to Mammoth Springs.[13] The prehistoric carriage that I hired together with two Americans to make this passage cost us the modest sum of ten dollars. It was take it or leave it. Actually, the money was not earned without some effort. This is a veritable breakneck route, with climbs to leave both man and beast breathless and descents so steep and rugged that the slightest false move could have reduced us to little bits. The wheels kicked up thick clouds of dust, and the carriage box gave itself over to a frenzied saraband, swaying right, swaying left, so that we thought it would upset at any moment. At times we were suspended over ledges so narrow that a swerve of only an inch would have precipitated us into the Yellowstone. The jolts made us bounce like peas on a drum. One after another, two springs on the rattletrap broke, to the serious detriment of its stability.

I shall always remember that frightful passage when we were tilting so far over the abyss that I felt the blood freeze in my veins. We held ourselves ready for the plunge, but a crack of the whip saved us. "It was a narrow escape!" one of my companions in torture cried with relief. In order to avoid the jolts, this good American used my person as a cushion, crushing me with the weight of his massive corpulence.

Fortunately, our route soon left the valley of the Yellowstone River and reached that of the Gardner River, which joins the Yellowstone from the south at the point where the latter turns sharply from the east toward the north in a right-angled turn.

As one ascends, the volcanic aspect of the country becomes more marked. One climbs a series of steep hills strewn with obsidians, agates, and jaspers and riddled with small lakes that appear to be ancient volcanic craters.[14]

As night was falling we arrived at a grassy plateau. At that very moment a storm that had been threatening us for a long time broke out. Never in my life have I witnessed a more sublimely awesome scene. Blinding flashes of lightning shooting out from all over the sky rent the air in all directions and crisscrossed above our heads, striking the peaks and illuminating their snows with a livid and sinister brilliance. Magnified by echoes from the mountains, the mighty voice of the thunder rumbled continuously like a horrifying cannonade. A glacial cold succeeded the stifling heat. Nothing shielded us in our carriage from the sky's cataracts. In vain did we encase ourselves as hermetically as possible in our coats and blankets, but the deluge was not long in soaking us to the bone.

The route seemed interminable to us. For two hours the rain fell in a downpour. We who had complained of the heat all during the journey were now accommodated far beyond our desires; we shivered while the horses labored at every step on a path transformed into a quagmire.

In this dismal equipage we made our entry into the National Park. At eight o'clock in the evening we discerned with a sigh of satisfaction some lights at the end of a valley lying at our feet. We were at Mammoth Springs.

An immense American-style caravansary, the National Hotel, has just sprung up in this wilderness as if by the wave of a magic wand. The hotel was as yet unfinished, the newly built walls oozed dampness, and by six o'clock in the morning the blows of workers' hammers awakened those still sleeping. But even so, electric lights were already illuminating the immense "hall" and the long corridors onto which open hundreds of rooms. The dining room is vast enough to seat three hundred guests. The walls are adorned with heads of bison, wapiti, and cougar. Mr. Hatch, the entrepreneur of this vast construction, wishes to make Mammoth Springs the headquarters for the legions of tourists that the Northern Pacific Railroad will soon disgorge into the confines of the National Park. Americans will be going to the Land of Wonders as easily as we go to Switzerland.

In 1883 the Mammoth Springs Hotel was still empty; as a matter of fact, it was the first one built in this new country, but before long hotels will spring up all across the Park, and roads will be built to enable visitors to travel comfortably through the Park in vehicles. Then the solitudes of the Rocky Mountains will have lost their principal fascination; gone will be the poetic attraction of the unknown and the exquisite freshness arising from the land in the first days after its birth.

Happy are they who have not waited to visit the Land of Wonders until it suffers the desecration of speculation and fashion! In places other than Mammoth Springs, I was still able to contemplate it in its glorious virginity, just as it appeared only a few years ago to the first explorers, when it was still completely unknown to men. I went through it the same way I went through Iceland, traveling on horseback, camping each night in a tent, and living the rough and healthy nomadic life, whose powerful charm causes man to regret so bitterly the loss of his first independence.

CHAPTER V

Mammoth Springs

General appearance of Mammoth Springs. — Their temperature. — Their deposits. — The nature of the substratum. — Where
is the Mammoth? — The Liberty Cap. — Appearance of the terraces. — Enchanted architecture. — Origin of the basins. — Enthusiasm. — Rich colors. — Algal growths. — Marvelous transparency
of the waters. — The last terrace. — Extinct geysers. — Decline of
the springs. — Forest decimated by the waters. — Extent of the deposits. — An extraordinary fishing incident. — Curative qualities
of the springs. — An interrupted bath.

I arrived at Mammoth Springs on a dark night.

Upon waking the next morning, I noticed from my window
a sort of frozen river standing out against the dark green of the
pines and sparkling under the fiery sun in its dazzling whiteness. At first sight I would have taken it for a glacier, had I not
been undeceived by the vapors that arose from its bosom. In
reality it was the terraces over which plunge the fountains of
boiling water so well situated at the threshold of the National
Park. Squeezed between grassy and wooded hills, these terraces descend the length of a ravine as a glacier would.

From my window I could see only the lower tiers, rising to a
height of about three hundred meters and spreading out across
an equivalent width. This was but a minuscule portion of the
prodigious monument built by the mysterious, slow, and continuous work of the thermal springs. For thousands of years,
they have carried along and dissolved saline substances while
working their way through the stratified rocks, and upon emerging at the surface, they deposit them in the form of geyserite.[1]

From the banks of the Gardner River to the upper extrem-

6. Mammoth Springs.

ity of the ravine situated close to two thousand meters above sea level, the mountain is covered with a white calcareous armor, whose shimmering the eye can scarcely bear when the sun's rays inundate it.

The springs differ in temperature and in the nature of their deposits. Their heat varies from human body temperature to the boiling point;[2] by some mysterious phenomenon, these differences occur in springs in close proximity. Some are rich in carbonates of lime, others in silicates. All emit much carbonic acid and a little hydrogen sulphide; they also contain soda, aluminum, and magnesium.

The speed with which the incrustations form is surprising. If one leaves a glass bottle, a horseshoe, or a basket in the thermal waters, these objects become covered in a few days with a white mineral deposit; even the line holding them becomes encrusted and turns into a stiff rod. Based on similar observations, one could calculate how long the deposits have taken to build the long succession of terraces descending from the summit of the mountain down to the river.[3]

The substratum from which these springs issue is made up of layers of carboniferous limestone, but one finds basalts and trachytes in the vicinity. The springs are dominated to the west by high volcanic peaks. It is to these igneous rocks that the subterranean waters owe their high temperature; it is from the calcareous subsoil that they derive their carbonates of lime.

I devoted two mornings to exploring the springs of Mammoth. Where exactly is the Mammoth? I would have searched for it in vain, and the first explorers did not find it either. Americans have a mania for comparing everything that seems to them gigantic or grandiose to some antediluvian animal.[4]

First I stopped before the Liberty Cap. It is a cone fifteen meters high, six meters in diameter at the base, which looms up at the very foot of the terraces and rests on the spongy and resonant crust covering this portion of the valley. Upon examining it closely, it is easy to convince oneself that this mausoleum is an extinct geyser.[5] It was built up by the discharge of waters expelled at the terminal orifice through the tube piercing it from top to bottom. As the deposits of geyserite accumulated, they formed innumerable compactly structured and very old sedimentary layers. This ancient monument is falling down from age; deep fissures furrow its surface, and the cone will eventually crumble completely. Perhaps it could be preserved from ruin by a conduit bringing in the thermal waters to which it owes its existence; by filling in the fissures, the calcareous deposits would restore the edifice.[6]

I set about to climb up the steps from whose heights the thermal waters fall. With what childish joy I went on my journey of discovery, running from terrace to terrace, touching the delightful, intricate patterns with my finger, dipping my hand in the warm water of the basins and cascades!

Seen from a distance, the Mammoth Springs resemble so strongly the Mer de Glace [Sea of Ice] of Chamonix [a glacier in the French Alps] that at first encounter they excite little astonishment; but when one approaches the edifice and examines the marvelous details of its architecture, one's sight is bewitched, and the enchantment passes quickly from the eyes to the soul. One feels oneself captivated all at the same time by the beauty, the grandeur, and the strangeness of the scene.

7. The Liberty Cap.

It was only upon reaching the first tiers that I observed how the work of the waters has hollowed out an infinite number of basins, which are like so many natural baths. Each perfectly level terrace is contoured as regularly as if built by the hand of man, and each is supported by massive stalactites similar to the alabaster columns that rest on the terrace below.

The hot springs originate in a thousand places and rush from terrace to terrace, from basin to basin, depositing the substances dissolved in them as they evaporate.

The eye loses itself among the multiple combinations of this magical architecture. How delicately are the sides of the basins chiseled! Their edges are outlined in scallops of an infinite richness of shape. Fountains in the most marvelous palaces born of the Oriental imagination would scarcely give an idea of these perfect bowls created by a caprice of nature; from them escape a thousand graceful cascades that lovingly bathe the sculptures of the stalactites and flow as pure and limpid as molten diamond. Since the waters cool as they descend, the bather may choose the temperature that pleases him.

How can one admire these marvels without wondering what mysterious cause has produced them and by what whim of nature the waters have thus fashioned a thousand elegant, crescent-shaped basins, rather than following a regular path? A mundane observation furnishes the solution to the problem. The thickness of the deposits being proportional to the depth of the liquid layer, it is precisely at the edges of the terraces, where this depth is greatest, that the deposit is most abundant. These edges thus build up gradually and fashion themselves into overturned shells, from which the water pours out in cascades.

Therefore, one imagines that if the hot waters loaded with saline constituents happen to spurt out from the bosom of a level surface, then at a certain distance from the point of emergence their deposits will accumulate, influenced by evaporation and cooling, such that with time a circular rampart will be built up around the spring.

And thus, little by little, the terraces are transformed into so many basins, whose depth varies from a few centimeters to almost two meters. Some overflow on all sides into lower basins, others are dried up. As long as water bathes the geyserite it is hard and resistant, but in drying out it becomes soft and friable, and a steel blade penetrates it easily.

The springs that feed the basins change position according to their whim; it is not unusual to find an active spring in the midst of debris abandoned by another one that is long dry, and it would be very difficult to say if any relationship ever existed between them.

I spent several hours climbing this crystal stairway. Not that the ascent is long and laborious, but so many wonders invite the gaze that one cannot resist the temptation to idle along the way. One must, as in a gallery of paintings, be content to admire a small number of masterpieces, while regretting having only a few fleeting hours at one's disposal to enjoy them and to fix an undying memory of them on the soul.

I could not take a step without crying out in surprise at this labyrinth of clear brooks and steaming basins, among which I ventured with care, not so much for fear of scalding myself as for fear of desecrating the work of centuries. The calcareous crust is often treacherous: in a good many spots it is so thin that one distinctly hears the sound of subterranean water. Here and there crevices permit one to follow the course of those torrents for a certain distance.

The terraces seemed to grow larger as I went up. Their scalloped edges and their dazzling stalactites built up like a series of frozen cascades above my head; the overall effect was of a striking majesty. I marveled as much at the splendor and variety of colors as at the delicate structure of these concretions. The deposits are arrayed in almost all the hues found in nature, and these colors are of a freshness and a brilliance that no paintbrush could reproduce. Here the streaming crystalline waters make the immaculate white of the silicates sparkle, while elsewhere the rock has the milky transparency of alabaster or borrows tones of vermilion red or golden yellow from sulphur and iron; in still other places it is a deep brown, a tender green, and occasionally a most delicate pink.

8. Terraces at Mammoth Springs.

The richness of the coloring is heightened still more by the carpet of algae that thrive in these hot waters. There are white, brown, yellow, red, and green ones; these algae take the form of long, silky filaments that dissipate in trailing fringes, undulating constantly in the running water. Sometimes the presence of sulphur makes them appear like a mesh of crystal, slender as needles. What a strange phenomenon is this luxuriant vegetable life in the midst of these boiling waters!

Almost at the top of the ravine, I finally reached the large plateau where the principal active springs supplying the basins of the lower levels well up. These springs spurt out from the bottom of vast, roughly circular reservoirs. Most of the basins have two centers of ebullition. I do not know how long I stayed on the margin of one of these wells, my eyes bewitched by the azure depths over which played the puffs of steam that a breath of air dispersed. The water is so transparent that there is not a single design on the interior walls of the basin that is not perfectly visible. Crystal or turquoise are comparisons too imperfect to give an idea of the wonderful purity of these ultramarine-blue waters. Such charming magic is the agitation that boiling produces on the surface of the liquid expanse! One's captivated gaze follows the little ripples originating at the center of the reservoir and sparkling with all the colors of the prism, refracting the sun's rays in their waves.

Continuing my climb, I finally reached the last terrace. An isolated spring arises there, one that now has only a rather meager discharge, but formerly other, more sizeable springs originated on this same terrace, as evidenced by the scalloped edges of the basins and the crevices from which sulphurous gases escape. One of these craters forms a cave whose mouth sends out scalding jets of hissing steam that deposit sulphur crystals on the rock.

Numerous cones of extinct geysers are found in the vicinity of the upper terrace; chipping away at them, time has transformed several into caverns, which have sometimes served as lairs for wild animals. In one of these caverns bones and tree branches carried in by animals have been found, and legions of bats have taken up residence there. In places where the crust is broken, numerous layers of sediment appear.

These vestiges of now-extinct hot springs and geysers attest that the activity of the Mammoth Springs is in the process of decreasing and that the subterranean forces no longer manifest themselves with the energy that they must have formerly displayed. The annual decrease that has been noted in the flow from the springs since their discovery shows that the decline is rapid.[7] A number of sinkholes that were formerly basins today provide a habitat for bushes. Cones that not long ago sent forth columns of boiling water today support pine trees more than a hundred years old that contrast, by their vigor, with the stunted bushes that grow in the vicinity of the active springs.

The forest is decimated across the entire course of the thermal waters; many trees stricken dead are still standing erect, extending their bare branches over the white layer of geyserite [actually, travertine], where they remain half buried. These trees, which obviously could not have sprouted in the midst of substances turned to stone, attest to the frequent displacement of the active springs. A great many terraces that are dry today support conifers whose age shows the antiquity of the sediments; some of them are not less than a meter thick, which would represent more than five centuries of growth.[8] And also one must take into account the years that passed between the disappearance of the springs and the moment when the trees could find sufficient soil to take root; but what are those years compared with the centuries represented by the unknown thickness of the sediments!

The calcareous deposits cover a surface area of three square miles, extending from the bank of the Gardner River to the head of the ravine. The region of active springs, limited to a part of this territory, occupies about eighty hectares [two hundred acres]. Many boiling springs gush out along the banks of the Gardner. Overlooking the river, a long series of terraces formed by vanished springs climbs back up the hill over the course of a mile and ends up at the present center of activity, whose decreasing intensity one can follow for a mile beyond

9. A bath at Mammoth Springs.

that, up to the dense pine forests that crown the summit of the mountain. The center of activity must previously have been found much lower down, about equidistant from the present center and the banks of the Gardner.

One of the most curious contrasts in this marvelous valley [below the terraces] is that springs of boiling water gush forth a few steps from the glacial waters of the Gardner. To catch a trout in the river and, without taking it off the hook, to plunge it still wriggling into a neighboring spring in order to eat it on the spot, there is a feat that seems as unlikely as those of Baron Münchhausen.[9] However, the experiment was carried out before my very eyes by two Americans, avid practitioners of this "exciting sport," who had undertaken a trip from New York to the Rocky Mountains chiefly with the goal of finding just such an ineffable pleasure. Since the river abounds with fish, they had soon put together the elements of a copious lunch, which they invited me to share. The poor trout passed instantly from river to pot, whence they emerged after five minutes only to pass into our stomachs. Perfectly cooked, they were found to be delicious, but Brillat-Savarin[10] would perhaps have made this qualification: they lacked salt.

The Mammoth Springs thermal waters have been known for too short a time and are not yet sufficiently analyzed for their healing virtues to have been tested. They do seem to be effective for skin ailments and rheumatic diseases. Perhaps one day the sick will hasten from all parts of the world to bathe in these beneficial springs.

I experienced supreme satisfaction plunging into a basin whose waters were an exquisite 30°C [86°F]. My bath was a meter deep. The siliceous efflorescence that lined the interior walls seemed like velvet cushions.

I remained perfectly still for a long time in this delightful bath, allowing my body to be pervaded by the invigorating influence of those waters, gentler to the skin than the softest comforter and as agreeable to the taste as to the touch.

While I was reveling in my bath, I became aware of the augmentation in water level following a sudden rise in level in a higher spring, and, to my great horror, I noticed a neighboring basin that had been completely dry was now flooded by the rise. Now, it was in that basin that I had put my clothes, my boots, my towels. One must have suffered a similar ordeal to understand what deep despair can arise from the smallest accidents. The proximity of the hotel consoled me in my misfortune.[11]

CHAPTER VI

The Gibbon River

Traveling companions. — The guide Jack. — Trip plan. — National Park roads. — Indian ponies. — The California saddle. — Delights of traveling on horseback. — President Arthur. — Terrace Mountain. — Lone Star Geyser. — In the forest. — Squirrels and snakes. — Wreck of the presidential wagon train. — Terrace Pass. — Quadrant Mountain. — Swan Lake. — A burned forest. — Obsidian rocks. — A glass road. — Sulphurous spring. — Beaver Lake. — Lake of the Woods. — The Gibbon River.

I had the good fortune to meet two Englishmen at Mammoth Springs who were en route to explore the National Park. One of them, Dr. Clarke, had visited Iceland in 1877. As a geologist, he proposed to compare the volcanic phenomena of the Land of Wonders with those he had observed in the Land of Ice. When he learned that I, too, had ridden on horseback across the lava fields of the great island of the north, he regarded me highly, introduced me to his friend Alexander, and invited me to join their expedition. The cost of the trip would be divided among the three of us, and we would sleep in the same tent. Needless to say, the prospect of traveling with some amiable gentlemen through a completely uninhabited country made me accept the proposition with enthusiasm.

We engaged a guide by the name of Jack. A typical Far West trapper, this man had never set foot east of Chicago. For eight years he had toiled as a miner in the placer gold mines of Colorado. He wore an outfit that was half Indian, half European: buffalo-skin trousers plunged into oversized yellow boots with Mexican spurs that jingled like little bells, elk-hide vest, colossal felt hat shading a bearded face, and on his belt an enormous American pistol in a leather holster. Under this ferocious costume, Jack was the best fellow in the world. The success of the expedition was due in large part to his unfailing good humor, energy, and intelligence. We left to him the task of finding us horses.[1]

Our plan was to go directly to the geyser region, in the south of the National Park. Next we would visit Yellowstone Lake, then the Mud Volcanoes and Sulphur Mountain. After admiring the Grand Cañon and the falls of the Yellowstone, we wanted to climb Mount Washburn, visit Tower Falls [sic],[2] and return to our point of departure by way of the Gardner River valley. About ten days ought to suffice for this expedition.[3]

The network of roads that will eventually cross the interior of the National Park had scarcely been started in 1883. A wagon route led from Mammoth Springs to the geyser region and the falls of the Yellowstone, but other parts of the region were accessible only by mule tracks or simple paths cleared through the forests. Besides, the wagon road was in as pitiable a state as the "royal roads" that I would later experience in Mexico; the surest way to avoid overturning on them was to travel on horseback.

The sum of $15,000 allotted annually by the United States Congress for maintenance of the National Park, from which must be deducted the salaries of the superintendent and the game warden, is obviously insufficient for the improvement of roads and trails; winter rains destroy the small amount of work completed during the summer. In the report of his expedition to the National Park in 1881, General Sheridan[4] proposes the allocation of a higher subsidy, the appointment of an engineering officer who would be responsible for the maintenance and improvement of roads, and the dispatch of one or two cavalry units, which would be stationed in the Park in summer to prevent forest fires and damage to the natural formations built up by the geysers.

Had we come a few months earlier, we would have been obliged to lead pack horses and carry in all our camping equipment, tents, buffalo skins, and provisions. But we had been assured that we would find tents, camp beds or buffalo skins, and even portable kitchens that the park superintendent had arranged to be set up for the use of visitors near all the most interesting points, pending the imminent construction of hotels.

Our little caravan therefore consisted of only four saddle horses. They were Indian ponies known locally by the name of "cayuses,"[5] excellent little animals with fine, vigorous legs. They seemed to have a lot in common with my cherished Icelandic ponies. On flat terrain they gallop as fast as the wind; in the mountains they display a marvelous sure-footedness. They skirt the most vertiginous precipices along narrow paths, and it is best to trust their instinct, without trying to lead them.

Our mounts bore California saddles fitted with a jumble of straps, a high pommel, and a back rising in a scroll like the Mexican saddle. The wooden stirrups are placed so they offer themselves easily to the toes. Less elegant than the English saddle, the California saddle is perfectly adapted to long rides in the mountains: the rider is more or less boxed into it. But woe to him if his mount should tumble; riveted to his horse, he will share its fate. Yet he can be reassured by the fact that the cayuse stumbles no more than the Mexican mustang.

Of all means of travel, the most appealing is incontestably horseback riding. I once met a musician who could find inspiration only when in the saddle. When the sensual pleasure of traveling along picturesque trails and breathing the pure, fresh air of high altitudes is added to the pleasure of horseback riding, one abandons oneself entirely to the happiness of living.

True, this delight is occasionally interrupted by passing afflictions. One is in turn roasted by the sun, drenched by storms, and whipped by the wind, and fatigue eventually overcomes even the most spirited horse and the most saddle-hardened rider. But these episodes are later recalled as inexplicably charming. One quickly forgets the well-appointed tables and soft beds encountered on a journey, but many years later one can still recall the places where one has slept on the ground or has gone hungry and thirsty.

On August 30, at eleven o'clock in the morning, our little caravan set off.

We left at the same time that an immense cavalcade of about a hundred people arrived at Mammoth Springs. It was the president of the United States, Mr. Arthur, coming to spend his summer vacation traversing the National Park in easy stages with his retinue.[6] We did not have time to offer him our respects.

It is said that Mr. Arthur is a "dude," which, when translated from Yankee into French, means that he is the most dandified of all the presidents who have succeeded to the White House. His stay in Yellowstone significantly disturbed his fondness for his toilette; therefore, the caricatures in the newspapers did not miss the chance to depict him as he might be upon his return to the White House, receiving his visitors in rustic Far West dress, with a pistol at his belt, his boots up on the desk, and rolling his eyes like a ferocious trapper.

The president's trip has become legendary in the American mind. For several days all of America was in mortal agony concerning his fate, following a sensational piece of news reprinted in all the newspapers of the Union under this thrilling headline:

"They Are after Arthur."

The dispatch, datelined from Hailey (Idaho) announced that a band of "desperadoes" from Texas had left for the Yellowstone Park. They had been seen camping on Willow Creek, and they appeared mysterious. One of them had divulged the goal of the expedition, which was nothing less than to capture President Arthur and all his entourage, to hold them captive in a cave, and to extort from the United States a ransom of a million dollars that would be drawn from secret funds and shared out among the bandits. The band was composed of sixty-five men, armed with repeating rifles and commanded by a "desperado" with a price on his head. During the night they had held a big confabulation on the prairie, and all had sworn by their daggers to do their duty. Sheriff Farcy had sent troops with orders to arrest the bandits. . . .

This was worth reporting as an example of the hoaxes on

10. The Lone Star Geyser.

which American newspapers thrive. Sheriff, troop deployment, bandits, ransom, cave—all were only a story, or to express it like a Yankee, a "humbug."[7]

So here we were, climbing the tiered terraces on the northeast slope of Terrace Mountain. The calcareous crust was reverberating with a sinister resonance under the horses' hooves. Mammoth Springs Hotel, the last vestige of civilization, quickly disappeared from our view.

After some time spent in a difficult ascent, we encountered some new mineral concretions similar to those at Mammoth Springs. An enormous cone of geyserite, completely isolated, rises to the left of the path. It is the crater of Lone Star Geyser, which erupts at irregular intervals.[8]

Farther on there is glorious Alpine scenery where one becomes intoxicated with the resinous scent of the pines, cedars, and larches.[9] Here and there are splendid vistas of the mountains, whose steep cliffs make them appear disproportionately high. The forest is filled with jays hopping from branch to branch. The friendliness of these birds proves they have not yet experienced man's malice: they let themselves be approached so closely that one can almost take them in hand.

Also abundant are pretty squirrels called "chipmunks"; a little larger than a mouse, they have brown backs and yellow bellies. Extraordinarily agile, these charming little animals frolic among the snakes that infest these forests and that, God knows, are numerous! There was one stretched out dead along the path; as thick as one's arm, it measured not less than two meters long. Jack assured us that it was only a grass snake, infinitely less formidable than the rattlesnakes that proliferate in this region.

The narrow, rugged trail is extremely arduous and overhangs frightful abysses. At the bottom of a ravine lay a wagon from the presidential retinue, with its wheels in the air. The plunge it took from high on the mountain the day before left it in a lamentable state. The sight of this wreck gave us pause. But, heavens! What a road! To climb this incline of less than three miles would take a four-horse team half a day.[10]

At one o'clock we reached Terrace Pass.[11] At this altitude of 2,250 meters there is a perceptible drop in temperature. The view from the top of the pass is somewhat limited. To the south, two snowy peaks loom up.

After crossing the pass, we reached a vast, circular basin with lovely grasses undulating in the breeze. Clumps of pine trees stand out like dark-green islands. Here and there the bleached bones of a bison or elk on the side of the road indicate that this country abounds in game. To the east, 2,675 meters high, rises the bare summit of Bunsen's Peak, its steep sides grooved with deep crevices. To the west the horizon is bounded by the strange mass of Quadrate [sic] Mountain,[12] dominating the landscape with its full height of 3,051 meters. Its four faces, delineated with geometric precision against an intensely blue sky, give it the appearance of a pyramid built by a vanished race, and the illusion is completed by the perfect regularity of the horizontal stratifications that score the sides of the mountain in bands of yellow, pink, gray, and black. This variety of colors stands out vividly against the background of the green plain and the azure sky. At the foot of this vast structure rises Castle Rock, which adds still more to the unexpectedness of the tableau. It is a pile of igneous rocks so oddly sculpted by the hand of time that it could be mistaken for the ruins of an ancient feudal castle.[13]

After we had passed little Swan Lake, slumbering among the reeds and marshes, we entered a mysterious, imposing forest. Renewing themselves from their own ashes for centuries, its pines attain gigantic proportions. In their shade reign a half darkness and a coolness, which were agreeably refreshing after our ride under the burning sun. Thousands of squirrels frolic in the tree branches.

It was there that we witnessed for the first time a scene that is quite common in these regions. An immense portion of the forest had been consumed by fire; as far as the eye could see, there were only charred tree trunks by the thousands, white on the windward side, smoke-blackened on the opposite side. Their bare branches reached out like the arms of a skeleton. It was a picture of supreme desolation that could have inspired the genius of Dante[14] and the pencil of Doré.[15] Inadequately extinguished campfires cause these fires, whose traces are so painful to see.

Coming out of the forest, we arrived at the foot of one of those curious "obsidian cliffs" that the first explorers took for mountains of glass, not without reason. More than fifty meters high, the cliff extends about three hundred meters in length. It is without doubt the largest known compact mass of obsidian. It has a most unusual appearance. The rock was crystallized by fusion, and it presents a magnificent cluster of six-sided prisms standing vertically, like the famous basalt colonnades on the coasts of Ireland and Scotland.[16] It is alarming to think that this prodigious mass of volcanic glass was spewed out as a molten mass from the depths of the earth. The rock is black, shiny like jet, and scored here and there with bands of yellow, red, and brown that indicate the presence of iron. Where it is of slight thickness, it acquires a transparency, proving that the colored matter has undergone a complete fusion into the silica.

Large blocks that have broken loose from the summit form a barricade of debris at the foot of the colonnade. The road had to be cut through this mass of fallen rock. To accomplish this job, Colonel Norris, former superintendent of the Park, devised a plan to light large fires: the obsidian blocks, expanded by the heat, were subjected to a sudden drop in temperature by being doused with cold water. They then shattered into small fragments easy to clear away. Thus a glass road was built, perhaps the only one on earth.

Obsidian seemed to me to be much more common in Yellowstone than in Iceland; it is found in almost the entire expanse of the area. Here, as in Mexico, the Indians used this substance to make arrowheads, spears, and implements of all sorts. They probably came to this very rock to seek it, because nowhere else can it be found so pure.[17]

At the foot of this rock, amid a carpet of moss, a deep spring of blue water gushes up. Leaving our horses, we clambered over the piles of fallen obsidian to examine it closely; the extremely cold water releases bubbles of carbonic acid and presents quite a pronounced taste of sulphur and alum. It sparkles and effervesces like champagne. The earth surrounding the spring is unstable mud, where one should venture only with caution.

Continuing our progress southward, we arrived at a strange, artificial lake, created not by the hand of man but by the trowel-shaped tails of beavers. These industrious masons have succeeded in blocking the course of Green Creek[18] by cooperative work and consolidation of capital. Their teeth have gnawed and felled the giants of the forest, their tails have converted mud into cement, and thus they have erected a series of dams describing elegant curves from one side of the body of water to the other.

These works have survived from the significant colony that trappers have pitilessly decimated. Was it necessary for the white man's destructive ingenuity to come to these wild and hidden places to wipe out that which the Redskin respected?

Beaver Lake is populated by legions of cranes, wild geese, ducks, and other aquatic birds that romp in perfect security, thanks to the danger posed to hunters by the unstable ground of the marshes.

Numerous hot and cold springs strongly impregnated with alum well up from the heart of the volcanic rocks that surround the lake.

After crossing the drainage divide between the basin of the Yellowstone and that of the Gibbon River, we soon found ourselves on the romantic banks of another body of water, sleeping like an emerald in the midst of a dense forest, at an altitude of 2,365 meters. This is the Lake of the Woods, and it is aptly named.[19] The slender columns of the pines are reflected in the clear, still waters and seem to plunge their verdant crowns into it. All is silent on the banks of this solitary lake; no breath of wind ripples the diaphanous surface that shimmers like a mirror. At certain times of year deer and elk come to its banks to drink, but in summer they seek altitudes closer to the eternal snows in order to avoid the attacks of mosquitoes that infest the valleys.

This enchanting site is followed by a strange contrast, a region riddled with sulphurous springs, probably old geysers on the wane, where gas bubbles up in water yellowed by sulphur deposits.[20]

A gentle descent brought us to the beautiful prairies watered by the Gibbon River.

CHAPTER VII

The First Geysers

The Gibbon Geyser Basin. — The encampment. — Boiling springs. — Muddy springs. — Feeling of dread. — Supper. — The campfire. — A concert in the woods. — A delightful evening. — Dryness of the atmosphere. — A storm. — Morning bath. — The geyser basin. — The Monarch. — The Minute Man. — The Constant. — The Twins. — The Emerald Pond. — A mud volcano. — The Steamboat Vent.

At five-thirty in the evening we reached the end of our first day's march. We had arrived at the Gibbon Geyser Basin,[1] the first group of geysers one encounters coming from the north.

On the banks of the Gibbon River we found a camp of eight A-shaped tents made of sailcloth, anchored with stakes driven into the ground. The largest served as a dining hall; in another a Chinese man conscientiously carried out the duties of chef; the six others were meant to shelter the station personnel and travelers, on whom exorbitant prices were levied. We took possession of one of them, where, to our great satisfaction, we found camp cots and warm wool blankets.

After unsaddling our horses, and while supper was being prepared, we hurried over to the hot springs southwest of the camp. The plumes of white steam we glimpsed between the trees showed us where they were. According to Hayden's not very poetic but apt comparison, the valley resembles an immense industrial city over which hovers the smoke of factories.[2]

At the end of several minutes' walk, we suddenly found ourselves at the edge of one of those basins that the first trappers who traversed this region took to be the openings of hell. With a surface area of about ten hectares [twenty-five acres] and a depth of eight to ten meters, the whole basin [Porcelain Basin] is an ensemble of boiling hot springs, pools, fumaroles, and solfataras that display the most bizarre assortment of colors and produce an unimaginably diabolic concert of hisses, sighs like the bellows of a forge, and raucous hollow-sounding roars. The overheated air is tainted with noxious gases, while the ground rumbles and shakes underfoot as if ready to open up. The sinister sound of boiling subterranean waters comes from underneath the treacherous crust, and one cannot venture onto it except with extreme caution.

The bottom of the basin, which is white streaked with yellow, is riddled with an infinite number of conduits spewing forth sprays of boiling water or jets of steam and lined with delicate, golden-yellow sulphur crystals.

There are also muddy springs of boiling clay; this slate-colored paste constantly heaves and sometimes spurts up several feet high, splattering the nearby area. The Americans designate these mud pots by the picturesque name of "paint pot."

One experiences an inexpressible feeling of horror in the presence of these convulsions of nature, on this ground palpitating like the chest of a sick person, before these somber outlets from where groans seem to escape. Nowhere else, not even in Iceland, had I felt such an impression of dread. And, despite that, this savage and grim poetry is fascinating. Illuminated by an admirable sunset, the scene had a marvelous, fantastic aspect that I shall never forget.

Upon our return to the camp, night was falling. As we had eaten nothing since eight o'clock in the morning, I will let you wonder whether we did justice to the elk roast we were served in the tent by the light of a candle stuck in the neck of a bottle. If, in Clarke's opinion, the coffee was not as good as that which we had so often happily savored in Iceland, to compensate, the icy water drawn from the nearby river was excellent.

After this copious repast we fraternized with a caravan of American travelers who had just arrived from the south; among them was an intrepid horsewoman. We made a circle in the open air around a large campfire fed by whole pine trees.

While we were conversing around the merry flames, our friend Alexander sent us distant echoes of Mendelssohn's "Wedding March" from deep in the woods, played on a perfectly portable little concertina that is the companion of all his travels. It was doubtless the first time that these lonely wilds had resounded with such harmonious chords.

This music in the bosom of the wilderness plunged me into a delicious reverie. No other evening has engraved itself more profoundly on my memory. Never have stars seemed to me to shine with such vivid brilliance: one might have said countless golden lamps dispersed in infinity.

I have always been vividly impressed by the beauty of the nights in these high northern regions of the Rocky Mountains. The brilliance of the stars is due to the great clarity of the air at these elevations; the atmosphere is so dry that all you need do is pass your hand rapidly over a bison pelt to make electric sparks fly. Nights are cold, and in the month of August frosty nights regularly follow blazingly hot days. But one is less aware than might be supposed of these extremes of temperature; the cold does not occur unexpectedly but gradually. Besides, it turns out that one feels the cold but little in camp life because one does not experience the abrupt variations of temperature caused by passing from the atmosphere of an apartment to the outdoor air.

That night we hardly slept at all. For barely an hour had I shared with Clarke the camp cot that served as our common bed, when an appalling thunderclap awoke us with a start. It was a proper storm. The flash of lightning dazzled us even in the tent, whose fabric crackled noisily under the torrents that fell all night. Happily, the tent withstood the downpour; not a drop of water came in.

At six in the morning we were up. A splendid sunshine had succeeded the storm. The temperature was biting, the air extraordinarily sharp and dry.

While breakfast was being prepared, we took a morning dip in the Gibbon River. Fed by the snows of nearby mountains, the water was freezing, so we took only a plunge.

The morning was spent in exploring the active geysers that

occupy the plateau southwest of the basin we had already visited. These geysers [in Back Basin] are hardly comparable to those of Iceland nor to those that we would admire later in the Firehole region; their eruptions are not very sizable, and they generally lack those magnificent basins whose classic structure complements the geysers, but they display phenomena that we would not find elsewhere. The geysers of the Gibbon River differ from their like in Iceland and the Firehole by the disposition of their craters, which generally open at the side of a rock.

American explorers have given these geysers various names. They paid their respects to the one that produces the highest column of water by naming it the Monarch. Not having seen it play, we cannot say if it deserves this honor. It is said that it erupts once a day with a spray thirty to forty meters high, which escapes through three distinct orifices.

Near the Monarch is a little geyser that passes for a model of exactitude and punctuality: regularly, once every sixty seconds, it shoots out a jet of several meters. It is the Minute Man [Minute Geyser]. Although we watched it for a rather long time, it did not deign to disturb itself for us. Probably the Minute Man has periods of slumber during which it forgets to carry out its duties.

The Constant [in Porcelain Basin] was nicer: every thirty seconds it offered us the spectacle of a small eruption, at the end of which the basin emptied completely only to refill right afterward.

The Twins, the Triplets, and the Fountain were likewise in perpetual activity.[3]

The Emerald Pond [Emerald Spring] seems to be the crater of a geyser, although it has never been seen to be active.[4] It is an unfathomable chasm, in which the scalloped walls are visible to a great depth through the marvelous transparency of the beryl-green water that fills it to the brim. By one of those contrasts so frequent in this enchanted land, next to these crystal-clear waters we found a mud volcano [Bathtub Spring], which, from one quarter hour to the next, throws up a pasty mass three or four meters high.

We were attracted elsewhere by a noise exactly resembling

11. The Minute Man.

the roaring of a steamship's funnel: it came from the Steamboat Vent, an enormous hole in the earth throwing out puffs
of superheated steam with a terrifying vehemence. Upon our
cautious approach, we saw that the chimney has two vents. The
hissing is so intense that a dozen locomotives together would
scarcely produce such a noise.

As Doctor Peale[5] remarked, everything points to this cavern
being of recent formation: sulphur and geyserite deposits have
not yet had time to accumulate around the vents, but the surrounding ground is covered with a layer of sand that seems to
have been thrown out by an eruption; the nearby trees are dead,
and some are lying on the ground half buried under the sand.

According to the testimony of Colonel Norris, the Steamboat
Vent[6] did not exist in 1875; but since 1878 it has thrown out powerful jets of boiling water. It is obviously a new geyser that has
just been born and whose developmental period will no doubt
furnish valuable data on the age of the geysers, their patterns
of behavior, and the formation of their deposits. A geyser in the
different phases of its existence, from its earliest infancy to its
decrepit old age, would indeed make a curious story.

CHAPTER VIII

The Firehole

Elk Park. — Encounter with hunters. — The Gibbon Paint Pot Basin. — The Blood Geyser. — New mud springs. — Chemical phenomenon. — Horses' instinct. — The Monument Geyser Basin. — Powerful steam jet. — Beautiful panorama. — The Gibbon Cañon. — A waterfall. — The Firehole River. — A log house. — The travelers' registry. — The valley of the Firehole. — Appearance of the geysers at dusk. — The campsite.

After having devoted several hours to examining these phenomena, we remounted and continued southward. The previous night's storm had transformed the trail into a quagmire, and our horses floundered at every step, each horse worse than the one before.

An hour later, Elk Park came into view. How refreshing was this verdant space, enclosed as it was by a magnificent ring of pine-forested mountains! The Gibbon River here winds through the meadows. This is wonderful country for big-game lovers, as its lovely pastures are the favorite haunts of the denizens of the Rocky Mountains. Here we came across a camp of hunters; they were traveling in wagons that converted to tents at night. These Nimrods[1] proudly showed us the results of their hunt: they had killed a superb moose and a bull elk.

Near the far end of Elk Park, amid the trees and not far from the entrance to the Gibbon Cañon, lies the Gibbon Paint Pot Basin [Artists' Paintpots]. We approached it along a barely discernible track through the dense undergrowth.

The appearance of this basin is extremely strange: over an expanse of two or three hectares the ground is riddled with hundreds of craters spewing out substances half solid and half liquid. The Blood Geyser shoots out a column of water so pronouncedly red that the stream flowing from it seems to flow with blood. This coloration is due to the layers of red clay through which the boiling waters pass. Muddy masses of all hues explode on every side, spurt up into the air with peculiar noises, and spread out along the edges of the craters, creating with their splatterings the most grotesque and unexpected forms. The mud paste, soft as velvet to the touch, could furnish the palette of a painter with the most vivid colors that exist in nature: crimson red sparkles next to ultramarine blue, and episcopal purple mixes with sienna yellow or chalk white. The ground surrounding the mud springs has the look of porcelain ready for molding by a potter. The innumerable fumaroles rising from the fissures form a dome of vapor above the basin.

What is the mysterious phenomenon going on in this natural laboratory? Noticing that the water and mud of these mud pots contain much alum, the chemist will reply that what is occurring is a decomposition of the aluminum silicates in the volcanic tuffs as they are subjected to the action of the sulphurous waters.

As we entered the Gibbon Cañon we took note of a signpost to the right of the road indicating the trail leading along the opposite bank of the Gibbon River to the Monument Geyser Basin. The countless springs of boiling water that spurt out on the banks of this portion of the river are responsible for the hot currents. Crossing the river, our horses knew to avoid them with that marvelous instinct characteristic both of Indian ponies and of their Icelandic cousins.

After twenty minutes of arduous climbing up the slopes of Mount Schurz,[2] we reached a basin lying three hundred meters above the river and extending over two hectares. Here are clustered a dozen half-extinct geysers whose cones resemble monuments erected by nature's patient handiwork, simulating sometimes a monstrous animal, sometimes a headless man, sometimes an ordinary chimney.

Each of these cones, which vary in height between two and

12. Cone built up by hot spring deposits [View of Soda Butte, not visible from Leclercq's route].

four meters, possesses an opening at the summit. Some are still emitting steam, but most seem to have earned the right to retire, and their walls, no longer consolidating new deposits of geyserite, are rapidly crumbling. There was a time when streams of boiling water gushed from their vents, but their present appearance indicates that the volcanic activity of this region is diminishing.[3]

This basin encloses all the usual appurtenances of geysers: hot springs, solfataras, and fumaroles. From one fissure a jet of steam escapes with a deafening whistle audible for a considerable distance, like the whistle of a locomotive. The noise alone reveals the presence of the vent, for the hot current is so dry as to be almost invisible. A pine branch, placed before the orifice, dries up, contracts, and splinters almost instantaneously.

The existence of this curious basin, lying in an isolated region, has been known only for a short time. Who can say how many unknown marvels this still barely explored land encompasses!

The view over Elk Park encompassed from here is most beautiful: the eye follows with pleasure the Gibbon River, tracing its capricious meanders among green meadows, framed by the magnificent setting of forests rising in tiers up the mountains.

Returning to the banks of the river we enter the Gibbon Cañon, a dark defile two leagues long where the river is narrowly hemmed in between high basalt walls deeply furrowed by erosion.[4] This imposing gorge would arouse admiration in the Alps or the Pyrenees, but here the mind is so occupied with the extraordinary geological phenomena bursting upon one at every step that one views the scenery only abstractedly.

The cañon has a wild beauty. The high, imposing walls lean toward one another; the road often merges with the stream; the blue sky can only be glimpsed as if through a long crack. How curious it is to watch the water ouzel[5] hunt its prey in the clear water of the river, only a few steps from the hot springs gushing forth from its banks.

Near the middle of the gorge the river forms a romantic cascade [Gibbon Falls]. It shoots over the top of a wall twenty-five meters high, and its snowy whiteness sets it off clearly against the dark green of the pines dangling from the imposing rocks that dominate the falls.

The cañon opens onto a beautiful, wide valley across whose grassy meadows winds a river fed principally by the countless boiling hot springs one sees welling up along almost its entire length. Hence it was given the characteristic name of Firehole River.[6] At this juncture two arms of the Firehole converge, one coming from the east, the other from the great geyser basin to the south.[7]

After fording one of these streams as they do in Iceland, we soon found ourselves before a good fire in a log house, the precursor of a comfortable building that will one day be erected here, known as the Firehole National Hotel.[8]

We dined on a delicious leg of elk, then remounted our horses to go camp that very evening some ten miles away, in the upper Firehole basin.

It was late in the day and we were in a hurry to reach our destination, so we did not tarry to visit the curiosities along the way, which we would explore later. This day we contented ourselves with hailing the geysers in the lower and middle basins from afar.

For two hours we rode along among the countless sulphurous springs that riddle the banks and even the bed of the Firehole. We never tired of admiring the brilliance of the conferva[9] that delight in these hot waters and the splendid colors of the mineral substances deposited on their edges.

As we advanced, the geysers became more numerous, so numerous that eventually our curiosity was blunted and we became accustomed to the sight, just as did our horses, who displayed not the least fear in walking alongside the pools of boiling water all along the trail. In this realm of fire, cold water appears an anomaly: a body of water not emitting steam would seem to be out of place.

As evening drew on, the cooler air noticeably increased the density of the columns of steam rising over the basins. In a charming illusion, the refracted colors of the prism decorated these white clouds, seemingly motionless in the evening calm. One would say that the thousand colors from the edges of the hot springs were reflected in these aerial mists.

Here at last was the famous plain that forms the upper basin of the Firehole. We had crossed almost its whole extent from north to south, greeting along the way the Grotto, the Giant, the Pyramid, the Castle, and other geysers with which we proposed to become better acquainted.

At six o'clock in the evening our campsite appeared before us. It was a group of tents lined up along the right bank of the Firehole,[10] in the vicinity of the Beehive, the Castle, and Old Faithful.

CHAPTER IX

Old Faithful

Characteristics of Old Faithful. — Appearance of the crater. — Fantastic panorama. — Vulcan's laboratory. — An eruption of Old Faithful. — Vandalism. — A cold night. — A false alarm. — Appearance of the upper basin of the Firehole. — Large number of hot springs.

Dismounting from our tired horses, we ran at once to Old Faithful, the most popular of all the geysers of the Firehole valley. It owes its name to the regularity of its eruptions: night and day, no matter what the weather, it goes into action every hour, with such clocklike precision that it could serve as a standard for watches.[1] It is the only geyser that never fails the awaiting camera.

The crater of Old Faithful opens out at the summit of a conical mass of siliceous layers arrayed in terraces. These tiers are pitted with a thousand little pools where warm, limpid waters slumber, overspread with the richest colors: charming mirrors set within the most delicate sculptures. The rock has the granular appearance characteristic of geyserite and is reminiscent of coral in the delicacy and complexity of its structure; from a distance it appears ash-colored, but at close range one finds exquisite shades of pink, orange, and saffron standing out from the gray background.

The entire valley becomes visible from the height of the crater. From this point one takes in the full extent of the basin.

The sight of this magical panorama in the slanting rays of the setting sun left us with an indelible memory. If there are more alluring places in the world, there certainly are none stranger or more fantastic. Lieutenant Doane,[2] the first person to describe the Firehole valley, did not at all exaggerate in setting

13. Crater of Old Faithful.

it above all the other wonders found in America, and one understands how stunned and overwhelmed the first explorers must have felt by the spectacles they witnessed. The Ancients would have placed Vulcan's laboratory in this basin where the earth covers a sea of boiling water[3]; Dante would have seen here one of his circles of Hell.[4]

But let each one judge for himself.

All along the Firehole are cratered mounds on whose summits thermal fountains open out. Above all these caldrons, aerial plumes [of steam] stand out like ghosts against the dark green background of fir groves.[5] These vapors impregnate the air with strong, sulphurous fumes. Undermined in a thousand places, the ground is shaken continually by muffled subterranean detonations resembling the rumbling of a distant storm.

From time to time the strange whistling of rockets of boiling water being shot into the air blends with these sinister noises; sometimes they are compact spouts of water shooting up in violent vertical jets, sometimes sprays of water opening out like a parasol in the midst of a cloud of foam and iridescent steam and then falling back to earth like a rain of diamonds.

While dispersing in the air, the sprays of water produce a sad murmur, like the monotonous song of wind in the forest.

Hundreds of rivulets feed the waters of geysers and thermal springs into the Firehole. The layers of geyserite accumulated on top of each other along the banks of the river form walls that reach as much as ten meters in height. The waters rush from the top of these cliffs in steaming cascades, creating a commanding scene.

One would have to have seen a landscape as extraordinary as this with one's own eyes in order to believe that such a thing could exist on our planet. If a man were to be suddenly transported to the middle of this valley he would believe himself in a fantastical world, far removed from our own, or else he would be persuaded that he was the victim of an illusion, so much does reality exceed fiction here, so greatly do the objects that affect the senses appear to belong to the supernatural and improbable.

We had been watching for scarcely a quarter of an hour when suddenly Old Faithful emitted several menacing hiccoughs, precursory signs of an explosion. We immediately positioned ourselves safely on a neighboring knoll to await events.

First the waters rose in the pool with muffled rumblings, then subsided, only to rise again. Only after three or four minutes did the column of water begin to spout up into space: it rose in fitful jets rapidly succeeding each other and ceased its continual ascent only when it had attained a height of about fifty meters.

At this moment it seemed a terrifying supernatural phenomenon. The powerful roars of the volcano resounded throughout the valley, and the great rockets of steam and spray shooting much higher than the mass of water seemed to want to surpass the nearby mountains in height.

After reaching its apogee, the column of water gradually subsided. Long after it had sunk underground there were still explosions of steam; then these last remnants of anger vanished, and we could without danger cast our eyes into the interior of the funnel. Several meters down, the water foamed furiously within the walls of its prison. "Pretty, Clarke! Pretty, Clarke!" cried Mr. Alexander, who was in the habit of expressing his admiration in this succinct fashion to his friend Clarke.

The watery eruption had lasted five or six minutes. We noted that a few moments before the phenomenon the temperature of the water inside the crater was 94°C [201°F]; immediately after, it was 77°C [171°F] in the shallow pools surrounding the crater. At that elevation the theoretical boiling point is 93°C [199°F]. The excess of temperature above the boiling point is doubtless caused by the superheated steam escaping from the bottom of the tube.

Old Faithful was already erupting hourly when discovered in 1870;[6] since then it has never failed to live up to its name. It would be impossible to say how long it has performed on its present schedule. If, as is believed, the activity of the American geysers is generally decreasing, such an observation cannot be applied to this one. This geyser must be quite old, to judge by the size of its cone, which is nearly four meters high, sixty meters in diameter at the base, and sixteen meters at the top.[7]

The crater of Old Faithful, just like that of the Great Geyser of Iceland, is already covered with hundreds of names carved by visitors on the smooth surface of the rock. In a few hours the inscriptions are covered with a siliceous coating, which preserves the most insignificant names.

The crude hand of vandals does not stop there; it is truly revolting to see them taking the brutal ax to the fragile and delicate concretions under the pretext of searching for specimens of geyserite. In building these admirable monuments, in artistically fashioning them, in sculpting and ornamenting them, nature has employed a slowness, a meticulousness, a patience of which men would not be capable, and it takes but one minute for irreverent hands to disfigure the work of thousands of years. There are few craters that have not been damaged by ax and spade, and, if care is not taken, they will gradually crumble to pieces under the attacks of these ruthless destroyers.

It is the duty of the American government to halt these devastations, to prevent the criminal profanations of a sanctuary

14. Eruption of Old Faithful.

wherein no mortal should enter without a religious feeling of respect. As long as the National Park found itself isolated from populated areas, it had but a small number of visitors; but from now on the railroads will bring legions of the curious here, and a vigilant police force will have to be organized against vandals. Perhaps it would be best to place the Park under the control of the War Department, as Captain Ludlow[8] and General Sheridan[9] recommended. The conservation of this marvelous natural museum would best be entrusted to military posts that would be established at important points, at Mammoth Springs, Yellowstone Lake, and especially the geyser basin.

It was after dark when we went to the tent for supper. The pine campfires burning in the valley illuminated the steam hovering above the geysers with a reddish glow; one might have thought them fantastical Bengal lights.[10] The sky was incredibly clear; the Great Bear and the polestar shone with a wonderful brilliance.

The night was extraordinarily cold. In the tent the thermometer dropped to 0°C [32°F]; outside it was freezing. Clarke and I shared our body heat with each other, buried under a mountain of coverings.

At about two in the morning we were dragged from slumber by frightful rumblings accompanied by earth tremors. It seemed to us that the ground would open up under our tent. The shouts of the camp watchman, "Beehive! Beehive!" told us that it was an eruption of the Beehive, the geyser from which we were separated only by the Firehole flowing between it and us.

When we had recovered from our initial fright, it took us but a moment to emerge from the covers and dash outside, to cross the footbridge thrown across the river, and to rush up to the geyser, at the risk of falling in the darkness into one of the holes of boiling water found in the vicinity.

All this trouble for nothing! The eruption came to an end just as we arrived on the spot. A little sheepish and pretty well chilled, we regained our cot. Alexander was much more sensible: having had no reaction to this untimely eruption, he had not stirred from his warm, snug bed.

The next day was spent diligently exploring the upper basin of the Firehole. It lies in a wide valley, dominated by basaltic hills five hundred to six hundred meters high that are covered with dark pine forests. Here and there meadows stand out like islands of greenery among vast spaces sterilized by invasions of white siliceous deposits. A milky-colored mist produced by the respiration of the geysers hovers perpetually over the region like an aerial shroud. The basin stretches over an area of about two square kilometers: its form is that of a triangle with the apex in the north, at the confluence of the Firehole and the Little Firehole. Old Faithful marks the southern extremity.

The area thus bounded is the great wonder of the National Park; it is here that erupt the most powerful known geysers. Nature has grouped them along the Firehole, which runs through the basin in a northwesterly direction. Sometimes their eruptions produce a boiling flood great enough to raise the level of the river suddenly and to increase its temperature noticeably. While one of these watery volcanoes was belching, we observed that a thermometer plunged into the river waters registered 4°C [7°F] above their usual temperature.

The various geysers scattered over the extent of the basin are by no means active at the same time. They gush forth only at more or less regular intervals, and their eruptions vary in length and in energy. Some are constantly at work, exploding from hour to hour and even from minute to minute, while others remain quiet for years at a time. A geyser that is very active today will become extinct in the near or distant future, while others will spring up, taking the place of those that have expired. Except for Old Faithful, the appearance of the geysers varies from year to year; thus one cannot furnish data in this regard with absolute precision.

There are more than fifteen hundred hot springs in the Firehole basin; many of them have been recognized as active geysers, but they have been known for so few years that many springs are certain to be elevated to the rank of geysers once they have been more thoroughly observed.

CHAPTER X

Beehive and Giantess

Eruption of the Beehive. — Appearance of the Giantess. — A mar-
velously beautiful basin. — A scalding armchair. — Eruption of the
Giantess. — Appearance of the basin after the explosion. — Specter
and halo. — A boiling shower. — Decline of the Giantess.

During our stay in this valley, we were fortunate beyond all our
hopes. The most powerful geysers, the very ones that erupt
only after long intervals, wanted to display their prowess for us.

The Beehive, which had caused a false alarm the first night,
was gallant enough to give us a double display. The first took
place at ten o'clock the following night, just as I was taking
notes in the tent, writing in my lap by the light of a candle; the
second occurred at seven the next morning.

What a splendid sight is an eruption of the Beehive! This
geyser does not spew forth in a halting, spasmodic way, as do
most of its fellows, but sends up a sustained, powerful, and im-
petuous jet. A compact column of water a meter wide bursts
exuberantly from its narrow orifice, rising so high in its superb surge that it disdains falling back to earth: the water column partially evaporates in midair and is transformed into
a dissipating cloud dispersed into space, carried away by the
breeze. Accordingly, the Beehive is the only geyser that one can
approach while it is in action, without fear of being scalded.
At the height of the eruption we saw a spectator hold out his
hat to the column of water; in less than a second, to the great
amusement of the audience, the hat was propelled as high as
the towers of Notre Dame and then fell back at the feet of its
owner.[1]

The eruptions of the Beehive last about as long as those of

15. Eruption of the Beehive.

Old Faithful. They have so much energy that they cause a violent shaking of the ground around the geyser, accompanied by subterranean cannonades that are particularly frightening at night.

The crater of the Beehive is so modest in appearance that one would hardly think it capable of such fury. It is a cone one meter high in the shape of a beehive, rising abruptly from the ground, without surrounding itself with those tiers of terraced deposits that complete the architecture of most geyser craters. The small quantity of water that falls back to earth during its eruptions is not sufficient to produce these deposits. From afar, the cone appears to be a bench placed there expressly for the comfort of visitors, and one would be tempted to sit there but for the scalding steam constantly escaping from it. Leaning over the edge of the orifice, one looks deep into the interior vent and discerns the waters boiling furiously at the bottom. Several open spouts around the cone allow the steam to escape; one of these faithfully announces explosions of the geyser by its violent whistling.

Nothing is more uncertain than the time of these explosions; they occur with absolutely no regularity. In 1871 Hayden noticed that the phenomenon took place around six o'clock in the morning. In 1881, during one of Colonel Norris's exploratory tours [as superintendent], the geyser spouted the first day at nine forty-five in the evening, the second day at two fifteen in the afternoon, and the third day at eight forty in the evening. We saw it erupt on September 1, 1883, at two o'clock in the morning and at ten o'clock in the evening and on September 2 at seven fifteen in the morning.

According to these data it would seem that the Beehive is active daily, but local people have assured us that it had not erupted for several days and that we were especially privileged to be honored by its gallantries.

Heaven favored us once more in allowing us to enjoy the much more rare and infinitely more impressive spectacle of an eruption of the Giantess, one of the most powerful geysers in the Firehole valley. Its dimensions are extraordinary. It is

16. Crater of the Beehive.

a magnificent basin, completely devoid of those crater-shaped projections surrounding most geysers.[2] Located in the neighborhood of the Beehive, equidistant from the Firehole and the hills dominating the valley on the north, it opens out at the summit of a large mound formed from deposits rising in a gentle slope. At its base, the mound measures two hundred meters in diameter. The nearly circular basin is thirty meters in circumference; its edges, made up of thin layers of geyserite, overhang the cavity.

The waters contained in this gigantic bowl are an ideal blue, and as they are as clear as crystal, one can gaze into the depths of the abyss and wonder at the beautiful structure of the inside walls. Beneath the azure water, the innumerable granular formations on these walls look like sapphires.

In Iceland there is no basin of such striking beauty. Its appearance is most animated and changeable: sometimes the steaming waters, completely at rest, display an unbroken surface as transparent as a mirror, and sometimes they are violently agitated by great bubbles that come up to burst at the surface. To provoke this bubbling, one need only toss in a stone.

17. The Giantess.

By plunging a sounding line into the chasm, we determined a depth of twenty-four meters.

At the edge of the basin rises up a rock of geyserite, where I had the unfortunate idea of sitting down. I learned at my expense, jumping up as if propelled by a spring, that in this country the rocks are burning hot. My friend Clarke, witnessing my misadventure, was much amused. He revealed to me clearly that what I had taken for an armchair was in reality the lid of a caldron, and a perfidious jet of steam escaping from it affirmed this only too well.

The local people had assured us that the Grand Geyser would be active in the afternoon that day. We therefore went there after lunch, when, at ten past two, repeated shouts caused us to run as fast as we could go toward the Giantess. In ten minutes we had covered the kilometer that separates the Giantess from the Grand Geyser. The eruption of the Giantess was at its fullest when we arrived at the site.

I shall never forget the magnificence of the great and awesome phenomenon taking place before our eyes. A column of water as wide as the orifice surged spasmodically from the bosom of the formidable caldron. This enormous mass of liquid rose as high as the tallest houses in Paris,[3] bulging at the top like a crystal dome, and fell back with all its weight to the ground, causing it to shake over a considerable radius. In the heart of the main column of water a passage of thinner jets opened up, and the most powerful of them rose as high as the Barrière de l'Étoile.[4] From where did these jets come? Undoubtedly from secondary vents abutting with the main tube at the point where the explosive force attains its maximum. Dreadful subterranean thundering mingled with the roaring of this deluge of boiling water as it rose into the sky.

Such an imposing scene would move the most blasé of men and cause the most intrepid to tremble. What, then, are the forces set in motion by man compared with the awesome physical agents that produce these stupefying phenomena?

We noticed that many small geysers in the vicinity of the Giantess participated in the activity of the overlord, with whom they evidently had connections. It was like a powerful tide lifting this entire subterranean sea, whose numerous spouts boiled and emitted puffs of steam. We had observed an oval crater a few paces from the Giantess at the summit of a dome of geyserite: its waters, which before the eruption were boiling most violently, had completely disappeared when we returned, and the crater was empty like that of its absorbent neighbor.[5]

The Giantess differs from other geysers in the long duration of its eruptions. It becomes active only at intervals of seventeen days, but the explosions continue for twelve to fifteen hours. It does not play continually like the Beehive but rather in bursts occurring every half hour and lasting about twenty minutes.

During the intervals between bursts we were able to approach the edges of the crater with impunity. This admirable basin, which a short while before was overflowing its rims with water blue as lapis lazuli, was now dry. We could look down into the empty chasm and discern the junction of the vent and the basin at a depth of eight meters. The subterranean waters remained invisible, but we heard them roaring in the depths of the earth. The inside walls, which had seemed blue under the water, had become whitish and had the granular look of geyserite.

From the bosom of this caldron thick puffs of steam were constantly escaping. When one of us placed himself between them and the sun, the projection of his shadow onto the vapors created a specter, and the sun's rays were concentrated around the head of this phantom like a sort of sparkling halo, similar to the nimbus of the saints.[6]

The eruptions of the Giantess occur as suddenly as a flash of lightning. I was leaning over the edge of the furnace during the interval between two bursts when a river of boiling water spurted out without giving me the least warning. I can boast of having executed the longest strides of which legs are capable in this critical circumstance, but I was scalded nonetheless, to the great glee of the onlookers. Thanks be to the broad-brimmed American hat that protected my head from the burning downpour!

Hayden reports that in 1871 the Giantess had two eruptions in the space of twenty-four hours.[7] One must conclude that the bursts were more frequent at that time but of shorter duration. If a dozen years were enough to have decreased the number of eruptions from two per day to fewer than two per month, then perhaps not many more years will pass before the noble geyser decides to retire completely from active life.[8]

CHAPTER XI

Along the Firehole

Excitement produced by the geysers. — The Sawmill. — The Grand
Geyser. — The Castle. — The Devil's Well. — The Washtubs. — The
Giant. — The Young Faithful. — The Grotto. — The Fan. — The
Splendid. — A bath in the Firehole. — A storm.

We spent two days in the valley that the Icelanders would call
Reykjadalr (Steaming Valley). The geyser eruptions kept us in
continual activity: sometimes they woke us during the night;
sometimes they tore us away from our meals. We ran like mad-
men, half-awake or with our mouths full, to gaze upon the phenomenon; but often it was abortive, and more than once we
returned crestfallen.

Each one of us wandered about as he pleased, according to
his curiosity, having no guide other than the map by Ludlow,
although it is very detailed and indicates the configuration
of the valley and the exact position of the principal springs.[1]
How interesting it is to roam thus across the fields of geyserite, where here and there emerge craters that take their names
either from the fantastical outlines of their cones or from the
caprices of their spouting waters.

A path runs along the Firehole, crossing a plain undermined
and riddled with caldrons where the subterranean waters boil.
How many times I went over it, impatient as a hunter lying in
wait to witness the beginning of an eruptive phenomenon that
could at any moment burst forth from under my feet!

At first one feels overcome by I know not what sense of vague
terror. All these bubbling and flowing waters, these steaming
fountains, these roaring jets warn you in their singular, oth-
erworldly language that you are in the formidable proximity

of the central fire. The crust on which you walk is not always reassuringly solid; sometimes it gives way beneath your footsteps, and the horrible idea of being engulfed crosses your mind. But these perils, which you get used to quickly enough, add to the charm and the mystery of this valley, which seems to possess the secret of what happens in the somber laboratories of the terrestrial core.[2]

With your permission, we will honor the principal geysers spread out along the Firehole's two banks with a moment's attention.

Here, ten minutes away from the Giantess, is a geyser in full play, for it spurts half the time: it is the Sawmill. Its crater, not more than six inches wide, opens up at the bottom of a bowl-shaped depression. The eruption plays in a most singular way: the column of water rises several meters high, and in falling back to earth it encounters new ascending jets that send it back up into the air, exactly as a [badminton] racket does with a shuttlecock.[3] The basin, ordinarily dry, fills with water at each eruption; the liquid mass is no doubt lifted up by the vapors mounting in the tube, since, just as the burst begins to quit, the water instantaneously reenters the crater.

A little farther on, the Grand Geyser comes into view. Despite the similarity of the name, it does not at all resemble the Great Geyser of Iceland. It does not rise from the top of a magnificent dome of geyserite, as does its cousin in the Land of Ice. In fact, its basin attracts so little attention that one would not find it at all were it not adjacent to a geyser whose prominent crater is reminiscent of the shape of a turban [Turban Geyser]. Its basin is just a simple depression having a very irregular appearance, not more than a foot deep at its center and lacking raised edges. Large, shapeless masses of geyserite frame the mouth of the vent.

We kept watch in vain near the Grand Geyser at the time when we had been assured it would start erupting.[4] It did not deign to give a show. We are told that its eruptions are analogous to those of the Giantess: they are produced suddenly, without any warning.

18. Crater of the Grand Geyser.

On the other bank of the Firehole, near the place where a torrent of boiling water rushes down, stands the Castle, the most imposing crater in the entire extent of the basin. Its appearance is reminiscent of an old, ruined, fortified castle. It crowns a knoll formed of whitish deposits covering about two hectares [about five acres] and rising to almost twelve meters above the river. The four-meter-high cone is made up of layers of geyserite, accumulated one upon the other. The silvery gray siliceous deposits are very hard. The geyser's orifice is bordered with orange-colored incrustations. Puffs of steam issue from it constantly, and jets of water spurt out from time to time, even in the interval between eruptions.

The Castle launches a column of water from ten to fifteen meters high. There is no doubt that this geyser was formerly the most powerful in the whole valley.[5] Information from travelers about its periods of repose and activity are rather contradictory: according to some, it erupts once in twenty-four hours; according to others, once in forty-eight hours. It is likely that its regime varies according to the time of year. Colonel Norris reported that Castle had an eruption on October 4, 1881, at three o'clock in the afternoon and another on the sixth at nine forty-five in the morning. In 1882 Mr. Haupt witnessed an eruption on August 25 about ten o'clock in the morning.[6] One can therefore conclude that this time period [late morning to midafternoon] is the most propitious for seeing the phenomenon, but we wasted our time waiting.

At a few paces from the Castle there is a spring called the Devil's Well [Crested Pool]. I would rather call it the Enchanted Goblet, for apart from the temperature of its waters, it has nothing to awaken the idea of hell. Imagine a lovely basin six meters in diameter and of unknown depth, perfectly circular and surrounded by a prominent border completely encrusted with an efflorescence that could be taken for pearls. The eye is fascinated by the astonishing transparency of its blue waters, overflowing its edges. Under the crystal liquid, the siliceous encrustations of the walls glitter like precious stones. The sun's rays cast magical prismatic colors, and one's gaze follows these dazzling sights down to the last visible, unfathomable depths of the well.

What then is this marvelous spring? An inexplicable mystery! It is very close to the Castle, but during the geyser's active periods it shows no disturbance. Usually the surface of the pool is as smooth as a mirror, and only at rare intervals does it present a light agitation near the center. To interrupt that state between placidity and anger, no other provocation is needed than to toss in a stone.[7] Then the waters boil violently for a moment and rush over the edges of the basin, scalding the feet of any impertinent person not quick enough in getting away.

Continuing our promenade along the left bank of the Firehole, we came upon the Washbowls. They are a group of small pools two or three meters in diameter, with solid tubing that connects them to the subterranean regions. Their strongly alkaline waters would please our laundresses: after remaining in the water a few minutes, linen comes out white as snow.[8]

Passing near this natural laundry, I could not resist the temptation to engage in a conscientious laundering. I ran to get everything that needed a soaping and plunged the bundle into the washtub; but at the moment when I was about to take it

19. The Devil's Well and the Castle [Devil's Well was one of Crested Pool's former names].

20. The Grotto.

out, I realized that the things were going down the central vent, drawn in by a mysterious suction, and before I could retrieve them the basin emptied out in the way that the convivial cup of Tours wine was emptied down the gullet of Grandgousier, *uno haustu*.[9] Unfortunately, I had no other course of action but to wait patiently for my pilfered things to be restored to me. When I returned two hours later, I found happily that I was dealing with an honest rogue. The linen was washed like new, and it was all there to the last piece. However, beware the Washbowls!

A little farther along, the majestic, broken crater of the Giant emerges from the bosom of the plain like a horn whose mouthpiece is turned toward the sky. This three-meter-high cone is breached from top to bottom on the north side, as if an exceptionally violent eruption had carried away a portion of it. The gap allows one to see the interior walls of the edifice, which display encrustations rather similar to inlaid work: it is a brilliant mosaic, resplendent with saffron yellow, crimson red, and emerald green. Leaning over the edge of the breach, one casts one's eyes down into a chasm that resounds with the noise of the waters boiling in its deep cavities.

An eruption of the Giant is an imposing phenomenon, according to travelers who have had the joy of witnessing it. This geyser projects a column of water sixty meters high and two meters in diameter straight into the air. One can appreciate the volume of water produced by an eruption of the Giant if one knows that the Firehole, with its very rapid current and width of thirty meters, is more than doubled by an eruption.

In the vicinity of the Giant there is a multitude of little springs that throw out water and steam. These springs cease their work only when their powerful neighbor is active. One might call them safety valves that are sometimes insufficient to their task. Among them is a little geyser known by the name of Young Faithful [Bijou]; opening up on the top of a mound of geyserite, it is constantly in a state of great agitation and throws out irregular jets in all directions, earning it the epithet "Stupid Spitter" from my friend Clarke.

A stone's throw away from the Giant is a crater that is by far the most curious of all that appear in the Firehole basin. It is called the Grotto. Under arches of a fantastic architecture open up caverns that function as lateral openings during the geyser's eruptions. Their interior walls are adorned with granular, opalescent concretions that evoke the image of a palace of pearls.

The insane inspiration to enter one of these caverns came to me. It is a good thing that all I did was take a quick glance, because no sooner was I again outside than the fountain began to erupt. How picturesque is the play of the Grotto's waters! Two quite distinct jets escape from different orifices; the larger one rises to eight or nine meters; both scatter into spray at a certain height, intermingling and falling back in a rain of droplets on which a rainbow projects its magical glitter. The phenomenon lasts about half an hour and repeats regularly at six-hour intervals.[10]

My admiration had not had time to cool when another geyser three hundred meters away on the other side of the river had an outburst in its turn. I dashed over to it, just in time to see the most graceful play of water that I had yet encountered. Its name is the Fan. Imagine a group of several small geysers whose separate vents have a common crater and discharge all at once. The different vents, diverging from the vertical to a greater or lesser degree, radiate toward a single center; as a result the sheet of water spreads out like a fan. This performance surpasses the most ingenious combinations of water in the fountains of Versailles.[11] During the eruption a small neighboring geyser launched an oblique jet as grotesque as the spray of the Fan is graceful.[12]

As I was returning to the campsite, the Splendid gave me a show of its eruption from a distance; its emotion calmed at the moment I arrived. This geyser is relatively recent. According to Hayden's account, in 1871 it appeared to be an extinct geyser, giving no other sign of life than a plume of steam. Since 1881 it has entered a new period of activity; rivaling Old Faithful in its regularity and in the height of its jet, the explosion oc-

21. The Fan.

22. The Comet.

curs at three-hour intervals and lasts five to ten minutes. The name Splendid was given to it by Colonel Norris; others call it the Comet or the Pyramid. Each traveler thus names the geysers according to his fancy, and a regrettable confusion results: sometimes several geysers receive the same name from different travelers.[13] In the Firehole basin there are two "Comets," three "Fountains," and I do not know how many "Paint Pots." One should keep to the designations of the Geological Survey.

A bath in the Firehole ended the day. By a superb sunset I plunged into the famous river of the Holes of Fire. It is well named, because even its bed is riddled with springs of boiling water,[14] as I learned at my own expense. While I was attending to my ablutions, I noticed more than once abrupt elevations of the water temperature when I encountered hot currents: thus it happened that I passed suddenly from 16°C to 45°C [61°F–113°F].

During the night one of those horrifying storms that are almost daily occurrences in this corner of the globe broke out. The wind and rain raged to the point where our tent would inevitably have fallen over had it not been equal to the test of the storm.

CHAPTER XII

Land of Wonders and Land of Ice

The geysers of America compared with those of Iceland.—Their common characteristics.—Their temperature.—They have an analogous cause.—Volcanic character of the Yellowstone crater.—Rapid decline.—Earthquakes.—Nature of hot springs.—Their different stages.—Origin of their waters.

Of all nature's phenomena, I know of none more magnificent, more captivating, than the eruption of a geyser. I had already been fortunate enough to witness this event in Iceland, and there remained with me one of those vivid and profound impressions that leave an indelible memory. But my curiosity was not completely satisfied. The only one I had seen in action was the Strokkur,[1] an erupting fountain of secondary importance whose spasms could always be artificially provoked. As to the Great Geyser, it had given me the slip, and I bore it some resentment. I felt avenged for its disdain by my stay in the Firehole basin: I was happy and proud to pay homage to more tractable geysers. I recalled what I had heard an American in Iceland say: according to him, the geysers of Iceland were pygmies, "mere puppets," in comparison with those of the Firehole. Since Americans possess an excessive national vanity, at the time I did not know what to think, and I came rather close to believing that the supposed wonders of the Yellowstone were "humbug," at the base of which was a good dose of exaggeration.

Now that I have been able to compare and judge, I must acknowledge that my American spoke only the truth. With respect to the phenomenon of geysers, Iceland is only a pale imitation of Yellowstone.

The erupting fountains of the Rocky Mountains exceed those of the Land of Ice in their number, in the volume of water they discharge, in the frequency of their eruptions, in the duration of their effervescent activity, in the amplitude and height of the columns of water they eject, and finally in the size and beauty of their deposits.

The geysers of the two countries do, however, have many characteristics in common: their eruptions display the same intervals and the same successive stages; their waters, subject to the same flows, have the same purity, the same splendid blue color, and the same petrifying properties. The specimens of geyserite that I collected in Iceland are very similar to those I brought back from Yellowstone. The shapes of the geyser pools and the patterns of ornamentation on their edges and walls bear such a surprising resemblance to each other in the two areas that one is tempted to wonder if nature has not repeated herself, unconsciously producing an echo of earlier work, like an artist whose inspiration is waning. This creator favors an oval or circular form for the contours of the pools of boiling water; she varies the appearance of the incrustations according to the type of flow of the thermal springs.[2] Most often the appearance is that of vegetation on little hillocks, so reminiscent of the flowerets of cauliflower; but in the quiet pools smooth surfaces appear instead, indented in festoons and extending toward the center of the pool like floating blocks of ice.[3]

Iceland's Great Geyser does perhaps transcend the geysers of Yellowstone by the simplicity and the perfection of its shape: its nearly circular basin opens with a wonderful regularity toward the central tube. I have not seen any in the Rocky Mountains that present a more classic example.

One finds in Iceland not only the same shapes but also the same coloring, so brilliantly rich that an artist's brush would hardly be capable of rendering it.

We see further similarities in the temperature of the erupting springs; in America as in Iceland it is extremely high, and one observes that it increases notably as an eruption approach-

23. Panorama of the Firehole Valley. 1. The Old Faithful. 2. The Castle. 3. The Giant. 4. The Grotto. 5. The Fan. 6. The Giantess. 7. The Beehive. [Giant Geyser is drawn next to the river near Grotto, but the numbers are reversed for Giant and Fan Geysers.]

es. In the Firehole valley and on the shores of Yellowstone Lake the geysers' water boils at a temperature of 92°C or 93°C [198°F or 199°F]. These regions are at a much higher elevation than Iceland: from sea level to the level of Yellowstone Lake[4] the boiling point drops by about eight degrees [14°F].

In Iceland the temperature of the Great Geyser has been measured at depths one cannot reach in the American geysers because of the irregularity of their interior walls. It was possible to plunge a thermometer to a depth of more than twenty-three meters into the Great Geyser. Ten minutes before an eruption, Bunsen[5] observed there the enormous temperature of 122°C [252°F] at a depth of about fourteen meters. In the Firehole basin the temperature rarely exceeds 93°C [199°F]; it has not yet been possible to observe the temperature of the waters at depth.[6]

The geysers of America and those of Iceland obviously have an analogous cause, since nature is subject to the same immutable laws everywhere on the globe. In both countries, geyser phenomena are the last vestiges of volcanic activity on the path to extinction. Intermittent springs are, moreover, true volcanoes, the only difference being that they eject water instead of ejecting molten materials. As in volcanoes, it is a gaseous substance, principally water vapor, that causes the eruptions.

During the Pliocene epoch the whole region of the upper Yellowstone was the setting for prodigious plutonian labors, of which the present-day eruptive activity in Iceland offers but a feeble reflection. Hayden considers the whole basin to be a vast crater formed by thousands of volcanic surface vents and fissures that discharged and dispersed innumerable quantities of lava, ashes, and igneous rocks. There still exist hundreds of volcanic cones, often rising more than three thousand meters above sea level. Mounts Doane, Langford, Stevenson, and a hundred other peaks that emerge around the whole expanse of the basin were themselves formerly centers of eruptions. In the present geological age hot springs and geysers have replaced volcanoes: they are the last manifestations of those subterranean forces that were so powerful in the past and that today are dying out.

If the volcanoes in the Yellowstone basin are long extinct, Iceland is still in full plutonian activity: it has twenty-two active volcanoes, and Hekla, the dreadful neighbor of the geysers, has had no fewer than twenty-one eruptions from 1114 to 1878.[7] It would therefore seem that the geysers of Iceland are of a more recent origin than those of Yellowstone and that they are destined to outlive their relatives in the New World. Even the appearance of the deposits of the American geysers evinces their greater age; these usually sizeable deposits are almost always surmounted by the ancient chimneys that are so characteristic of the Firehole springs and distinguish them at first glance from those of Iceland.

Because of their greater age, the geysers in America seem to be diminishing more rapidly than those in Iceland. According to Hayden, there is no doubt that these eruptive springs have been constantly declining since they became the surface vents of previously much more active volcanic forces, and they will

24. Geyserite deposits at the Castle.

continue to wane until they entirely disappear. In their present state the number of extinct springs is at least equal to the number of active ones; one can therefore affirm that the network of geysers and hot springs as it exists today is no more than a diminished manifestation of those great subterranean forces that were deployed with such an astonishing intensity during the periods of plutonian activity. Over the course of centuries the gradual cooling of the volcanic rocks beneath the earth's surface will cause the hot springs to cool, for, as Hochstetter[8] remarked, these springs are themselves but a transitory phenomenon in the eternal metamorphosis of all created things.

Like Iceland, the basin of the upper Yellowstone is subject to terrestrial shocks that seem closely connected to the geysers. Hayden reports that while he was camping on the northeast shore of Yellowstone Lake he felt several violent earthquake shocks. Mountain men assured him that these shocks are frequent and sometimes very intense, and it is indeed for this reason that the Indians never dared to settle in this part of the country.[9]

In Iceland the intermittent springs are siliceous; they lixiviate palagonites and palagonitic tuffs that contain 50 percent silica.[10] In America, sometimes siliceous substances and sometimes calcareous substances predominate in the incrusted springs. Those of Mammoth Springs are calcareous, although they also deposit silica;[11] those of the Firehole, to the contrary, contain no trace of lime but are very rich in silica: their deposits contain 85 percent silica as well as a slight amount of magnesium chloride.

In the Rocky Mountains as in Iceland, the hot springs display three distinct stages: some are constantly boiling; others are agitated only periodically; still others are permanently placid. Geysers belong to the second category of hot springs: their waters, usually tranquil, become agitated only when an eruption is about to take place; then they start to boil and release steam, their level gradually rises in their pool, and finally they shoot into the air.

Exploration of the American geysers has convinced me of the accuracy of a remark made in Iceland by Commodore Charles Forbes.[12] This English traveler was struck by the fact that in that land there is not a single intermittent spring that is not close to a river or lake. He therefore concluded that the hot waters of the geysers are supplied not by subterranean springs but by expanses of surface water seeping through fissures deep into the earth, where they become heated upon contact with volcanic rock. The combined action of the expansive force of steam and of hydrostatic pressure causes them to rise toward the surface, where they reappear in the form of geysers or of simple hot springs. If, therefore, the neighboring waters were diverted and the geysers abandoned to the supposed subterranean springs alone, they would become extinct from lack of nourishment.

The American geysers fully confirm this observation. In the Rocky Mountains as in Iceland, all the hot springs originate near a river or lake: they are spread out along the Firehole and on the shores of Shoshone and Yellowstone Lakes, and they often originate even within cold surface waters. It therefore seems very likely that they are the result of the contact of surficial currents with heated surfaces. I would be most surprised if analysis of these thermal waters did not demonstrate such an origin.[13]

Theory of Geysers

Iceland, the classic land of hot-water volcanoes, has given us the name by which we call the geysers. It is an old Icelandic word meaning "to gush." According to Professor Peale's definition, a geyser is a hot spring with intermittent or periodic eruptions that project a column of water into the air. Numerous theories have been proposed to explain its mechanism. We will summarize them according to Professor Peale's exposition in a recent United States Geological Service publication.[1]

The oldest theory is that of Sir George Mackenzie,[2] who visited Iceland in 1810. It postulates the existence of a tube coming out at the top inside the basin and communicating below with a subterranean chamber, where waters of meteoric origin enter through fissures.

The walls of this cavern are heated by a nearby seat of volcanic fire and also receive heat from steam entering through fissures at the bottom. This steam, having an extremely high temperature, heats the water in the cavity to the boiling point; the space between the surface of the water and the roof is filled with steam under high pressure. This pressure is sufficient to sustain the column of water at a certain height in the tube and the basin. But if there is a sudden addition of heat, steam will accumulate within the cavity until the instant when its expansive force expels the waters, forcing them to escape through the tube. This is when the eruption occurs. The shaking of the ground and the subterranean noises are produced by the movement of the steam within the cavity, caused by the sudden rise in temperature.

Mackenzie admitted that his theory could only be a partial explanation of the phenomena; Bunsen[3] thought that it would account for the action of the Little Geyser but not that of the Great Geyser [of Iceland].

In his *Researches on the Internal Heat of the Globe*, Bischof[4] adopts the theory of Krug Von Nidda,[5] which is strongly analogous to that of Mackenzie. It takes for granted that these hot springs derive their temperature from the aqueous vapors rising from below. When these vapors are able to rise freely, the water at the different depths must have a constant temperature equal to that at which water would boil under the pressure existing at the respective depths. Thus the constant ebullition of perpetual springs is explained, as is their temperature, which is that of boiling water.

If, on the other hand, the vapors be prevented by the complicated windings of its channels from rising to the surface; if, for example, they be arrested in caverns, the temperature in the upper layers of water must necessarily become reduced, because a large quantity of the water is lost by evaporation at the surface, which cannot be replaced from below. And any circulation of the layers of water at different temperatures, by reason of their unequal specific gravities, seems to be very much interrupted by the narrowness and sinuosity of the passage. The intermittent springs of Iceland are probably caused by the existence of caverns in which the vapor is retained by the pressure of the column of water in the channel that leads to the surface. Here this vapor collects and presses the water in the cavern downward until its elastic force becomes sufficiently great to effect a passage through the column of water. The violent escape of the vapor causes the thunder-like subterranean sound and the trembling of the earth that precedes each eruption. The vapors do not appear at the surface till they have heated the water to their own temperature. When so much vapor has escaped that the expansive force of that which remains has become less than the pressure of the confining column of water, tranquility is restored, and this lasts until such a quantity of vapor is again collected as to produce a fresh eruption. The spouting of the spring is therefore repeated at intervals depending upon the capacity of the cavern, the height of the column of water, and the heat generated below.

According to the theory of the famous chemist Bunsen, the mechanism of the geysers is found quite plainly in a system of siliceous deposits that, as they accumulate, eventually build a very deep tube, like a chimney. A spring whose waters are not alkaline remains a simple thermal fountain, never being able to rise to the rank of geyser; but if its waters are alkaline it will hold some silica in solution and will deposit it on its sides. Little by little the deposits will build up in the shape of a tube. As long as the circulating layers of water maintain an approximately equal temperature in all parts of the tube, the spring will not have violent eruptions. But when the tube becomes deeper and when the circulation is impeded, an ever more noticeable difference in temperature between the deep waters and the surface waters will be produced, so that at the surface the waters will be relatively cold, while below they will reach the boiling point. Then the sudden expansion of great masses of steam produced by the extraordinary heating of the column of water in the lower part of the tube will determine the explosion, which will recur intermittently for a great many years. The eruptions will cease only when the ever-lengthening tube presents an obstacle to the formation of steam.[6]

Bunsen lays out the following three principles:

1. The temperature in the geyser tube increases as we descend.
2. At no point does the water in the tube attain the temperature of ebullition that it should have under the pressure to which it is subjected, but the temperature depends on the time that has elapsed since the last eruption. As a great eruption comes near, it approaches the boiling point.
3. At a depth of about forty-five feet the difference between the temperature of the water and the calculated boiling point for that pressure is the least.

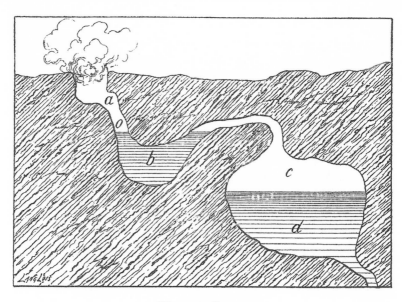

25. Diagram of a geyser.

Professor Müller[7] of Freiburg has succeeded in demonstrating Bunsen's theory by constructing an artificial geyser.

The American professor Comstock,[8] who accompanied the 1873 expedition of Captain Jones[9] to Yellowstone, thinks that Bunsen's theory does not entirely explain geyser phenomena. Nor does it, in his opinion, account for all the differences between geysers and hot springs, and he proposes a structural hypothesis that combines Bischof's and Bunsen's theories. He pictures a subterranean chamber *d* containing water.

> By constant accessions of heat from below, the vacant passage above is finally filled with vapor, and by degrees the water in the bent passage *b* becomes heated, and steam also expands in *o*. After a time the expansion of the vapor in *c* is able to overcome the combined pressure of the water and vapor in *b* and *o*, when the latter is forced out, followed by a portion of the water in the reservoir *d*. The force thus expended, a vacuum is produced in *c* by the receding of the column of water, and the foregoing operations are indefinitely repeated. The passage *b* may be kept filled with water by means of the surplus which falls back into the bowl.[10]

26. Appearance of a geyser after eruption.

According to Baring-Gould,[11] a bent tube is sufficient to explain the action of Iceland's Great Geyser. To demonstrate his theory, he took an iron tube and bent it at an angle of 110°, keeping one arm half the length of the other. He filled the tube with water and placed the short arm in a fire. For a moment the surface of the liquid remained quiet, and then the pipe began to quiver; a slight overflow took place, without any sign of ebullition, and then suddenly the whole column was forced high into the air. With a tube, the long arm of which measured two feet and the bore of which was three-eighths of an inch, he sent a jet to the height of eighteen feet. Steam is generated in the short arm and presses down the water, causing an overflow until the steam bubble turns the angle, when it forces out the column in the long arm with incredible violence.

Of these theories, perhaps no one is adequate to explain all the phenomena of geyser action. According to Professor Peale, Bunsen's theory is the most rational: in the simplest kinds of geysers it is a sufficient explanation. The variations and modifications in the geyser tubes and subterranean water passages must undoubtedly be important factors entering into any complete explanation of geyser action. We can easily see what the conditions are at the surface, but in our experiments we can only penetrate to a very inconsiderable distance. We have, therefore, no data, and Mr. Peale proposes to provide it by the means within our power, namely, to construct artificial geysers and to make different modifications in the shape of the tubes until we arrive at results analogous to those we observe in the natural geysers.

"If water in a glass tube be heated with rapidity from the bottom," says Mr. Peale,

it will be expelled from the tube violently, and if boiled in a kettle which has a lid and a spout, either the lid will be blown off or the water will be forced out through the spout. The first case is an illustration, in part at least, of Bunsen's theory, and the second exemplifies the theories that presuppose the existence of subterranean cavities with tubes at or near the surface. According to the former we must suppose that the layer of rock, extending seventy-five to seventy-seven feet below the surface, contains sufficient heat to account for the geyseric phenomena, or else that the geyser tube has some opening either at the bottom or on the sides, by which steam and superheated water have access to it from a considerably greater depth, where the temperature is very high. At these depths caverns probably exist.

In *Frost and Fire*[12] it is stated that in the tube of the Great Geyser of Iceland, at a depth of forty-five feet from the surface, there is a ledge which was first discovered by Mr. Bryson,[13] of Edinburgh. From beneath this ledge steam bubbles rise while the geyser tube is filling, and a thermometer sunk a few feet below it was lifted and driven about and when brought to the surface was found to be broken. The conclusion is that steam or hot water or both enter the tube from the side just beneath this ledge, for when the thermometer was sunk lower it remained quiet. Here, then, we have an explanation of the quiet and safe condition of Bunsen's thermometer at the bottom of the geyser during a great eruption. Strokkur[14] has openings on opposite sides of its tube, and when empty, water and steam can be seen pouring into it from both apertures. The Great Geyser is usually full of water, and consequently its internal construction cannot readily be examined, but there is little doubt that it is similar to that of Strokkur, i.e., it consists of a tube with a conduit or conduits leading to subterranean cavities. That such cavities exist is more than probable.

It is my belief that all geysers are originally due to a violent outburst of steam and water, and, under such conditions, irregular cavities and passages are more likely to be formed than regular tubes. As a fact, geyseric action on a small scale, dependent on an arrangement of cavities and tubes, may be simulated by heating water and plaster of Paris together in a tin pan.[15]

In view of what we have just written, Bunsen's [second] conclusion would have to be modified somewhat. His conclusion was that at no point in the tube did the water attain the temperature of ebullition that it should have attained under the pressure to which it is subjected. As far as this relates to the straight tube in which his temperatures were taken, it may be so; but if he could have taken temperatures in the side conduit, I have little doubt he would soon have reached a point where the temperature would not only be at the boiling point for that depth but even exceed it. In the Yellowstone Park we obtained a number of temperatures *at the surface* that were above the boiling point. In the main, I am inclined to accept Bunsen's theory, especially as it seems to me to require subterranean cavities in which the water must be heated. Whether these are caverns, enlargements of tubes, or sinus channels, appears to me to be of no consequence, except as the interval or period of the geyser might be affected by the form of the reservoir.

Almost all observers of the geysers of the Yellowstone National Park have been inclined to regard the action of many geysers as sympathetic. In the opinion of Professor Peale this sympathy is only apparent and the synchronous action only a coincidence, because certain geysers behaved totally differently for him than for other travelers. Furthermore, he recognizes that more numerous observations are necessary to determine whether the geysers situated in close proximity are in sympathy with each other. The same uncertainty on the subject is noted with respect to the Iceland geysers, some observers thinking them entirely independent of each other, while others believe that they are connected. Mr. Peale admits that there can be subterranean connections in the water supply, but he considers it improbable that the action of a geyser is dependent upon that of its neighbor. Horrebow[16] wittily demonstrated this alleged sympathy with the following experiment: if water from the geyser be put into a bottle, whenever the geyser has an eruption the water in the bottle will also be agitated, and if it be corked it will burst.

In summary, here are the three essential conditions for the existence of a geyser, according to Mr. Peale:

1. The presence of igneous rocks that still retain their heat at a considerable distance below the surface
2. The presence of meteoric waters, which, when carried near burning-hot rocks and heated upon contact with them, are partially converted into steam
3. A tube, by means of which this heated water, with other meteoric water, can reach the surface and appear as a geyser.

CHAPTER XIV

Excelsior

The middle basin. — The Devil's Half-Acre. — Excelsior Geyser. — The largest geyser in the world. — Formidable eruptive force. — A lake of boiling water. — The lower Firehole basin. — Enthusiasm. — The Mud Caldron. — A post office.

On September 3 we turned back toward the north with the aim of visiting the geyser groups known as middle basin and lower basin.

At a distance of eight or nine kilometers we reached the middle basin, located halfway between the two others.[1] We picketed our horses and explored the portion of this infernal country known by the meaningful name of the Devil's Half-Acre.

Crossing a fragile wooden bridge spanning the river, we climbed the high ramparts of geyserite dominating the left bank of the Firehole, and we soon found ourselves before the enormous, gaping crater of the geyser Excelsior.

Peering into the abyss, one cannot avoid an unspeakable terror. We were at the edge of the most powerful eruptive spring not only in America, but probably in the entire world; next to it, the Giant, the Giantess, and the Grand Geysers are nothing but dwarves![2]

Formidable in appearance, the orifice of the basin measures more than seventy-five meters in diameter. Its vertical walls have a layered structure that attests to its recent origin. The edges of the crater are so undermined by eruptions that they overhang the chasm. We ventured near only with much circumspection for fear that the siliceous crust, yielding under our weight, would drag us down into the dreadful caldron. The waters are in a state of violent boiling; one feels the ground tremble underfoot, and one instinctively recoils in dread.[3]

Hot puffs of steam escape from the chasm, and it is only when the breeze disperses them that one can catch sight of the blue expanse rippling like a sea six or seven meters deep.

The crater opens out at the riverbank, giving issue to the immense sheet of boiling water that pours over the terraces in an infinity of rivulets filled with fine, silky, bright-yellow filaments, which the current agitates in a vibratory motion. This vegetation, formed by sulphurous deposits, is so delicate that it crumbles away between the fingers.

How marvelous are the various hues assumed by the layers of geyserite: scarlet red, pink, and yellow gold blend against a snow-white background.

At the spot where the waters escape from the basin we measured a temperature of 80°C [176°F]; it was impossible for us to determine the prevailing temperature in the center of the basin, which must be much higher.

In 1880 Excelsior revealed itself to be a stupendous geyser. Since no one had seen it play previous to that date, it was thought to be a simple hot spring. Hayden, who visited it in 1871, gave it the name of Caldron without suspecting that it was an eruptive spring.

Colonel Norris, superintendent of the National Park in 1880,[4] reported the first eruption of Excelsior. He was more than two leagues away when he heard the noise of the explosions. He arrived in the area too late to witness the phenomenon, but he was able to observe its staggering effects: the flood of boiling water had so swollen the Firehole that several bridges located downstream had been swept away and were adrift.

That year the eruptions were exceptionally violent. They caused earthquakes and covered the whole valley with a haze of dense vapors. This period of activity lasted several months. The phenomenon took place daily. The first times it happened around ten o'clock in the evening, but since it occurred later each day by several minutes, at the end of nine months it was

27. Excelsior Geyser [Steam and environs of the geyser crater].

28. The large, boiling spring [Grand Prismatic Spring].

twelve hours later—at ten o'clock in the morning—that the explosion occurred.

The eruptive force of Excelsior Geyser is hardly believable. According to the testimony of Colonel Norris, a column of water would spout one hundred to three hundred feet high and with such a volume of water as to render the Firehole, which is nearly one hundred yards wide at this spot, a foaming torrent of steaming water. The geyser would hurl chunks of rock weighing up to one hundred pounds into the air, scattering them far afield.

On August 28, 1881, General Sheridan witnessed an explosion of Excelsior:[5] a column of water forming a compact mass sixty to seventy-five feet in diameter was projected to the prodigious height of three hundred feet, and the vapors rose more than one thousand feet into a pure, cloudless, azure sky.

One year later, on August 22, 1882, Messrs. Haupt and Eccleston[6] had the good fortune to arrive in front of Excelsior at the very moment when the geyser was preparing to erupt. Dull subterranean rumbles warned them of the phenomenon, and they prudently kept at a distance. Suddenly, they saw a column of water shoot up with a noise of an underwater explosion, rising to several hundred feet. After some seconds they heard the crash of chunks of rock falling back to earth and saw an enormous cataract of boiling water rush down the sides of the crater and descend into the river. The eruption lasted only a few minutes.

In 1883 Excelsior seemed to have retreated into a period of repose.[7] According to the testimony of local people, it would spout only every now and again. Quite rare are those who have been able to see the power of this formidable aqueous volcano. Of all the geysers spouting on the banks of the Firehole, there is none whose eruptions have more terrible effects. The walls of its tube, being of a less compact rock than that of other geysers, break up under the influence of the explosive force. It is for this reason that Excelsior has the dangerous habit of belching out chunks of rock: the ground is strewn with them to a radius of more than two hundred meters surrounding the crater.

Almost beside the biggest geyser in the world, nature has placed her most gigantic hot spring [Grand Prismatic Spring]. It occupies the summit of a mound formed of siliceous deposits tiered in lamellate terraces on the left bank of the Firehole, as high as fifteen meters above the level of the river.

As we were climbing these terraces, walking gingerly between the pools and the cascades of boiling water, we were struck by the extraordinary resonance of our steps: it seemed as if the ground were completely undermined.

What an unexpected scene was revealed when we reached the top of the terraces! We were facing a lake of boiling water extending over not less than half a hectare [a hectare is about 2.5 acres]! Mute with amazement and astonishment, we gazed upon this expanse of steaming, sapphire-colored water so surpassingly transparent that the thousand fantastical forms on the festooned walls could be distinguished under the crystal liquid. The aqueous layers take on a more and more intense blue color as the eye penetrates deeper into the abyss. Several meters from the edge one loses sight of the bottom of the basin, and the dark color of the water indicates unfathomable depths that are concealed from view. Toward the center of the basin the water rises several inches high as it boils; agitated by an undulating motion, it regularly spills over from all sides above the reddish and curiously festooned siliceous ring that slightly protrudes around the basin. The suspended mineral matter is constantly being deposited, forming a succession of terraces in an incomparable richness of color.

An extensive mist of hot vapors rises continually from the bosom of this marvelous expanse of water. Nary a bird glides above it; no tree grows on its banks. Words fail to describe the country surrounding it, sublime in its desolation and nakedness. And yet I need only close my eyes to see it again, for it is unforgettable.

Continuing on our way, toward noon we reached the lower basin of the Firehole, a large valley, two leagues wide, totally riddled with springs of boiling water. Hayden estimated their number at 693 and counted 17 active geysers in addition. The average elevation of the basin is 2,205 meters, and wooded hills of two to three hundred meters overlook it. There we observed phenomena that held no more novelty for us, who had just been contemplating the most beautiful geysers in the world. Bedazzled, intoxicated on marvels, and inured to astonishment and enthusiasm, we had only a distracted and disdainful eye for the springs and geysers grouped in the lower basin.

The Mud Caldron alone was able to reawaken our blasé curiosity. This curious basin [Fountain Paint Pot] contains a sort of white siliceous paste rather reminiscent of plaster in the hands of the molder. The paste, half solid and half liquid, is in extreme agitation; it swells up and splashes in bubbles constantly bursting at its surface, and this bubbling activity produces a thousand bizarre figures: globules, sugar loaves, and rings. Sometimes masses of paste are even projected into the air, but their weight prevents them from rising very high like the light showers of the geysers; they fall heavily back, spattering the edges of the caldron. All around this singular laboratory the ground resembles porcelain paste.

29. The Mud Caldron [Fountain Paint Pot].

We supped at the log house next to the lower basin, at the confluence of the two branches of the Firehole. We were pleasantly surprised to find a post office there run by the travelers themselves:[8] always practical, these Americans! I took advantage of it to let my family know that I was in wonderful health deep in the Land of Wonders.

The place from which I dated my letter is the very site where a caravan of travelers was attacked by Indians in 1877. It is one of those stories that trappers of the Far West are fond of telling around a campfire, and it constitutes one of the most moving pages in the history of the explorations of the National Park.[9]

CHAPTER XV

The Indians in the National Park

Security of the National Park in peacetime. — Peregrinations
of the Nez Perces in 1877. — The Radersburg caravan surprised
by the Indians. — Chief Looking Glass. — Prisoners. — The attack. — The slaughter. — Carpenter's story. — The peace pipe. — The
rescue. — Unbelievable adventures of Cowan. — The Helena caravan. — The attack on the camp. — Roberts's story. — Death of
Dietrich. — Six years later.

In the peregrinations of their nomadic life, the Indians seem
to have always carefully avoided the Land of Wonders. For very
good reasons they have never established residence there: these
fiery domains inspired a sort of superstitious terror in them.[1]
Although one must always be armed against possible encounters with nomadic Indians in other parts of the Rocky Mountains, in peacetime the area of the National Park affords perfect security. It was only when the Indians were on the warpath
that they were sometimes forced to take refuge in these solitudes to escape pursuit by federal troops.

In the month of August 1877 the hostile Nez Perce tribe, led
by Chief Joseph[2] and pursued by General Howard,[3] bypassed
the colonized parts of Montana and Idaho, entered the National Park by way of Henry's Lake, passed through the geyser region, crossed the Yellowstone near the mud volcanoes, and escaped by the pass located near the sources of the Clarks Fork
River. Along their march these ferocious warriors encountered
some peaceable caravans of travelers. The events occasioned
by these encounters inspire dramatic interest, and the memory is still alive among the people of Montana. The account by
travelers who escaped the massacres has been published in the

Helena newspapers, and Mr. Edwin Stanley has added details that he gleaned directly from several survivors in his *Rambles in Wonderland*.[4]

On August 6, 1877, an eight-person expedition left Radersburg[5] to visit the National Park. It was composed of Mr. and Mrs. George Cowan and Mr. Charles Mann, of Radersburg; Miss Ida Carpenter and Mr. Meyers, of Missouri Valley; and Messrs. William Dingee, Albert Oldham, and Frank Carpenter, of Helena.[6] Traveling in wagons, they went by way of Sterling and up the Madison River (Firehole) as far as the Lower Geyser Basin. Here they made their permanent camp and left their vehicles, making the rest of the tour on horseback. They visited the Upper Geyser Basin and three members of the party pushed on as far as the lake and the falls of the Yellowstone. It was as cheerful a party as ever went through the Land of Wonders. They lived well; in the evenings they assembled around the campfire, playing violin and guitar, little dreaming that an enemy was so near.

The night of the twenty-third they returned to their campsite and prepared to start homeward on the morrow. Toward five in the morning, while Arnold and Dingee were making the campfire, they observed the approach of three Indians, who came up to them and alighted from their horses.

Soon everybody was gathered around the newcomers. To the questions posed to them, the Indians responded after some hesitation that they were from the Nez Perce tribe, that their chief was Looking Glass,[7] that Looking Glass was a friend of the white man, and that he did not seek combat with anyone except soldiers of the federal army. They said that his band of two hundred warriors was camped in the woods a short distance away. Indeed, at that moment the goings and comings of a large number of Indians could be seen. The travelers consulted with each other and resolved to strike camp immediately.

The horses were saddled, and the expedition started out without even taking the time to prepare breakfast. But it was not long before they were surrounded by a large troop of warriors, who told them that it was dangerous for them to trav-

30. Indian chief.

el on that road because there were hostile Indians in that direction, who would massacre the entire caravan if they came upon it. They then told the tourists that what they had better do was turn back and accompany them under their protection. In that way they would not be attacked by hostile Indians, and they could soon reach the white settlements.

While the travelers were consulting each other about which direction to follow, the Indians, who were all well armed, surrounded them and compelled them to fall into their line of march.

After traveling for a while up the east fork of the Firehole [now called Nez Perce Creek] they had to abandon the wagons, which could not get over the trees fallen across the road. The horses were unhitched and saddled for Mrs. Cowan and her sister Ida.

Then Frank Carpenter declared that he would go find Looking Glass to ask his permission for them to return home. In exchange for six cartridges, he hired an Indian to take him to the chief. He found Looking Glass eight miles farther along, at the foot of a steep mountain west of Mary Lake. He shook his hand and asked if he was a friend. The chief replied in the affirmative.

While Frank was telling him about the caravan, another Nez Perce chief, White Bird,[8] came up. He was accompanied by Shively,[9] who had been captured the evening before and forced to act as guide for the Indians. White Bird invited Frank into his tent and asked him who they were, where they were from, and where they were going. Frank replied to all these questions.

In the meantime, the Indians had brought their captives to White Bird's camp. This dignitary informed them that they could return home but that he found it necessary to keep their horses and their arms and ammunition. He told them that he would give them other horses in exchange, other guns, and three cartridges per gun. He kept his word.

The chiefs then struck camp, and the march resumed. The captives received the order to return from whence they had come, and they obeyed without hesitation. They were nonetheless terrified to see that they were followed by forty or fifty savages of ferocious demeanor. Had not White Bird even confessed that he could no longer control his men? They became insolent, seized their weapons and blankets and made the woods resound with their hideous yells. About this time Dingee and Arnold sneaked away into the thicket and escaped.

For a time the savages closely followed the travelers, then they ordered them to stop and to retrace their steps. It now became obvious that they meant mischief and that the object of these marches and countermarches was to let the other chiefs get farther away. The warriors then took the captives back to a place near a thick woods, not far from where White Bird had left them, and there they began their bloody work.

Cowan and his wife were riding in advance when two Indians came dashing down the hill in front of them. The savages halted; one of them raised his gun and fired. The bullet passed through Cowan's right thigh. He slipped from his horse and, being unable to support himself on his wounded leg, sank to the ground. His wife instantly flew to his aid and bent over him, when two Indians came up, one pointing his revolver at Cowan's head intending to finish him off. Seeing this, Mrs. Cowan threw her arms about her husband's neck and, shielding him with her body, implored the Indian to kill her first.

Without listening to her, the Indian seized her right hand to drag her away, but with her other hand, the unfortunate woman clung with heroic strength to her husband's neck. Cowan's head was then exposed to the other Indian, and he discharged his revolver into his left temple. The unfortunate man was left for dead.

When the carnage began, the members of the expedition had scattered, and several of them had succeeded in escaping into the brush. Albert Oldham was wounded in the face, the ball passing through his tongue but not inflicting a mortal wound. Left for dead, he wandered for four days and five nights in the wilderness without food or shelter and was found by the Howard expedition. Charles Mann escaped into the forest, his hat pierced by a bullet. He was taken in by some scouts of the friendly Bannock Indian tribe and returned with Howard to search for the other members of the expedition, who were believed to be dead. Meyers, though suffering severely with a scalded foot, outran the Indians and succeeded in getting several miles ahead of them to join the soldiers. Dingee and Arnold, who had fled before the massacre, spent five days and nights in the mountains without food, fire, or coverings, and they were ready to succumb to despair when they joined the Howard expedition near Henry's Lake [west of Yellowstone Park].

During the firing Frank Carpenter saw a young chief aiming at his breast. Thinking his hour had come,[10] he made the sign of the cross; seeing this, the Indian threw down his gun and cried, "Come quick, me no kill, — me save you!" Before Cowan had been wounded in the head, Carpenter had run to where his sister was bending over her husband in order to assist them. However, the chief took him aside and ordered him to stay quiet behind a bush. Carpenter implored the chief to spare the women, and the Indian promised him he would.

When the carnage was over, Mrs. Cowan was torn away from her husband's body. She and her sister were each lashed on a horse behind a savage and led into captivity with their brother.

The next day White Bird called together a council of the chiefs present, in order to decide what should be done with the prisoners. The council consisted of seven chiefs. White Bird spoke on behalf of the prisoners. His principal argument was that, if they were killed, the citizens of Montana would take revenge by killing the Nez Perces. Another chief got up and spoke for a long time. He pawed the ground and gesticulated fiercely. He wanted to kill Carpenter and make his sister his "squaw." White Bird lit a pipe, took a few puffs, and passed it around the circle. Those who smoked expressed in this way the opinion that the prisoners should be let go.

"Never in my life," said Carpenter, "did I experience such delight in seeing a person smoke!" Twice the pipe passed around the circle. Four of the chiefs smoked the pipe, and three refused. The council dispersed. White Bird informed Carpenter that he could return home with his sisters. He escorted them about a mile away and left them, saying,

"Go home—go quickly! You will not meet Indians on the trail—they have gone back to Henry's Lake to fight the Lewiston soldiers. I do not want to fight Montana citizens or soldiers. You tell the people of Bozeman, the people of Montana, if Montana soldiers fight us any more, we will kill all the white women, children, and citizens—everybody! We will kill them all, and not let them go! We are going to Shoshone country. You will get to Bozeman in three days. Good-by."

The most dramatic narrative is that of Cowan. You will remember that he had received a bullet to the head and that he had been left for dead. But he was not born to be killed by a bullet. The bullet bypassed the skull without piercing it. The wounded man remained insensible for about two hours. When he came to, he ascertained that his wounds were not fatal.

Believing himself alone, he drew himself up by the boughs of a tree, and was standing on his feet when he discovered an Indian approaching him with rifle in hand ready for use, twenty yards away. Cowan ran toward a bush; as he turned around to see how closely he was pursued, the Indian fired; the bullet struck Cowan in the left hip and exited by the abdomen. The poor wounded man fell on his face in the high grass about twenty yards from the trail and remained perfectly still, thinking his situation hopeless now and every moment expecting to see the Indian come complete his work. But the Indian did not come. About twenty minutes elapsed, when a hostile band passed along the trail but did not discover the wounded man.

Cowan remained in place for another half hour. Darkness had fallen; a profound silence reigned. He cautiously surveyed the scene and, finding himself alone, took a new inventory of his injuries, which gave him some hope. Finding himself incapable of standing on his feet, he commenced to crawl, reached a place of greater safety, pondered his situation until midnight, then lay down waiting for day.

Bearing three serious wounds, suffering from cold and hunger, exhausted by loss of blood, abandoned in a vast wilderness among ferocious beasts and savages, incapable of walking, distraught by the thought that his wife had been murdered or was in captivity, Cowan was indeed worthy of pity. But he was not a man to give himself over to despair. He recalled that his companions had dropped some matches and spilled a small amount of parched coffee at the camp in Firehole basin; he also recalled that an empty food can had been left there. If he found the matches, the coffee, and the can, he could make a fire and procure some nourishment to sustain him until he was rescued.

The former camp was some twelve miles away; resolutely Cowan undertook this perilous journey. When on the way he encountered the abandoned wagons, he crawled around them searching in the vain hope of finding some garment to ward off the cold. There he found his faithful hunting dog, watching and waiting patiently for its master's return. The dog was delighted to see him, lavished the greatest signs of tenderness upon him, and was his traveling companion from then on. Finally, after dragging himself for four days and four nights on his hands and knees through dense forests, on Tuesday evening Cowan reached the camp where the expedition had been captured. There he found the matches and the grains of coffee scattered in the dust. He then considered himself saved, because he had fire to warm himself, coffee to drink, and a dog that he could kill and eat, if necessity required.

The next day he was found by General Howard's scouts. The following day the advance guard arrived with Arnold, who was the first to tell Cowan that his wife was healthy and unharmed. Cowan was placed in a wagon and taken with the expedition to the Yellowstone [River]; accompanied by Arnold, whose solicitude for his friend was unceasing, he was sent from there to Bozeman. He encountered his wife on the way, and after several other misadventures arrived safely and received congratulations from a large number of friends who had given him up for dead.[11]

The adventures of the Helena expedition were equally as stirring as those of the Radersburg expedition. This caravan was composed of Messrs. Frederick Pfister, A. J. Weikert, Richard Dietrich,[12] Joseph Roberts, Charles Kenck, Jack Stewart,

August Foller, Leslie Wilkie, L. Duncan, and Benjamin Stone, colored cook.

On the morning of 25 August the travelers left the falls of the Yellowstone to camp that night at the Mud Geysers, nine or ten miles away; but when they reached the summit of Sulphur Mountain, they saw in the distance a moving body that they took at first for a band of elk, then for a large caravan of tourists, but they finally ascertained that it was a troop of Indians. They soon came upon the Indian camp on the east bank of the Yellowstone. The whole caravan immediately returned to within three miles of the falls, rode a mile west of the path, and camped in a small clearing near a brook that flows into the Yellowstone. They were not disturbed in any way during the night. No one knew to what tribe the Indians they had observed belonged.

The next morning Weikert and Wilkie volunteered to act as scouts. It was understood that if danger threatened, they would fire their guns, which should be the signal for the caravan to seek safety in flight.

At about eleven o'clock the cook was preparing dinner and most were sleeping or lounging about camp, when the crack of a gun aroused everyone. Immediately a volley of bullets was fired into the camp by a band of savages, who then rushed in, firing their guns and making the woods ring with their ferocious war whoops. Kenck was killed outright; Stewart received a severe wound to the hip, but he managed to get away. The rest of the party scattered and ran for the woods, followed by a shower of bullets, and succeeded in making their escape.

The scouts were retracing their steps, having failed to find the Indians on account of the haze. When they were about two miles from the camp, they discovered the savages lying in ambush and wheeled their horses to retreat. In the midst of a hail of bullets, Weikert was wounded in the shoulder. They were able to escape pursuit by the Indians and reach the camp.[13]

In camp, the broken guns, the provisions, and the camp equipment piled on the smoldering fire told the story of the terrible events. Starting homeward, they came upon Stewart and Stone. Stewart was gravely wounded, and Stone was look-ing after him. Both were exhausted. The noble-hearted scouts gave their horses to their comrades in distress and trudged along beside them all night.

They arrived the next morning at Mammoth Springs, hav-ing covered forty-five miles in one stretch since the attack. There they found Carpenter and his sisters, who had just ar-rived. During the day, all the survivors of the Helena caravan came back, with the exception of Roberts and Foller.

These young men, one scarcely twenty and the other seven-teen years of age, managed to reach the forest. They crossed the mountains in a northwesterly direction, trudging through the woods and hoping thus to avoid the Indians, whom they believed to be hard on their heels.

Lost amid these dreary solitudes without guide or compass, destitute of food and clothing, their feet bleeding, it is a mir-acle that they were able to escape death and rejoin their fam-ilies. Stanley has given young Roberts's curious story.[14]

Weikert and McCartney[15] returned to the site of the attack to search for the missing, bury the dead, and transport the wound-ed. Dietrich, a man by the name of Stoner, and the Negro Stone remained at Mammoth Springs to care for the wounded who would be brought back. All the others left for Bozeman. A troop of Indians made their appearance and opened fire. Stoner and Stone succeeded in escaping to Doane's camp,[16] but Dietrich was killed. Weikert and McCartney buried Kenck's body; they were returning to Mammoth Springs when they were attacked by the same Indians, from whom they escaped only by a mira-cle. One of the scouts had his horse shot out from under him.

One can imagine the mourning that spread through the en-tire Montana Territory when the telegraph carried the news of these tragic events. It was at first believed that all the travel-ers had been scalped or taken captive. Only two had died. The salvation of the others was miraculous.

Six years later, we found a vast hotel at Mammoth Springs, at the very spot where Dietrich was killed. The Indians were only a distant memory. In America time moves quickly!

CHAPTER XVI

Yellowstone Lake

Morning departure. — Firehole Falls. — Norris Pass. — The backbone of America. — Arrival at Yellowstone Lake. — Altitude of
the lake. — The nature of its waters. — Appearance of the landscape. — Hot springs. — In the forest. — Bluff Point. — Scorched
forests. — The natural bridge. — The campsite. — Appearance of
the lake. — A glorious night.

The same evening of our expedition to the Lower Geyser Basin found us back in our tent near Old Faithful.

On September 4 we mounted our ponies in that glorious
Rocky Mountain sunshine that we greeted so enthusiastical-
ly every morning. At this early hour the steam[1] thrown up by
the geysers and hot springs was extraordinarily dense. Rising
like clouds of incense, the white of the vapors stood out against
the dark background of the wooded mountains, and the valley
appeared to be an immense, steaming solfatara.

We took the road to the southeast toward Yellowstone Lake,
casting one last glance back at the geyser craters, seeking to
fix forever in our memories the bizarre silhouettes and strange
colors. Old Faithful graciously acknowledged our departure by
sending into the air her beautiful column of water and steam.

Following a rough mule path wending its way along a picturesque cañon floor, we reached the Firehole Falls [Kepler Cas-
cades] in half an hour. In cutting a narrow passage in the basalt
rocks, the river has formed a gorge through which it writhes
and roars like a rushing stream in the Alps. The falls are composed of a series of successive cascades rushing into an abyss
dominated by vertical walls.

Continuing to climb through pine forests, we soon arrived

31. The Yellowstone Lake.

at Norris Pass, which leads from the Mississippi basin to the Pacific basin.[2] A narrow defile, it opens onto the crest line of the Rocky Mountains, as the Brèche de Roland opens onto the crest line of the Pyrenees.[3]

The sides of this enormous portal rise vertically in two parallel walls for a distance of more than three hundred meters.

One league farther on, to the right we passed little Shoshone Lake,[4] in the region where the sources of the Firehole arise. Forgoing an exploration of the geysers that erupt on its shores, we followed an excessively arduous track to recross the backbone of America at an altitude of 2,500 meters, where lies a pond [Isa Lake] that gives rise to two streams: one rushes down the west side of the Rocky Mountains to lose itself in the Pacific; the other heads east to swell the Yellowstone and disappear into the Atlantic with the Mississippi. The view is much more limited than one would suppose, because of the thick forests obscuring the horizon; only toward the south is there a distant vista of the Red Mountains and the valley of Lewis Lake.

The country has a conspicuously volcanic character: the rocks are all of igneous origin, and in many places we observed masses of pure obsidian.

Having arrived toward the middle of the day at the far western end of Yellowstone Lake, we experienced the same enthusiasm that captivated the first explorers when they pitched their tents on the shores of this broad and splendid expanse of water. The staid geologist Hayden, in a moment of poetic elation, cried that this was one of the most beautiful scenes he had ever beheld and that such a vision was worth a lifetime.[5] Sparkling like a burnished steel mirror, the lake rests at the foot of snowy peaks, at an altitude of 2,358 meters above the two oceans. It is adjacent to the sources of the three great rivers[6] that flow through North America. It measures about thirty leagues around.

There is no other lake as large in North America at such an altitude. If one could plunge the Rigi into it so the base of the mountain were at sea level, its summit would still be drowned more than half a kilometer under the surface of the water.[7]

The lake is very deep. The Hayden expedition brought along a small boat to take soundings, and they recorded depths of three hundred feet.[8] When the wind stirs up the waves navigation is not without danger, and because the water is very cold in all seasons, hardly rising above 15°C [59°F], even the most able swimmer could not long survive. The lake is traversed from south to north by the Yellowstone River, of which it is merely an expansion. It receives numerous torrents laden with mineral substances from the neighboring mountains. Its shores and even its bed are riddled with alkaline, aluminous, and sulphurous springs, which sully the waters in many places, although everywhere else they are of admirable clarity. A healthy marine vegetation is growing there. Hayden warrants that after a strong north wind, the waters along the shoreline are often covered with little fragments of vegetation broken up by the waves. Different species of plants grow underwater as deep as six or seven meters.

This vast expanse of water has a very irregular shape; like the fiords in Iceland, it is incised with deep bays that are reminiscent of the extended fingers of an open hand. We approached the lake at the west bay, which forms the thumb of the hand.

In this place, where one day a hotel will probably be erected, the landscape is of a robust beauty. On the grassy and perfectly flat plateau standing six or seven meters above the waters grow pines of a gigantic size, whose thick shade protected us from the broiling rays of the noonday sun beating down on our heads. The forest extends to the foot of the plateau. From there to the edge of the water stretches a wide, smooth beach covered with little pebbles and fine sand, where waves stirred up by the west wind come to break. Extended before us was a beautiful blue expanse, framed by green forests and overlooked by a rocky point that interposes its long white lines between the blue of the lake and the blue of the sky. From the south the high peaks of the Rockies rise up noble and majestic, covered with a shining armor of ice. Dominating all the peaks, the superb mass of Mount Sheridan rises to 3,165 meters, deeply cut by glaciers and avalanches.

Nothing demonstrates better how much geyser phenomena need a proximate surface body of water, lake or river, than the large number of hot springs or erupting geysers on the shores of the west bay of Yellowstone Lake. In leaving the upper basin of the Firehole we had thought we would no longer encounter boiling waters, but here we found them to be even more numerous and more active than ever. They emerge all along the shore, and for more than a league the earth is honeycombed like a kitchen skimmer with cavities where waters boil as in thermal baths or are tossed about as in fountains. The action of underground forces is realized in all its forms: geysers, jets of steam, mud volcanoes, and simple hot springs.

Here nature has assembled a collection of all the thermal phenomena, and she appears to be amusing herself by putting cold and hot in intimate communion. Immersed in the glacial waters of the lake are many tubes that give issue to boiling waters; spreading out on the surface, the hot waters raise the temperature of the upper layers of the expanse of water, while the lower layers become successively colder. In one dive, the bather can thus cover the whole thermometric range.

A crater completely surrounded by water rises up in the lake at a rather great distance from the shore. From the edge of this calcareous island a fisherman can catch a trout and fry it in the central basin without even taking it off the hook.[9]

Other craters are half in the lake and half on the shore. At every step on this gently sloping terrain extending into the distant woods one encounters wells filled with incredibly clear and seemingly unfathomable water. The reflection from the silvery-white, sedimentary coping that borders these wells noticeably lights up the interior of their basins; I do not know what strange clarity it is that reigns even in their most profound depths. A stone dropped in remains long visible as a luminous object in the clear crystal waters.

One of these fountains is especially notable for the marvelous effulgence shining from the depths of its abyss. Its walls seem to converge rapidly near the bottom, like the circumference of a funnel, so that one would think it possible to touch with the end of an oar. But optical illusions are common in this enchanted land: a sounding line plunged into this would-be funnel reveals a well 107 meters deep.[10]

It is hardly astonishing that such a long cylinder has the form of a cone! But who can explain why no bubble of steam troubles the calm of these indigo-blue waters? Their temperature is very close to the boiling point, but still they remain calm in their mysterious prison. Who again can explain why such a deep thermal well is not a geyser?[11]

Everything in this region is strange. Pools situated only a few paces from one another seem to have no connection. They differ in level, temperature, color, and regimen; some are entirely quiescent, others boil constantly, and still others have intervals of convulsive pulsations, after which they emit puffs of steam. Only rarely do two neighboring springs have identical waters and deposits; sometimes they are green as emeralds, sometimes blue as sapphires or lapis lazuli; there are white, red, and yellow ones, depending on the nature of the mineral substances on their walls.

The deposits present a thousand varieties of form and design: some resemble coral, others fish scales, honeycombs, crystal,

32. Mud spring crater.

or cauliflower. According to whether they are calcareous or siliceous, they have the delicacy of a light duvet or the hardness of diamonds.

In their depths many pools harbor caves of marvelous construction, underground palaces that might have been built by the naiads;[12] their silvered walls encrusted with pearls sparkle and shimmer in the limpid waters.

Innumerable rivulets empty into the lake, their waters spilling over from all the boiling reservoirs: they present the same fantastical colors as the edges of the springs. Everywhere the rivulets flow, the shores of the lake are covered with a calcareous shell of considerable thickness. The edges of this travertine[13] are cut sheer by the action of the waters.

Mud springs, called "paint pots" by the Americans, are also abundant in this region. Some present little mounds in the form of craters, others open like funnels where floats a viscous and boiling pink material containing a mixture of calcareous and siliceous substances, as well as some iron and alum. Pasty spurts spatter the edges of these strange boiling basins.

We had to make a strong effort to tear ourselves away from

this unusual and varied spectacle. Only hunger acted as a damper to our rapture.

After a light lunch on the edges of the western bay, we set off to camp fifteen miles farther on at the northern extremity of the lake.

Spreading out at the edge of the hot springs region is one of those splendid pine forests that have never known the woodcutter's blade. Thousands of squirrels frolic in the high branches of the noble conifers that for centuries have been springing up from their own detritus. We rode for an hour in their shade, finally emerging abruptly on the promontory of Bluff Point, which overlooks the western bay from a height of about a hundred meters.[14]

Before us shimmered a blue sea, smooth as glass, in the center of which emerges Carrenton [Carrington] Island with its dark-green forests.[15] To the south stretches a long expanse of steep rock covered by a chevelure of pines. To the north extends a little bay, which we justifiably compared to the Bay of Naples, as it seems in fact to be its very likeness in miniature; as if to complete the resemblance, the crater of a boiling spring, a little aquatic Vesuvius,[16] rises at the end of the bay, stirring up a plume of vapors.

Beyond Bluff Point, we turned off toward the east. Two imposing bowlders seemed to bar the route: they are Rock Point and Sand Point. From between them opens a distant view of the east shore of the lake, which is hardly three leagues wide at this point.

Leaving the shores of the lake, we climbed the high plateaus covered with vast grassy meadows and woods, the abode of elk, antelope, and moose. We crossed through the remains of several forests that had been burned by the poorly extinguished fires of hunters camping in this game-filled country. It is impossible to imagine a more desolate scene than these thousands of blackened trunks and charred branches that not long ago gave deep shade but that now afforded us no protection from the broiling sun. It is frightening and gloomy to see these skeletons of trees, even in full daylight.

A true marvel has recently been discovered at the bottom of the valley as one emerges from these dreary solitudes: it is an arch of trachyte, spanning a gorge, at whose base winds a torrent. This natural bridge, ten meters long, is perfectly negotiable by carriages in spite of a long, gaping hole in the middle of the arch.[17] A trail used by inhabitants of the forest confirms that they do not fear to pass over it. A sturdy pine grows practically in the middle of the bridge. The structure is covered with a rich vegetation of moss, lichen, and ferns. Downstream and upstream the river forms a series of cascades whose snowy white color stands out against the dark green of the fir trees: it would be impossible to imagine a more romantic site.

This aerial structure, suspended more than twenty meters above the torrent, must once have formed the top of a waterfall; but by undercutting the rock, the waters succeeded one day in making a hole in it, forming the perfectly semicircular arch under which they now rush.

We arrived at the campsite near six o'clock in the evening, happy to set our feet on the ground after a rough horseback ride of thirty-four miles along arduous tracks, across forests and mountains. The campsite is located at the spot where the Yellowstone River flows out from the lake after traversing its whole length from south to north.

We stretched our legs on a beautiful beach where one can find agates, carnelians, and other precious stones intermingled with lavas and obsidians.

The view from this beach encompasses the magnificent ensemble of all of Yellowstone Lake and the mountains overlooking it. In the background toward the south, the bold silhouettes of the Red Mountains are outlined in the clear air of these high altitudes.

Near the center of the lake, large Frank Island partly obscures the view of the mountains to the south that form the dividing line separating the two oceans. Toward the southeast, the eye loses itself in the depths of a mountain gorge forming the extension of one of the southerly arms of the lake. Behind Signal Hills[18] on the east shore rise the snowy summits of Mount

Stevenson (3,175 meters), Mount Doane (3,265 meters), and other as yet unnamed peaks. At the foot of Signal Hills, three leagues distant, one can easily distinguish the wisps of steam from a group of geysers [Brimstone Basin]. To the west soars a promontory overlooking the lake from a height of 335 meters.[19]

Because of the surrounding landscape, this lake very much reminds one of Lake Lucerne[20] but is significantly larger.

Receding one behind the other at sunset, the jagged mountains take on warm, velvety violet colors; the snowy peaks become tinged purplish-pink and are surrounded by attendant clouds that drift past them and become illuminated by their splendid colors. Each time I see the beautiful lake in my mind's eye, it is at the moment of this magical sunset, and I hear once more the soft chords of our friend Alexander's concertina that plunged us into a delicious reverie.

The night was cold and clear. The Milky Way was exceptionally luminous. Were we under the influence of that religious emotion so natural to man faced with the magnificent scenes of nature and surrounded by marvels that seem beyond human understanding? I don't know, but never had the sky seemed to us so beautiful; never had we read more clearly the sublime name of God in the innumerable stars that twinkled in the infinite depths of that resplendent night.

We slept perfectly well, with no physical disturbance to remind us that we were camped at the same elevation as an average Alpine peak. It is true that in Mexico I slept soundly at four thousand meters above sea level.

CHAPTER XVII

Remarks on Fishing and Hunting

Morning bath. — Trout in the lake. — Indian artifacts. — The grizzly bear. — The cougar. — The wolf. — The fox. — The elk. — The
moose. — The deer. — The antelope. — Remedies to prevent the
extermination of game.

The next morning we took a dip in the lake, which sparkled
like a molten ruby in the light of the rising sun. Pelicans were
treading carefully among the reeds, stretching out their pouches
as traps for the innumerable trout living in those cold waters.

Surely there is no place in the world where trout proliferate
as in Yellowstone Lake; their number is prodigious, and since
they greedily snap up the grasshoppers offered as bait, in one
hour a fisherman can catch enough to exhaust a dozen cooks.
But eating them is a different matter: although it is true they
are as large as they are appetizing and seem to make exquisite fare, we were careful not to eat any when we learned that
most of them were infested with long white worms the size
of a knitting needle that live not only in their intestines but
also in their flesh. This worm (*Dibothrium cordiceps*),[1] previously mentioned by Hayden, was described by Professor Leidy,[2]
who considers it to be completely different from the parasites
found in European salmon; they are found only in fish caught
in the lake and in the part of the Yellowstone River extending
from the lake to the falls. Beyond the falls, the trout are perfectly healthy. It therefore seems certain that the presence of
the parasite is due to the waters of the lake.

The solution to this problem is best left to ichthyologists. It
is a strange fact that has as yet no satisfactory explanation. A
fish afflicted with this malady does not die of it; after a time

33. Rocky Mountain bear cubs.

it sloughs off the parasite, as evidenced by the scars borne on its sides, usually near the pectoral fins.[3]

Speckled trout is the only species sustained by the waters of the lake. But what a variety of birds! It is enough to drive an ornithologist crazy. For a long time the ducks, swans, geese, and other representatives of the aquatic tribe lived in peace in their undiscovered domains, but hunters have flushed them out of their retreat, and the golden age for these shore dwellers is over.

And yet, who knows for how many centuries these poor birds were acquainted with arrows before they made the acquaintance of lead! This beautiful lake with its game-filled shores must have been visited from time immemorial by indigenous people.[4] When the first explorers visited its islands, in the middle of jungles that served as retreats for bears, they found evidence indicating that the red man formerly hunted in these solitary regions: they collected lances, obsidian arrowheads, and other tools that had belonged to a now-extinct aboriginal race.

Today firearms have wakened echoes in this country so long unknown to man. In the solitudes around Yellowstone Lake you can still hunt big carnivores and large ruminants; in the forests and jungles you can give yourself a scare by going on a bear hunt. If you are only a beginner at this kind of sport, settle for the black bear or brown bear (*Ursus americanus*); if you aspire to great exploits, dare to measure your prowess against the gray bear, the terrible grizzly (*Ursus horribilis*) [now *Ursus arctos*], the largest and most ferocious of the species. You will have no trouble finding him, for he is everywhere within the boundaries of the National Park, and occasionally I have caught sight of his freshly made trail from horseback. Had I encountered him, I would have ceded him the path with as much alacrity as I would have for a nobleman. Moreover, he rarely attacks man, but when he is wounded and pursued he becomes formidable and falls upon his aggressor with dreadful vehemence. Then it is he who becomes the hunter, and woe to the hunted if he has not got a good Winchester!

The first explorers, Clark and Lewis, had more than one encounter with the grizzly in which they nearly lost their lives. Still, he is often well behaved, especially in very hot weather. Mr. Stanley[5] reports that one day a grizzly was shamefully killed by stoning. This happened in the Madison Valley. The heat was stifling, and while on his rambles, the bear became lost on the prairie. An inhabitant of the valley noticed him, gave the alarm, and gathered a "posse." In their haste, the assailants forgot their guns, and the poor bear was ignominiously roped with a lasso, then stoned as punishment for the numerous misdeeds he had committed against the herds of that country.

The grizzly is not always such easy prey. Colonel Norris recounts[6] that a young horse, somewhat lamed by scalding in the "fire holes," having been left near Obsidian Cañon, was killed by a grizzly that, in devouring the carcass and game in the vicinity, continued to haunt the place. Trailing him some weeks afterward, the colonel killed two large elk he found a few meters apart and, it being nearly night, he removed their entrails and camped alone near them, confident that the bruin would visit them before morning. In fact, the grizzly soon arrived and

34. Cougar.

began to drag the two elk so near together as to leave only a space for a lair of boughs and grasses between them. As the bear worked to finish this lair, the colonel opened fire at a distance of a hundred yards with a Winchester rifle loaded with fourteen ordinary bullets and a dynamite shell. He first hit him in the shoulder with the dynamite, which exploded and severed the main artery beneath the backbone. The grizzly fell but instantly arose with a fearful snort or howl of pain and rage; before he could get his bearings he received four additional ordinary .44-caliber bullets, fell almost as many times, then charged his attacker. Hastily inserting another dynamite shell, the colonel aimed from a distance of fifty yards and sent his projectile into the chest, where the explosion obliterated his lungs, again felling him; the animal made an effort to rise, but a new charge broke his neck. The hide of this terrifying specimen was 8¾ feet long from tip of snout to roots of tail and 6 feet, 7 inches at its widest place. From his blubber, thirty-five gallons of grease or oil were extracted.

35. After the hunt.

Very little is known about the habits of the grizzly.[7] One thing that seems certain is that the young are born around January 15, hardly larger than a young dog.

Another formidable carnivore living in the jungles and caverns of the Yellowstone is the cougar (*Felis concolor*), a species of panther referred to in the Rockies as a "mountain lion." Though it is rarely seen, still a few are killed in the mountains every winter. When hunted in its own domain it becomes fierce. Mr. Everts, whose lamentable adventures I have recounted,[8] was pursued by a cougar and managed to escape only by climbing a tree.

The skins of the cougar were formerly imported in large quantities from the east and from California for purposes of trade with the Indians. A few years ago a good skin was sometimes sold for seven or eight buffalo robes, but at present they have little or no commercial value.

Other felines haunt the solitudes of the Yellowstone, such as the wildcat (*Lynx rufus*) [now called bobcat], abundant in the mountains, and the Canada lynx (*Lynx canadensis*).

Of the canine species, there is the gray, or timber, wolf (*Canis occidentalis*) [now called *Canis lupus*]. Wherever buffalo are abundant one is sure to find Lord Wolf, often in large packs. At night one can hear them howling around the camps.

Wolf hunting is an established industry in Montana, known as "wolfing": pursued only in winter, it gives employment and support to a large number of teamsters, steamboat hands, and others who are necessarily idle at this season. The method is rather simple. The "wolfer" first kills a deer, a buffalo, or some other large animal and, thoroughly poisoning it with strychnine, leaves it for a day or two. When he returns to it he finds a dozen wolves or foxes lying dead about the carcass, poisoned. As wolf skins bring on average two and a half dollars, it is not unusual for two men to make $1,000–$1,500 at this work in a winter.

Almost all the dogs seen among the Assinaboines, Crows, and Gros Ventres of the prairie appear to have more or less wolf blood in their veins and many of them would be taken for true wolves were they seen away from the Indian camps.

The prairie wolf, or coyote (*Canis latrans*), is much more common on the prairie than in the mountains. It is found mostly in the plains, where there are deep ravines to which the animals may retire during the day, and in holes in the sides of which the young are brought forth. Mr. Grinnell[9] recounts that when searching for fossils in such places he often came upon an old female lying at the mouth of a hole in the bank and surrounded by her half-grown litter. At sight of the stranger the whole family would spring to their feet, stare at the scientist for a few seconds, and then two or three of the young would dart into the hole, as many wildly scramble up the bank, and the rest of the group would start off up the ravine, looking back every few steps as if there were a constant struggle between their fears and their curiosity. The Ludlow expedition[10] captured a pup perhaps three months old at their Crooked Creek camp. He had taken refuge in a hole in the bluffs and was dug out and brought to camp. Although so young, he was utterly wild and vicious, snapping at anyone who ventured to touch him and refusing to eat. His unceasing efforts to escape were at length successful, and one morning they found that during the night he had gnawed off the fastenings and departed.

The prairie fox (*Vulpes alopex macrurus*) is abundant everywhere. It is often found lying dead near the carcasses poisoned for wolves.

Another fox, called by the Americans "swift" or "kit fox" (*Vulpes velox*), is common on the prairies of Dakota and Montana; as it has but few enemies, it is often quite tame. Mr. Grinnell sometimes came upon one of these pretty little animals as it lay sleeping in the sun at the mouth of its burrow: he was amused to see the fox examine him briefly, then stretch, yawn, and with its tail held straight up in the air, and an appearance of the utmost unconcern, trot slowly into the hole. This has generally two openings; and sometimes, while you are examining one entrance, the little fox may be seen inspecting you from the other.

If the mountains and jungles are the favorite territory of the carnivores, the beautiful pastures, dense forests, banks of rivers, and shores of lakes are hospitable to the proliferation of ruminants. The king of the ruminants is the bison, the noblest representative of American fauna. The mountain bison (*Bos americanus*) [now *Bison bison*] differ somewhat from the plains bison. They are abundant in certain regions of the Yellowstone; they roam in herds of two or three hundred on the plateaus and in the large valleys.

Another noble species of game is the elk (*Cervus canadensis*) [now *Cervus elaphus nelsoni*, or Rocky Mountain elk], also occasionally seen in herds of several hundred. They are found over the entire extent of the National Park but especially on the grassy sides of mountains, which provide them with excellent grazing. At the commencement of the rutting season, elk meat makes a delicious dish. The elk rut in September, and the young are brought forth late in May or early in June. The cry of the elk is heard only for a few days during the early part of September. It is made up of several parts and is so peculiar a cry that it can hardly be described, much less imitated. The first part consists of a prolonged, shrill whistle, which seems to come to the hearer from a long distance, even though the animal uttering it be quite near at hand. This is followed by a

36. Rocky Mountain moose.

succession of short, grunting brays or barks, three or four in number, and the call is completed by a low, smooth bellow. The cry is an odd one, and one that once heard will always afterward be recognized.

The moose (*Alce americana*) [now *Alces alces shirasi*],[11] although a member of the elk family, is of a much larger size. It is found in remote areas of the National Park. Like all the large game, it has been driven away from the neighborhood of the trail by the constant passage of travelers. Grinnell saw signs of its presence in the Bridger Mountains and was told that there was a famous country for moose about sixteen miles from the mouth of Trail Creek. The only living specimen that he saw was a young calf that had been captured by a settler: it was very tame and would come at the call of its owner.

Like its European cousin that I saw in a domesticated state in Lapland, the American moose,[12] of which I saw only a stuffed specimen, is one of the most ungraceful creatures in all creation: an ugly head reminiscent of a mule, mounted on a short, thick neck; small eyes; pendulous ears; a monstrous nose; a prodigious lip that flaps over the mouth; long, thick, and bristling

37. Rocky Mountain deer [white-tailed deer].

hair; and finally, on the male, enormous webbed horns as grotesque as the total aspect of the animal. It is easy to approach
a moose if one stays downwind, but once it bolts, it stays on
the alert for several hours. Launched into a trot, it can outrun
the fastest horse.

The black-tailed deer (*Cervus macrotis*) [or mule deer, now
Odocoileus hemionus] roams in the valleys and lower regions of
mountains, where it finds dense forests; it is also found along
rushing streams and brooks. This animal is quite unsuspicious;
it will often permit the hunter to fire two or three shots at it
before thinking to take flight. Like all large game in that section of the country, it is at present most recklessly slaughtered
for the hides alone, and Grinnell maintains that unless some
means are taken for its protection it will soon be unknown in
the regions where it is now so plentiful.

The antelope [pronghorn] (*Antilocapra americana*) is everywhere abundant on the plains and, according to Grinnell, is one
of the most pleasing features of those barren wastes. They are
very unsuspicious and quite curious. The female sometimes
has horns and is sometimes without them. Grinnell's obser-

vations led him to conclude that the horned does are always barren.[13]

Yellowstone country sustains not only large game; a great variety of small fur-bearing animals can also be found there: marten, sable, ermine, otter, beaver, muskrat, badger. . . . What marvelous country for hunting!

Is it necessary to say that neither regulations for carrying arms nor the presence of game wardens are known in this divine sportsman's paradise? It is true that the act of Congress[14] establishing the Land of Wonders as a public park states that the secretary of the interior, under whose control this domain is placed, will take measures against the unnecessary destruction of game. But despite this legislative constraint the National Park, where firearms never resounded before the arrival of the whites, has been invaded since then by legions of hunters and trappers, who every year commit an enormous slaughter of wild animals. They devote themselves to their exploits especially in winter, when the elk and the bison become easy prey in heavy snows. Captain Ludlow states that in one single winter about two thousand elk were massacred within a fifteen-mile radius of Mammoth Springs. Only the skins of these animals, representing a value of two to three dollars, are sought after; the rest is abandoned to the wolves.[15] Mr. Haupt[16] maintains that in the winter of 1881 to 1882 five thousand elk skins were sent to markets in the East, not to mention the beaver skins and other furs that were captured in the same proportions. I heard a sportsman in Chicago brag of having killed six female elk in two days, simply for the satisfaction of hunting.[17]

The continuation of this carnage will rapidly and inevitably result in the extermination of game. It is time to put an end to it by dispatching several companies of soldiers who would become the Park Police. Is not this domain the only territory in the Union where animal life has the right to government protection? Is not the inoffensive existence of interesting animals one of the main charms of this park, which has been reserved for the pleasure of visitors and for study by scientists? The Yellowstone basin, long unknown to man, owes to its isolation the richest and most varied animal life of North America. It is perfectly suited to the conservation of interesting species of animals that have disappeared from other countries of the New World when confronting the invasion of civilization. Surrounded on all sides by a ring of high mountains, these plateaus provide excellent grazing grounds for elk, moose, deer, and bison; it would be infinitely regrettable for science if these noble animals were not protected against fur hunters in the very domains that nature seems to have prepared for them in order to save them from definitive extinction.

The fauna of the National Park was carefully studied by Mr. George Bird Grinnell, one of the scientists accompanying Captain Ludlow's expedition, which was organized under the auspices of the Department of War. His report presents a table as comprehensive as possible of the mammals and birds characteristic of this region.[18]

CHAPTER XVIII

Sulphur Mountain

Along the Yellowstone. — The Giant's Caldron. — The Nez Perces.
— Icelandic landscape. — Sulphur Mountain. — Clarke's misadventure. — A dangerous climb. — Ruins of old craters.

Early in the morning we started out on the wagon trail that
leads from the lake to the falls of the Yellowstone, situated sixteen miles to the north. For this whole distance we followed
the west bank of the Yellowstone, which courses out of the lake
that bears its name. The noble river, dotted with islets, flows in
a picturesque valley surrounded by high, wooded mountains;
pelicans and wild ducks abound on its banks, and one can see
multitudes of trout sporting in its calm, clear waters.

One of the principal curiosities along the way is the mud volcano that the first explorers baptized with the name of the Giant's Caldron [now called Mud Volcano]. From a gaping hole that
opens on the side of a hill, enormous puffs of steam rise into
the atmosphere. Intermittently the volcano throws up masses
of mud that splatter its walls; in an instant the crater is filled
almost to the brim with a thick, slate-colored paste, but suddenly, in one draught, the monster sucks down everything it
has just disgorged, and the paste abruptly disappears. At the
end of several seconds it begins again: another disgorgement,
another sucking down. It is a ruminant consuming its life in
the eternal and laborious work of digesting and belching. Its
spasms emit frightening roars that are heard a kilometer away
and that shake the earth for a considerable area around.

Dr. Peale,[1] one of the first explorers to visit this curious place,
observed that the trees near the chasm were covered with a
layer of mud. At first he concluded that this geyser sometimes

projected its contents high enough to reach the branches of the neighboring trees, but his later investigations proved that the mud spring never erupted. The mud covering the trees is carried along by the force of the steam that is constantly escaping from the caldron. To verify this fact, it suffices to place several dead branches in direct contact with the steam vapor: in several hours they become coated with mud.

If this mud volcano was ever an active geyser, it must have been in a far-distant era: trees ten meters tall that are rooted in the deposits adequately prove that its current state dates from long ago.

Several paces away from the caldron is a wonderful boiling hot spring emitting sulphurous vapors [now called Dragon's Mouth Spring]. Its basin, from which emerge hoarse, cavernous sounds, fills and empties by turns with pulsations that shake the earth. While all the neighboring springs contain a horrible black paste, this one holds turquoise-blue waters.[2] An inexpressible and inexplicable contrast!

At this place there is a ford across the Yellowstone where the Nez Perces crossed when they were being pursued by General Howard[3] in 1877. Still visible are the ruins of the parapet behind which the Indian Chief Joseph was entrenched.[4]

We then reached a high plateau from where the view embraces a veritable Icelandic landscape; the sky, at this moment dark and austere, enhanced the illusion. The Yellowstone, flowing at our feet, recalled the rivers Clarke and I so often crossed on the backs of ponies in the wilderness of the Land of Ice. The high, white, snow-capped summits rising on the horizon could easily be mistaken for the polar *yokulls*.[5] The expanse of Yellowstone Lake, shimmering in the distance to the south, took us back to the shores of Lakes Thingvalla and Myvatn.[6] Only the verdant hillsides covered with forests reminded us that we were no longer in that Icelandic country, completely devoid of trees.

We soon arrived at the foot of Sulphur Mountain, which to all appearances overlies a region of past geyser activity. Imagine a group of hills forty to fifty meters high made up of a cal-

38. Sulphur Mountain [also called Crater Hills].

careous material so impregnated with sulphurous deposits that
the overall color of these formations is a rather pronounced
yellow. The deposits are very pure; in places they have accumulated to form brilliant crystals. It is a sulphur mine of ines-
timable value, from which several wagonloads of the mineral
could be extracted. The deposits constantly renew themselves;
a large number of small solfataras are in constant action, and
the vapor they emit affects the respiratory passages disagree-
ably. To venture among them is not without danger; Clarke
was almost burned alive for having approached too closely. In
breaking through the surface crust, his horse caused a jet of
sulphurous steam to issue from the ground, and the poor beast
would have been grievously scalded if, wild with terror, it had
not suddenly shied, nearly unseating its rider.

We prudently dismounted in order to climb one of the hills.
The terrain on which we were walking is treacherous: it is a
burning, flaky, calcareous crust that sounded hollow under our
feet and is riddled with an infinity of little vents from which
escape sulphurous gases that sublime to form very beautiful
crystals. In many places the heat is so intense that the rock

bulges, and it needs only the slightest pressure of the foot to cause a considerable amount of vapor to gush forth.

At the summit we found ruins of old craters that today are filled with debris. There must formerly have been hot springs here, maybe powerful geysers; today all the springs have retreated to the base of the slopes. They are sulphurous to the highest degree: their edges are covered with magnificent deposits of crystallized sulphur; their waters are whitish and boil with extreme violence: they emit enormous quantities of vapor and have a temperature higher than the boiling point. At this altitude (2,325 meters) water boils at 92.3°C [198°F].

CHAPTER XIX

The Falls of the Yellowstone

The encampment. — The painter Brown. — Geological aspect of the region. — The Upper Falls. — The Lower Falls. — Wondrous beauty of the cataract. — The Grand Cañon. — Sublime scenery. — Lookout Point. — Eagle's nest. — Origin of the falls. — Hayden's theory. — In the tent.

We arrived about one o'clock at a comfortable camping site in a grassy crater circumscribed by wooded slopes, from the top of which opens out the Grand Cañon of the Yellowstone.

From time to time a faint and indistinct rumble reached us from the depths of the pine forest. Failing that distant murmur, nothing would have led us to suppose that we were in the neighborhood of one of the most beautiful scenes of nature, the Grand Cañon and the falls of the Yellowstone.

I personally feared that this new marvel might prove to be a disappointment for travelers who, after several days, were sated with marvels from morning till night. At Mammoth Springs I had encountered the English painter Brown[1] from Newcastle, who had just spent several days at the Grand Cañon. He had shown me his canvases, where I had noticed a riot of violent colors that had seemed to me as improbable as they were inharmonious. It was thus with a certain mistrust that I set out with my companions on the rough path that climbs through the forest toward the falls.

The geological aspect of this region is rather complicated, and one must be aware of it in order to understand the scene.

The Yellowstone's cataracts form two different waterfalls a mile apart. From the place where it leaves Yellowstone Lake to the Upper Falls, the river cascades rapidly and impetuously

39. Upper Falls of the Yellowstone. [The engraver of this Jackson
photograph mistakenly took the large bare area in the foreground
(probably denuded of trees by a landslide) for the waterfall. Upper Falls
is the small white area between wooded hills in the left background.]

through a wide, grassy valley between low hills. Its dull, blue-green waters neither encounter any obstacle nor form any rapids.[2] But then a mountain barrier rises up before it as if to prevent it from pursuing its quiet course northward. The valley suddenly narrows, the river contracts and, with untamable energy, triumphantly overcomes all obstacles that oppose its flow. It then foams amid rocky places, forms a series of eddies and rapids, and finally hurls itself in two successive leaps, one of forty meters, the other of one hundred meters, into the immense crevice nearly ten leagues long that it has dug across a mighty ramification of the Rocky Mountains.

At the point where the river makes its first leap it is squeezed between basalt walls, and its waters, gathered into a compact mass, hurl themselves into space with all the speed acquired in the rapids preceding the falls. Instead of pouring as a sheet of water over the rocky crest that dominates the abyss, they leap far out and execute a dizzying trajectory into the void. Falling with all their weight into the basin below, they provoke an enormous and furious surge, a struggle between monstrous waves, white foam, and spray. The vaporized waters seem to want to return from the bottom of the abyss toward their source at the top of the cataract, and as they disperse, the magical colors of the prism transform their watery dust into a sparkling rain of precious stones.

One can hardly find a waterfall in our Alps comparable to the Upper Falls of the Yellowstone, and yet how inferior they are to their rival, the Lower Falls! Having passed my companions, I was the first to arrive at the rocky promontory that overlooks them. From my first glance I was enthralled by the wondrous beauty of the scene. My companions soon joined me; the same emotion overcame them, and they lacked words to express their feelings. We all stood silent before that divine tableau.

The Lower Falls of the Yellowstone is the jewel of America. Anyone who has contemplated it will forever be able to evoke that splendid image. It is not the largest in the world, but no other unites so many elements of beauty. I might long have forgotten Niagara Falls while I would still remember Yellowstone Falls.

The magnificence of a cataract does not depend only upon the dimensions of the sheet of water and the impetuosity of the leap but also upon its harmony with the setting. Here the grandeur is above all in the setting, in the phenomenally high walls that loom above the falls, flanked by towers, pinnacles, and buttresses. The river, strangled between those huge masses, is no more than 40 meters wide at the moment it falls in one uninterrupted leap into an abyss 120 meters deep.[3] This abyss is the Grand Cañon.

I have always thought the most beautiful places in the world were the famous Cirque of Gavarnie in the Pyrenees and the Grand Cañon of the Arkansas River in Colorado's Rocky Mountains,[4] and I did not imagine that the sublimity of these scenes could be surpassed. But now that I have seen the Grand Cañon of the Yellowstone, I do not hesitate to say that it is there that the boldness of the creative hand has wrought the greatest works. All the forces of nature have been brought into play: hot springs, snows, avalanches, torrents, rains, winds, and storms — and from all these combined efforts has resulted the most marvelous construction ever contemplated by the human eye.

Here are outlines of Gothic cathedrals with spires and little steeples, fortified castles with pierced walls and impregnable turrets, half-ruined towers, and light, airy pinnacles supporting eagles' nests.[5] How unexpected are these fantastic apparitions from the Middle Ages in the heart of the New World! It seems as if the castle builders from the banks of the Rhine had come here in search of inspiration.

Springs of boiling water add something unexpected to the setting; one of them sends up its steam through a hole at the top of a pinnacle. In bathing the walls of the gorge century after century, these thermal waters have covered them in the most vivid colors. Streaks of the purest white or borders of the most delicate pink stand out from a brilliant yellow background, scarlet needles rise up alongside orange or violet spikes, white

40. Lower Falls of the Yellowstone.

41. The Grand Cañon.

ghosts appear abruptly upon brown walls. It is a fairyland of colors impossible to describe, and it had appeared implausible to me on the canvases of the English painter I had encountered on my way here. These shades of color, which become violent and discordant under the paintbrush, harmonize admirably in nature. The very high basaltic walls display so clearly the lines of demarcation separating their successive strata that one would believe them built by a race of giants.

To obtain an overall view of this great work of centuries, one must leave the point of rock that overlooks the waterfall and make one's way along a ledge overhanging the gaping crevice where the Yellowstone has cut its course. One passes through a forest of ancient pines, where the strong voice of the cataract is lost, and after an hour's walk one reaches the summit of Look Out Point [now Lookout Point], a sort of watchtower that juts out over the precipice.

We arrived at the top of this rocky point at sunset. Practically suspended in space, the spectator lets his gaze wander to the cataract, whose sound barely reaches his ears from the opposite extremity of the gorge, over a panorama extending for three leagues. The Yellowstone roars a thousand feet below; this river, having just made such an imposing fall, is now only an emerald ribbon twisting within the embrace of giant rocks. The rocks are vertical, and their walls, eaten away by the seething waters, support aerial ledges that overhang the chasm. Stones hurled down from the height of these ledges travel through space a long time before shattering on the ground.

Immediately below Lookout Point's pinnacle an inaccessible peak looms up, where two eagles, at this moment majestically tracing orbs above the falls, had built their aerie. Their piercing call responded to the plaintive cries of the young eaglets who called to them from their airy dwelling place. This nest, already mentioned by Langford,[6] may have been there for centuries, and the pair that inhabited it were undoubtedly the same as seen by the first explorers, since the longevity of eagles is well known.

The eye is fascinated by the imposing cataract: it follows the

42. Eagle's nest in the Grand Cañon.

water's trajectory and watches it plunge into the depths, half veiled by the spindrift that rises up along the rocks. The sheet of water stands out white as snow against the deep green of the conifer forests that spread across the background mountains.

I saw this tableau illuminated with the ideal hues of a sunset and fixed it in an indelible image in my memory before it was obscured by nightfall.

Hayden declares that if the falls of the Yellowstone prevail in beauty over those of Niagara, the Grand Cañon is without parallel and no words can express its astonishing majesty.[7] With the exceptional eye of a geologist, he has tried to explain the origin of this marvelous landscape. He believes that the entire basin of the upper Yellowstone was formerly an immense lake whose shores were formed by the surrounding mountains, of which today's lake is merely a vestige. This lake existed in the epoch when this region was the scene of prodigious eruptive activity.

The underlying rock is a dense and very hard basalt that the elements do not easily wear down. The volcanic products and the deposits of hot springs have leveled out the extremely irregular surface of the original ground. Above the Upper Falls, across a course of sixteen miles from the point where it leaves the lake, the Yellowstone flows over a basaltic bed. Then an abrupt transition occurs between the hard basalt and the softer bed of volcanic products, in such a way that the river was easily able to hollow out a channel. This is shown by examination of the vertical walls seen below the first falls.

The second waterfall was formed in the same way; the entire mass of water plunges into a circular basin cut into the hard rock, in such a way that the rebound of the waters is not the least element of beauty in the scene. Below the second falls, the gorge's walls allow one to see the materials of which they are composed. There, where the river has cut a channel through the hard basalt, one distinctly sees the irregular fissures that no doubt continue on toward the fiery underground regions.

From the two sides of the Yellowstone one sees local deposits of silica coming from former hot springs, sometimes reaching a thickness of four to five hundred feet. They form the material of the aerial pinnacles with which the almost vertical walls bristle and which present such numerous and picturesque forms. The silica was originally as white as snow, but in many places over time it has taken on the richest and most varied shades. The walls are furrowed with irregular fissures crisscrossing the basalt and communicating with the deposits from former springs. From one end of the cañon to the other, from the falls to Tower Creek, the walls present the same appearance: first, irregular basaltic masses, then volcanic debris or multicolored formations from hot springs, then more recent, horizontally stratified deposits, coming from the former lake. Hayden concludes that, even if the Grand Cañon has the appearance of an enormous crevice, it is in reality only a channel cut by the river after the former lake bed dried out.[8]

We returned to the encampment as night fell; it was just in time, because at that very moment lightning struck a stone's throw from us with a boom that froze us with terror. While blinding flashes of lightning cleaved the sky and a torrential rain inundated the valley, we were comfortably sheltered under the big tent that served as dining room and kitchen and was perfumed by the resinous fragrance of the young pines that decorated it. Since it was cold, a big stove hummed in the middle of the lodge.

We supped on the classic leg of elk, in the company of two American tourists who were traveling like Far Western trappers, dressed in Indian costume of deerskin, wearing immense felt hats, shod in enormous muddy boots, and armed with an arsenal of guns and pistols. Under their bandit outfits, we discovered gentlemen of the "high life." In vain did we offer them the traditional "cock-tail," as they were confirmed nephalists,[9] who drank no sparkling drink other than "soda-water" and "ginger-beer."

CHAPTER XX

Mount Washburn

Along the Grand Cañon. — A broken saddle girth. — The virgin forest. — Mount Washburn. — Origin of the Yellowstone basin. — Sublime panorama. — Precious stones. — Fossil forests. — The effects of sunstroke. — Tower Fall. — Souvenir of the Nez Perces. — A log house. — A night on a bison pelt. — Return to Mammoth Springs.

The next day we set out at an early hour, wanting to climb Mount Washburn that day and to sleep that evening in a log house near Tower Fall.

After greeting the falls one last time, we passed Lookout Point, and we rode along the edge of the Grand Cañon. This huge gorge, at the bottom of which roars the Yellowstone, begins at the falls and ends twenty-four miles to the north, at the confluence with the East Fork [Lamar River], the eastern arm of the river. At the falls the elevation of the plateau is 2,377 meters. At the top of the Upper Falls the level of the river is only a few meters below the plateau. The two falls deepen the chasm successively. From the foot of the Lower Falls to the confluence with the East Fork, the river drops four hundred meters. Over the course of twelve miles, the river continues to descend, while the plateau rises and the cañon digs farther down: it attains its greatest depth at the foot of Mount Washburn. Farther on, this depth decreases rapidly. At the top of its high walls, the width of the cañon varies from four hundred to sixteen hundred meters.[1]

For an hour we rode along the western cliff. The path is suspended three hundred meters above the Yellowstone, which winds through the basalts, making the immense gorge ring with its raucous and cavernous voice.

Faced with this dizzying abyss, our horses were wonderful. Suddenly my saddle girth broke, my saddle turned. I escaped a terrible tumble only by throwing myself expeditiously between my horse and the rock face. I never saw death loom so near. But over there in the Rocky Mountains one becomes so accustomed to hair-raising horseback trips that after a few days one is indifferent to the danger. Besides, it is certain that nothing renders one fearless like the pure atmosphere of the mountains.

It is as impossible to ride along the rim of the Grand Cañon as it is to go along its bottom, due to the innumerable indentations that cut back the cliffs, the spurs that jut out like theater scenery, and the ravines scoured out by tributaries of the Yellowstone.

We had no choice but to turn left and enter the woods in whose depths the powerful roarings of the Yellowstone were lost. We saturated our lungs with the strong scents of the virgin forest. The grayish trunks of the pines, forty to fifty meters high and as thick as cathedral pillars, are carpeted with lichens of a great variety of colors, and from the high branches hang moss beards that proclaim the age of these veterans of the plant world. All this grandeur inspires grave and religious thoughts.

From the far end of a clearing, we caught sight of the powerful mass of Mount Washburn for the first time: seen from there, it had the aspect of a grayish pyramid with a bald façade.

Toward noon we reached the foot of the mountain, which we climbed under a white-hot sun. Eagles whistled above our heads, describing majestic orbs in the air. The slopes are so gentle that the ascension was entirely feasible on horseback: a mountain climber would not dare pride himself on such an easy expedition.

Mount Washburn, which owes its name to the head of the 1870 expedition, is obviously a former volcano. The mountain is composed entirely of igneous rocks. The summit, of a grayish trachytic rock, is covered with blocks of basalt; the slopes are strewn with volcanic debris. Chalcedonies and agates are to be found there.

At the end of an hour and a half of continuous climbing we reached the top, at an elevation of 3,151 meters above sea level. Although it is below the perpetual snow line, it is above the tree line, and nothing obstructs the view.

The panorama is overwhelmingly magnificent. The imagination, as also the eye, loses itself in such a chaos.[2] One takes in the entire extent of the National Park. One soars over a mountainous relief spreading out more than forty leagues around. The most distant summits are outlined with an unbelievable clarity in the pure atmosphere. We were almost at the summit of a continent, and at our feet were the sources of the largest rivers of America. I would not dare claim that there exists anywhere else a view so incredibly vast. The circular canvas of the horizon is circumscribed everywhere by enormous swells of peaks, the greater portion of which have as yet no names. These peaks, today sparkling with ice and snow, were in a recent geological epoch so many formidable volcanoes, throwing out flames, ashes, and smoke. Their burning lavas were extinguished, hissing in the waters of the immense lake that then covered the whole basin of the upper Yellowstone.

According to Hayden,[3] this intense volcanic action, of which we see everywhere such unmistakable indications, occurred at a very modern geologic period, not further back than the Pliocene period and perhaps even not older than Quaternary times. In that period waters surrounded and perhaps covered even the highest mountain peaks,[4] as is shown by the rounded rocks found on even the highest summits and also by the conglomerates and volcanic tuffs arranged for the most part in horizontal stratifications. Several of the highest peaks on the west [sic] side[5] of the lake are seemingly huge volcanic cones composed of compact trachyte but surrounded by stratified conglomerates jutting up against the sides and sometimes reaching the summits. Some of the highest peaks are apparently made up of conglomerates. We may conclude not only that the carving out of the channel of the Grand Cañon was a very modern event but that the deposition of the entire material that forms it is, in a geological sense, quite a modern occurrence.

The drainage of the country commenced long before the excavation of the present watercourses. How was this great drainage brought about? Hayden explains it by a general elevation of the entire country that would gradually have expelled this immense body of water. Thus it is not entirely to the phenomenon of erosion that the origin of the wonderful Yellowstone basin must be attributed, but in part to the phenomenon of uplift. This phenomenon would have prevailed all over the northwest of America, perhaps all over the Rocky Mountain region, the waters flowing westward into the Pacific and eastward into the Atlantic.

As the waters slowly subsided, they were separated into different lakes of greater or lesser size. Then came the excavation of the Grand Cañon, which slowly drained the great lake basin situated above the falls, of which Yellowstone Lake is but a small vestige. Scattered about in the vicinity are other small fragments, which now form reservoirs for the local drainage. The same series of remarkable physical events would have occurred in Oregon, California, and the Idaho and Washington Territories, and perhaps in Mexico. The hot springs, which today are slowly dying out, are the last phenomena of this series of events. The evidence seems clear that all over the American West during this great period of volcanic activity the hot springs and even geysers were very numerous. We find vestiges of them everywhere in all the states and territories west of the Mississippi.[6]

To describe conscientiously the panorama from Mount Washburn, one would have to name one by one the principal peaks that loom up across the expanse of the National Park, in which this magnificent belvedere occupies the center. On this relief map spread out at our feet as big as nature, we recognize the entire region we have passed through. In the northwest we make out Terrace Mountain, Sepulchre Mountain, Electric Peak, and Bunsen Peak, which dominate Mammoth Springs, the departure point for our horseback trip. Over there in the southwest, at an enormous distance, white columns of steam rise toward the sky. That is the geyser region, and maybe at this very moment Old Faithful is erupting. In the south beyond Sulphur Mountain the blue surface of Yellowstone Lake sparkles in the sun, like a mirror set in a dark border of mountains. Behind the lake looms the mother chain of the Rocky Mountains, and even farther away is the massif of the Red Mountains, dominated by the superb peak of Mount Sheridan. That wide silver ribbon that has its source at the northern extremity of the lake and snakes through the midst of prairies and forests is the Yellowstone, the marvelous river that begins its epic journey across the most disordered landscape in the New World. In following it from its source, we see it suddenly swallowed up by an enormous crevice, where it disappears from sight; that crevice, gaping open almost under our feet, is the Grand Cañon.

We had to tear ourselves away from these splendors. The descent of the mountain would have been an agreeable ride if it had not been for the fearsome sun that beat down on our heads. Beyond Mount Washburn we entered a country of prairies that we galloped through on our horses.

In this region abound different varieties of precious stones, agates, sardonyxes, malachites, chalcedonies, and amethysts. Had our time not been limited, we would have gone on for several miles on the other side of the Yellowstone to explore the famous fossil forests of Specimen Ridge. Trees that are silicified, opalized, turned into agate are found there in great number and in an admirable state of conservation. The ground is littered with trunks and branches of trees changed into hard white agate; in a great many places the trunks are still standing, like the columns of a ruined temple. At Mammoth Springs people sold us curious specimens of these petrifactions.

Around four o'clock we took a break in a romantic valley at the edge of a clear stream flowing between the trees and rocks. While the horses grazed, we sat on the grass eating the provisions we had brought. Mixed with whiskey, the water of the torrent was exquisite.

Alexander hardly shared our satisfaction at all: the ascension of Mount Washburn had afflicted him with sunstroke.

He had no appetite, and it was pitiful to see him lying on the grass, racked with fever.

Just a few paces on, the torrent that waters the valley forms Tower Fall, one of the most curious waterfalls in the world. The igneous rocks, from the top of which rushes the mass of water, are extremely hard, and the combat between the rock and the liquid element has resulted in the formation of a group of towers and turrets of an extraordinarily imposing aspect. The chute is dominated by two enormous basalt columns, svelte and slender, that rise from the bottom of the chasm, and between them hurtles the cataract, like the gigantic portal of a Gothic cathedral. The forest of pinnacles that rises behind the twin towers completes the illusion. In an uninterrupted leap of fifty meters, the cataract plunges into a circular chasm. It is a gripping spectacle. I remember that we saw the falls from the height of a rocky outcrop so narrow that there was only room for a single spectator, and then he had to cling to a tree suspended over the abyss. One can recommend this place to those who want to take lessons in vertigo. But the view is worth braving the danger, for it embraces the cascade and all the surrounding country at the same time. Three hundred meters away the Yellowstone flows at the bottom of its cañon, whose yellowish walls at this point form natural palisades laid out with such art and symmetry that one would take them for military constructions. In the distance one makes out the hazy, velvety blue summits of the cordillera [Beartooth and Absaroka Mountains].

Leaving Tower Fall, we passed through a desolate region. At the side of the road we noticed the bleached skull of a horse: we were in the very place where Weikert and McCartney were attacked by the Nez Perces in 1877. I remembered that one of them had his horse shot out from under him. The gloomy aspect of the country fits this lugubrious memory well.[7]

At seven in the evening we finally greeted the log house where we had resolved to spend the night that would conclude our wanderings. After the several nights we had just passed in a cold tent, we were delighted to be sleeping this time in an enclosed and well-heated dwelling.

43. Tower Fall.

44. Basalt walls of the Grand Cañon.

Think of a crude construction made of rough-hewn tree trunks and not draft proofed, admitting the wind through its chinks. It reminded me of the *saeters*, or shepherds' huts, in the Norwegian mountains. As in Iceland, the interior comprises a single room serving all at one time as kitchen, dining room, and bedroom. Also as in Iceland, the animals sleep with the people. Upon entering, we were greeted by large black dogs more inclined to jump at our throats than to welcome us.

The old recluse who lives in this cabin survives on charges collected from the travelers and miners who use "Jack's bridge," thrown across the Yellowstone for the exploitation of the gold and silver mines situated a dozen leagues to the east. He was formerly a miner himself; but one day, following a powder explosion, fragments of rock and a piece of his felt hat penetrated his brain; he endured a long illness, during which he lost a portion of his cranium. Finally he healed, and today he is perfectly healthy in body and mind.[8] He served us trout on a filthy hammered-iron plate and a cup of coffee. We supped seated on barrels by the light of a candle.

Foul bison skins spread on a floor that has never seen water served us as beds for the night. Not counting the two dogs, we were at least a dozen sleepers in this narrow room, since some miners had also come seeking hospitality. This whole crowd slept scattered about in all the corners. The temperature was suffocating. The candle was blown out at nine o'clock, and the room was lit only by the dying embers of the logs. Before closing their eyes, these "rough people" told a thousand episodes from their adventurous lives in the nasal accent so characteristic of the Yankee. Then profound silence, soon followed by a phenomenal concert of snores.

The darkness was complete. I too would very much like to have snored, but in the mystery of the darkness strange things were happening to keep me awake. What then was the warm contact tickling my feet? Was it the feet of a neighbor? No, it was one of the two hounds trying to devise a means to reach his master, sleeping behind my head; the animal hesitated a long time to step over the compact row of sleepers; he finally jumped on my body, then on my face, lay down close to me, and all night long I was obliged to listen to his breathing. My knapsack, serving as a pillow, soon began to stir under my cheek; since I had put my billfold in it, my first movement was to search for a criminal hand in the gloom, but I only encountered emptiness; upon opening the sack, I observed the escape of some sort of beast. Was it a rat? Was it a snake? What did I know? I am not even mentioning the spiders and other horrible insects that were running over my body. The door closed poorly and, since the air was cold outside and hot inside, I found myself in the path of an air current that afflicted me with a cold. Good God! What a night! How good it would have been to be in the tent! And with what relief I saw the day dawn at five in the morning! My companions confessed to me that they had never spent such a long, sleepless night in such a black hole.

After a new edition of trout and coffee, we left at seven-thirty in the morning to complete the last stage of our journey. We climbed up the mountain in an already burning heat. In these valleys of the northwest the days are as scorching as the nights are freezing. What splendid nature! What luxuriant vegetation! The dark green of the pines contrasts with the pale green of the willows, which imitate so well the birch with their silver trunks and their ethereal foliage.[9] The profound silence of these majestic solitudes is disturbed only by the strident call of the eagle. As we climbed, the horizon broadened; a sea of hazy peaks receded behind us in the morning mist. At the top of the slope we encountered a caravan of hunters. They were leading a great many packhorses that carried chests arranged in the Icelandic manner.

Arriving on the high plateau we let ourselves be carried for three hours by the infernal galloping of our cayuses, who already seemed to sense the pastures of Mammoth Springs. At eleven o'clock we began to make out, at the end of the valley, the calcareous terraces that from afar resemble an enormous glacier. Although they seemed to be only a gunshot away, it took us another hour of galloping to reach them. We arrived at the National Hotel at noon, in a fearsome storm.

CONCLUSION

The next day we had to say goodbye to the Land of Wonders. I surprised myself when departing by sighing the *never* of the poet.[1] *Never oh! Never more!* — Will we not see it again, "nevermore"?

How many times since have my recollections evoked splendid images of the Land of Wonders! How many times have my thoughts flown to the shores of Yellowstone Lake, to the edges of the Firehole's basins of boiling water, or to the peaks that overlook the cataracts of the Grand Cañon!

Like Iceland, with which it has so many features in common, this region attracts the imagination in a powerful way, and the traveler takes away a momentous impression that he will never forget.

One returns from there better, humbler, and profoundly touched by that reverence through which the mysteries of nature and the grandeur of creation inspire our feeble understanding.

With regret I parted from my amiable companions at Livingston. They were going to Mormon country. As for me, I took the road to faraway Mexico, whose frontier I reached eight days later, having covered a thousand leagues by Pullman car and traversed from north to south the immense territory of the United States.

WORKS TO CONSULT

Author's Note: This list was compiled almost entirely from the bibliographic appendix annexed to the report of Professor A. C. Peale in the Twelfth Report of the United States Geological and Geographical Survey of the Territories. Works published before 1870 that make only vague reference to the Yellowstone geysers have been omitted.

Translators' Note: For the convenience of the contemporary reader, the translators have modernized the format of Jules Leclercq's bibliography and corrected misspellings and incorrect references. The original version, "Ouvrages à Consulter," was arranged chronologically by the year in which the author visited the park rather than in alphabetical order.

Ackermann, Hermann W. "Yellowstone National Park." In *Sitzungsberichte* [Transactions], 49–64. Dresden: Naturwissenschaftliche Gesellschaft Isis [Scientific Society Isis], 1876.

Austen, Peter Townsend. "Note on the Siliceous Pebbles from the Geysers of Yellowstone Cañon." *American Chemist* 3 (February 1873): 288–90.

Barlow, John Whitney. Letter from the secretary of war accompanying an engineer report of a reconnaissance of the Yellowstone River in 1871, by Capt. Barlow and Capt. David Porter Heap, of Corps of Engineers. S. Exec. Doc. 66, 42nd Cong., 2nd sess., 1872, 1–43.

Bradley, Frank H. "Report of Frank H. Bradley, Geologist of the Snake River Division." In Hayden, *Sixth Annual Report*, 190–271. Eight illustrations, two maps. Chapter 3 contains descriptions of geysers and springs of the Firehole and Shoshone Lake basins.

Brockett, Linus Pierpont. "Yellowstone National Park." Chap. 22 in *Our Western Empire; or, The New West Beyond the Mississippi*, 1227–65. Philadelphia: Bradley, Garretson & Co., 1882.

Brown, Robert. "The Wonderland of America." In *The Countries of the World*, 2:91–99. London, Paris, and New York: Casell, Petter, Galpin & Co., [1876?].

Bunce, Oliver Bell. "Our Great National Park." In *Picturesque America; or, The Land We Live In. . .* , edited by William Cullen Bryant, 1:292–316. New York: D. Appleton and Co., 1872. Eighteen illustrations.

Champlin, John D., Jr. "Geysers." In *Appleton's American Encyclopedia*, 7:783–89. New York, 1876. Contains a description of the Yellowstone geysers.

Comstock, Prof. Theodore B. "Geological Report." In *Report upon the Reconnaissance of Northwestern Wyoming, Including the Yellowstone National Park, Made in the Summer of 1873*, by William A. Jones, Captain of Engineers, U.S.A., 85–291. Washington DC: Government Printing Office, 1875. Chapters 9–13 describe the springs and geysers of Yellowstone National Park.

———. "On the Geology of Western Wyoming." *American Journal of Science and Arts*, 3rd ser., 6 (December 1873): 426–32.

———. "The Yellowstone National Park." *American Naturalist* 8 (February–March 1874): 65–79, 155–65.

Conger, Patrick H., superintendent. *Report of the Superintendent of the Yellowstone National Park to the Secretary of the Interior, for the Year 1882*. Washington DC: Government Printing Office, 1882.

Coulter, John Merle. "Report on Botany of Firehole Basin." In Hayden, *Sixth Annual Report*, 747–92.

Dana, Edward S. "Mineralogical Notes, no. 4. On the Association of Crystals of Quartz and Calcite in Parallel Position, as Observed on a Specimen from the Yellowstone Park." *American Journal of Science and Arts*, 3rd ser., 12 (1876): 448–51.

Dana, James Dwight. "Hot Springs and Geysers." In *Manual of Geology, Treating of the Principles of the Science with Special Reference to American Geological History*, 2nd ed., 719–22. New York: American Book Co., 1875.

de Lapparent, Albert August. *Traité de géologie* [Treatise on geology]. Paris: F. Savy, 1883. The Yellowstone geysers are described according to Hayden's reports.

de la Vallée-Poussin, Charles, professor at the School of Sciences of the University of Louvain. "Les explorations géologiques à l'ouest des États-Unis" [Geological explorations in the western United States]. Extract from *La Revue Catholique* [The Catholic Journal]. Louvain, Belgium: Ch. Peeters, 1873. Paragraphs 4 and 5, pages 24–42, contain a description of the Yellowstone National Park taken from American publications.

Doane, Lieut. Gustavus Cheney. Letter from the secretary of war communicating the *Report of Lieutenant Gustavus C. Doane upon the So-Called Yellowstone Expedition of 1870*. S. Exec. Doc. 51, 41st Cong., 3rd sess., 1871, 1–40.

Eccles, James. "On the Mode of Occurrence of Some of the Volcanic Rocks of Montana, U.S.A." *Quarterly Journal of the Geological Society of London* 37 (August 1881): 399–401.

———. "The Rocky Mountain Region of Wyoming and Idaho." Read before the Alpine Club, June 3, 1879. *Alpine Journal* (London) 9 (August 1879): 241–53.

Ellsworth, Spencer. *A Pilgrimage to Geyserland; or, Montana on Muleback*. Lacon IL, 1883.

Everts, Truman C. "Thirty-Seven Days of Peril." *Scribner's Monthly* 3, no. 1 (November 1871): 1–17.

Folsom, David E. "The Valley of the Upper Yellowstone," by Charles W. Cook. *Western Monthly* 4 (July 1870): 60–67. This article, whose author is Mr. David E. Folsom, appeared erroneously under the name of Mr. [Charles W.] Cook. It is probably the first detailed description of the Yellowstone geysers. [Park historian Aubrey L. Haines clarified the confusion about who authored the original Cook-Folsom article by quoting Cook's 1922 statement that "we had prepared an amplified diary by working over both the diaries made on the trip, and combining them into one." Furthermore, Cook wrote in the *Western Monthly*, "the editor cut out portions of the diary which destroyed its continuity, so far as giving a reliable description of our trip and the regions explored." Haines, *Valley of Upper Yellowstone*, 45, 46.]

Gannett, Henry, M.E. "Geographical Fieldwork of the Yellowstone Park Division." In Hayden, *Twelfth Annual Report*, 455–90.

———. "Report on Astronomy and Hypsometry." In Hayden, *Sixth Annual Report*, 795–807. Includes elevations of peaks, topographical information, and meteorological observations.

Gauilleur, Henry. "Souvenirs d'un voyage à cheval dans le désert américain" [Recollections of a horseback trip across the American wilderness]. *L'exploration, revue des conquêtes de la civilisation, recueil géographique hebdomadaire* [Exploration, journal of the conquests of civilization, a weekly geographic collection] (Paris) 14 (1882, 2nd half of year). The Yellowstone National Park is described in nos. 294 and 295.

Geikie, Prof. Archibald, L.L.D., F.R.S. "Geysers." In *Text Book of Geology*, 236–39. London: MacMillan and Co., 1882.

———. "The Geysers of the Yellowstone." *MacMillan's Magazine* (October 1881); the same in *Appleton's Journal* 11 (December 1881): 538–47; also the same in *Geological Sketches at Home and Abroad*, 206–38. New York: MacMillan and Co., 1882.

"Die Geyserregion am Oberen Yellowstone" [The geyser region of the Upper Yellowstone]. *Globus* 27 (1876): 289–94, 305–9, 321–25, 337–41.

"A Gigantic Pleasuring Ground. The Yellowstone National Park of the United States." *Nature* 6 (September 12, 1872): 397–401; (September 26, 1872): 437–39. This description of the park was apparently taken from Hayden, *Preliminary Report*; it is illustrated with eight figures from that report.

Gregory, Col. James F. "Report of Col. James F. Gregory." In *Report of Lieut. Gen. Philip Henry Sheridan, dated September 20, 1881, of His Expedition through the Big Horn Mountains, National Park, etc., Together with Reports of Lieut. Col. James. F. Gregory, A.D.C., Surgeon William Henry Forwood, and Capt. Sanford Cobb Kellogg, Fifth Cavalry*, 10–23. Washington DC: Government Printing Office, 1882.

Grinnell, George Bird, and Edward S. Dana. "Geological Report." In *Report of a Reconnaissance from Carroll, Montana Territory, on the Upper Missouri, to the Yellowstone National Park, and Return, Made in the Summer of 1875*, by William Ludlow, 93–137. Washington DC: Government Printing Office, 1876.

Haupt, Herman, M.D., PhD. *The Yellowstone National Park. A Complete Guide to and Description of the Wondrous Yellowstone Region of Wyoming and Montana Territories of the United States of America.* New York and Philadelphia: J. M. Stoddart, 1883.

Hawes, J. W. "Wyoming." In *Appleton's American Encyclopedia*, 16:751. New York, 1876. Gives a description of the Yellowstone National Park.

Hayden, Dr. Ferdinand Vandiveer, United States geologist. "The Grotto Geyser of the Yellowstone National Park." Washington DC: Government Printing Office, 1876. Descriptive note, one illustration, one map.

———. "The Hot Springs and Geysers of the Yellowstone and Firehole Rivers." *American Journal of Science and Arts* ser. 3, 103, no. 14 (1872): 105–15; 103, no. 15 (1872): 161–76. Maps. See also *Petermanns Mittheilungen* 18 (1872): 241–51, 321–26.

———. "The Hot Springs of Yellowstone National Park." In *The Great West: Its Attractions and Resources*, 32–38. Bloomington IL: Charles R. Brodix, 1880.

———. *Preliminary Report of the United States Geological Survey of Montana and Portions of Adjacent Territories. Being a Fifth Annual Report of Progress* [for 1871]. Conducted under authority of the Secretary of the Interior. Washington DC: Government Printing Office, 1872, 59–139. In chapters 4 to 7, inclusive, Dr. Hayden describes the Yellowstone National Park. His report is accompanied by fifty-four illustrations and five maps.

———. *Sixth Annual Report of the United States Geological Survey of the Territories, Embracing Portions of Montana, Idaho, Wyoming and Utah. Being a Report of Progress for the Year 1872.* Conducted under the authority of the Secretary of the Interior. Washington DC: Government Printing Office, 1873, i–ix, 1–844. Sixty-eight wood cuts, twelve plates, five maps, and three diagrams. Chapters 2 and 3, by Dr. Hayden, relate to the Yellowstone National Park.

———. *Twelfth Annual Report of the United States Geological and Geographical Survey of the Territories: A Report of Progress of the Exploration in Wyoming and Idaho for the Year 1878.* In two parts. Part 2. Washington DC: Government Printing Office, 1883.

———. "Wonders of the Rocky Mountains. The Yellowstone Park. How to Reach it." In *The Pacific Tourist: Williams' Illustrated Guide* to the Pacific Railroad, California, and Pleasure Resorts across the Continent. New York: Henry T. Williams, 1876.

———. "The Wonders of the West. More about the Yellowstone." Scribner's Monthly 3, no. 4 (February 1872): 388–96.

———. "Yellowstone National Park." In Johnson's New Universal Encyclopedia, 4:1526–30. New York: Alvin J. Johnson & Co.,1878.

———. The Yellowstone National Park and the Mountain Regions of Portions of Idaho, Nevada, Colorado, and Utah. Boston: Louis Prang and Co., 1876. Two maps, fifteen chromolithographs.

Hayden, Dr. Ferdinand Vandiveer, Lieut. Gustavus Cheney Doane, and Nathaniel Pitt Langford. "Le parc national des États-Unis" [The national park of the United States]. In Le Tour du monde [Round the world], extracted from American publications and translated by Emile Delerot, 289–352. Paris: Hachette and Co., 1874, 2nd half of year. Forty-nine engravings and a map.

Heap, Capt. David Porter. Letter from the secretary of war accompanying an engineer report of a reconnaissance of the Yellowstone River in 1871, by Capt. John Whitney Barlow and Capt. Heap, of Corps of Engineers. S. Exec. Doc. 66, 42nd Cong., 2nd sess., 1872, 42–43.

Heizmann, Dr. Charles Lawrence, assistant U S A surgeon. "Report on Mineral and Thermal Waters." In Report upon the Reconnaissance of Northwestern Wyoming, including the Yellowstone National Park, made in the summer of 1873, by William A. Jones, captain of engineers, U.S.A., 293–307. Washington D C: Government Printing Office, 1875. Appendix. [The U.S. assistant surgeon general's name is spelled "Heigmann" in the Philadelphia Medical Times article; however, many modern sources use the spelling "Heizmann."]

———. "The Therapeutical Value of the Springs in the National Park, Wyoming Territory." Philadelphia Medical Times 6, no. 222 (May 27, 1876): 409–14.

Holmes, William H. "Fossil Forests of the Volcanic Tertiary Formations of the Yellowstone National Park." Bulletin of the United States Geological and Geographical Survey of the Territories 5, no. 1 (February 28, 1879): 125–32. Washington D C: Government Printing Office. One illustration.

———. "Glacial Phenomena in the Yellowstone National Park." Amer-

ican Naturalist 15 (March 1881): 203–8. Illustrated with map and [geologic] section.

———. "Notes on an Extensive Deposit of Obsidian in the Yellowstone National Park." *American Naturalist* 13 (April 1879): 247–50.

———. "Report on the Geology of the Yellowstone National Park." In Hayden, *Twelfth Annual Report*, 1–57.

Joly, Charles. *Note sur le Parc National de Yellowstone aux États-Unis* [Note on the Yellowstone National Park of the United States]. Paris: Imprimerie G. Roughier et Cie., 1884. Brochure of fifteen pages, taken from American publications.

Jones, Capt. William A. *Report upon the Reconnaissance of Northwestern Wyoming, Including the Yellowstone National Park, Made in the Summer of 1873.* Washington DC: Government Printing Office, 1875, i–vi, 1–331. Appendix. Pages 1–81 are by Captain Jones, as well as pages 323–26 of the appendix.

Langford, Nathaniel Pitt. "The Ascent of Mount Hayden." *Scribner's Monthly* 4 (June 1873): 129–57.

———. Report of the superintendent of the Yellowstone National Park for the year 1872. S. Exec. Doc. 35, 42nd Cong., 3rd sess., 1873.

———. "The Wonders of the Yellowstone." *Scribner's Monthly* 1 (May 1871): 1–17; 2 (June 1871): 113–28. [Author not attributed.]

Le Conte, Prof. Joseph. "Geysers." In *Elements of Geology*, 94–104. New York: D. Appleton and Co., 1878. Contains a description of the Yellowstone geysers, with illustrations taken from Hayden's reports.

———. "Geysers, and How They Are Explained." *Popular Science Monthly* 12 (February 1878): 407–17. This article is taken from Joseph Le Conte's *Elements of Geology.* New York: D. Appleton and Co., 1878.

Leffmann, Dr. Henry. "Analyses of Some Geyser Deposits." *Chemical News* (London) 43 (March 18, 1881): 124. Contains the analysis of deposits from the Yellowstone National Park.

Leffmann, Dr. Henry, and William Beam. "Contributions to the Geological Chemistry of Yellowstone National Park." "I. Geyser Water and Deposits," by Henry Leffmann, "II. Rocks of the Park," by William Beam. *American Journal of Science*, 3rd ser., 25, no. 146 (February 1883): 104–6.

Le Hardy, Paul. "La Terre des Merveilles. Souvenirs d'une exploration au bassin de la Yellowstone" [Wonderland. Recollections of an exploratory trip in the Yellowstone Basin]. *La Revue de Belgique* [Belgian Journal], 1875. The author participated in the expedition of Captain Jones in 1873.

Leidy, Prof. Joseph. "Notice of Some Worms Collected during Professor Hayden's Expedition to the Yellowstone River in the Summer of 1871." In Hayden, *Preliminary Report*, 381–82. Describes the worms found in trout in Yellowstone Lake.

Ludlow, Capt. William. *Report of a Reconnaissance from Carroll, Montana Territory, on the Upper Missouri, to the Yellowstone National Park, and Return, Made in the Summer of 1875*. Washington DC: Government Printing Office, 1876.

Maguire, Henry N. Chap. 13 in *The People's Edition of the Black Hills and American Wonderland, from Personal Explorations*, 298–301. The Lakeside Library 4, no. 82. Chicago: Donnelley, Loyd & Co., 1877.

Merriam, Clinton Hart. "Report on the Mammals and Birds of the Expedition." In Hayden, *Sixth Annual Report*, 661–715. Gives a list of birds of the Firehole basin on page 712.

Mitchell, Dr. Silas Weir. "Through the Yellowstone Park to Fort Custer." *Lippincott's Magazine* 25, no. 150 (June 1880): 688–704; 26, no. 151 (July 1880): 21–41.

Nealley, Edward B. A. "Gold Hunt on the Yellowstone." *Lippincott's Magazine* 9 (February 1872): 204–12.

Norris, Philetus W., superintendent. *Annual Report of the Superintendent of the Yellowstone National Park to the Secretary of the Interior, for the Year 1880*. Washington DC: Government Printing Office, 1881, 1–64. Index, map, and five plates. [U.S. Serial Set 1960:573–631.]

———. *Fifth Annual Report of the Superintendent of the Yellowstone National Park*. Conducted under the authority of the Secretary of the Interior. Washington DC: Government Printing Office, 1881, 1–81. Map and thirty-four illustrations. [U.S. Serial Set 2018:749–819.]

———. *Report on the Yellowstone National Park to the Secretary of the Interior*. Washington DC: Government Printing Office, 1877, 1–15. Map. [U.S. Serial Set 1800:837–45.]

———. *Report upon the Yellowstone National Park to the Secretary of the Interior for the Year 1878*. Washington DC: Government Printing Office, 1879, 1–20. Map. [U.S. Serial Set 1850:979–96.]

————. *Report upon the Yellowstone National Park to the Secretary of the Interior for the Year 1879*. Washington DC: Government Printing Office, 1880, 1–31. One map and one plate. [CIS U.S. Executive Branch Documents, 1789–1909: microfiche no. I, 137-1.]

Norton, Harry J. *Wonder-Land Illustrated; or, Horseback Rides through the Yellowstone National Park*. Virginia City, Montana [Territory]: Harry J. Norton, 1873.

O'Neil, Howard. "The Falls of the Yellowstone." *Southern Magazine* 9 (August 1871): 219–23.

Parry, Dr. Charles Christopher. "Botanical Observations in Western Wyoming." *American Naturalist* 8 (January 1874): 9; (February 1874): 102; (March 1874): 175; (April 1874): 211.

————. "Botanical Report." Appendix. In *Report upon the Reconnaissance of Northwestern Wyoming, Including the Yellowstone National Park, Made in the Summer of 1873*, by William A. Jones, captain of engineers, U.S.A., 308–14. Washington DC: Government Printing Office, 1875. Contains a list of the plants from the Yellowstone National Park.

Peale, Dr. Albert C. "Account of the Grotto Geyser, with Analysis of its Deposits." In Hayden, "Grotto Geyser." Descriptive note, one illustration, one map.

————. "Report of A. C. Peale, M. D." In Hayden, *Sixth Annual Report*, 99–187. Twenty-one illustrations. Chapters 3 and 4, pages 125–50, as well as a part of chapter 5, describe the hot springs of the park. The report also contains a catalogue of thermal springs.

————. "Report of Dr. A. C. Peale on Minerals, Rocks, Thermal Springs, etc." In Hayden, *Preliminary Report*, 165–204.

————. "The Thermal Springs of the Yellowstone National Park." In Hayden, *Twelfth Annual Report*, 63–454.

Poe, Col. Orlando Metcalfe. "Report of Colonel Orlando Metcalfe Poe, United States Engineers, Aide-de-Camp to General William Tecumseh Sherman." In *Reports of Inspection Made in the Summer of 1877, by Generals Philip Henry Sheridan and William Tecumseh Sherman, of Country North of the Union Pacific Railroad*, 59–110. Washington DC: Government Printing Office, 1878. Four illustrations and five maps.

Porter, Robert P., special agent; Henry Gannett, geographer of the Tenth Census; and William P. Jones, corresponding member of the American Geographic Society. "The Yellowstone National Park." In *The West, from the Census of 1880: A History of the Industrial, Commercial, Social, and Political Development of the States and Territories of the West, from 1800 to 1880*, 425–29. Chicago: Rand, McNally and Co.; London: Trübner and Co., 1882. Map and diagrams.

Porter, Prof. Thomas C. "Catalogue of Plants." In Hayden, *Preliminary Report*, 477–98. Gives a list of the plants of the Yellowstone National Park.

Raymond, Rossiter W. "Wonders of the Yellowstone." In *Camp and Cabin: Sketches of Life and Travels in the West*, 153–207. New York: Fords, Howard and Hulburt, 1880.

Richardson, James, ed. *Wonders of the Yellowstone*. New York: Scribner, Armstrong and Co., 1872. Another edition appeared in 1873.

———. *Wonders of the Yellowstone Region in the Rocky Mountains, Being a Description of Its Geysers, Hot Springs, Grand Cañon, Waterfalls, Lake, and Surrounding Scenery, explored in 1870–1871*. London: Blackie & Son, 1874. Illustrated. An earlier edition appeared in London in 1872.

Rutley, Frank. "The Microscopical Characters of the Vitreous Rocks of Montana, U.S.A." *Quarterly Journal of the Geological Society of London* 37 (August 1881): 391–99. Contains a description of rocks from the Yellowstone National Park.

Seguin, Augustin. "Dix jours aux sources du Missouri" [Ten days on the headwaters of the Missouri]. *Le Bulletin de la Société de Géographie de Lyon* [Bulletin of the Lyon Geographical Society] 4 (1881): 59–84.

Sheridan, Gen. Philip Henry. "Expedition through the Big Horn Mountains, Yellowstone Park, etc." In *Report of Lieut. Gen. Philip Henry Sheridan, Dated September 20, 1881, of His Expedition through the Big Horn Mountains, National Park, etc., Together with Reports of Lieut. Col. James F. Gregory, A.D.C., Surgeon William Henry Forwood, and Capt. Sanford Cobb Kellogg, Fifth Cavalry*, 3–9. Washington DC: Government Printing Office, 1882. Map.

Sherman, Gen. William Tecumseh, and staff. "Tour of Inspection Across the Continent along the Line of the North Pacific Railroad." In *Reports of Inspection Made in the Summer of 1877, by Generals Philip Henry Sheridan and William Tecumseh Sherman, of Country North of the Union Pacific Railroad,* 27–58. Washington DC: Government Printing Office, 1878. Two illustrations. A series of letters from General Sherman was also published in the *New York Herald* in the summer of 1877.

Stanley, Edwin James. *Rambles in Wonderland; or, Up the Yellowstone and among the Geysers and Other Curiosities of the National Park.* New York: D. Appleton and Company, 1878.

Strahorn, Robert E. *The Enchanted Land; or, An October Ramble among the Geysers, Hot Springs, Lakes, Falls, and Cañons of the Yellowstone National Park.* Omaha: New West Publishing Co., 1881. Illustrated.

———. *The Resources of Montana Territory and attractions of Yellowstone National Park.* Helena [Montana Territory]: Montana Legislative Assembly, 1879.

Strong, General William Emerson. "A Trip to the Yellowstone National Park in July, August and September 1875." In *Journal of General W. E. Strong,* 1–143. Washington DC, 1876. Illustrated.

Trumbull, Walter. "The Washburn Yellowstone Expedition." *Overland Monthly* 6 (May–June 1871): 431–89.

United States Department of the Interior. "The Yellowstone National Park." H.R. Rep. 26, 42nd Cong., 2nd sess., 1872. Report to accompany bill H.R. 764. [The entire act establishing Yellowstone can be found in *United States Statutes at Large* 17, chap. 24:32–33.]

———. "Yellowstone National Park." Letter from the secretary of the interior transmitting a letter from Nathaniel Pitt Langford, recommending an appropriation for wagon roads and the opening of the Park, etc. H. Exec. Doc. 241, 42nd Cong., 3rd sess., 1872.

———. "Yellowstone Park." Letter from the secretary of the interior, transmitting a draught of a bill amendatory of and supplementary to the act entitled: "An Act to Set Apart a Certain Part of Land Lying near the Headwaters of the Yellowstone River as a Public Park." H. Exec. Doc. 147, 43rd Cong., 1st sess., 1874, 1–8.

Winser, Henry Jacob. *The Yellowstone National Park. A Manual for Tourists. Being a Description of the Mammoth Hot Springs, the Geyser Basins, the Cataracts, the Cañons and Other Features of the Land of Wonders.* New York: G. P. Putnam's Sons, 1883.

"Wonders of the Yellowstone Region." *Chambers' Journal of Popular Literature, Science, and Arts* (London) 51 (ca. 1883): 315.

Wyndham-Quin, Windham Thomas, Fourth Earl of Dunraven. *The Great Divide: Travels in the Upper Yellowstone in the Summer of 1874.* Illustrations by Valentine W. Bromley. London: Chatto and Windus, 1876, i–xvi, 1–377. Fifteen illustrations and two maps.

"The Yellowstone Park." *Nature* 5 (March 21, 1872): 403. This article is mainly a reprint of reports to Congress in relation to the creation of the National Park.

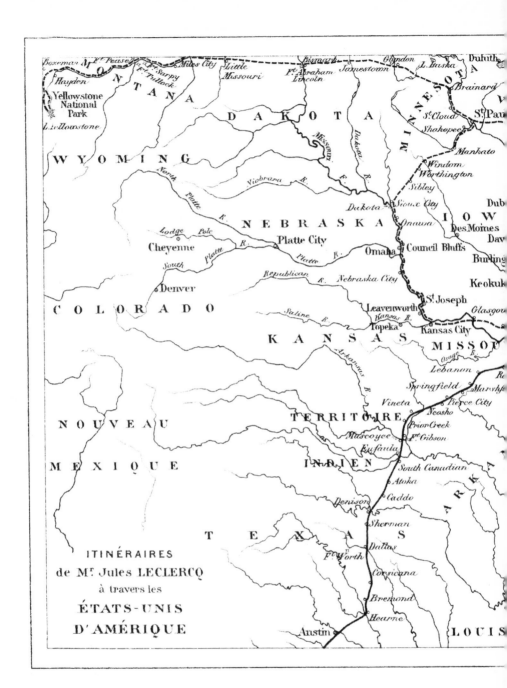

MAP 1. Itineraries of Jules Leclercq.

Lac Supérieur
CANADA
MICHIGAN
WISCONSIN
Lac Michigan
Lac Huron
Toronto
L. Ontario
Hamilton
Rochester
Chutes du Niagara
Buffalo
Saginaw
Détroit
Lac Érié
NEW-YORK
Walley
Baraboo
Madison
Milwankee
CHICAGO
Joliet
Toledo
Cleveland
PENSYLVANIE
NEW-YORK
Jersey-City
Brooklyn
Altoona
Allegheny
Harrisburg
Lancaster
Philadelphie
NEW-JERSEY
Steubenville
New-Philadelphia
Pittsburg
Bloomington
La Fayette
OHIO
INDIANA
ILLINOIS
Quincy
Springfield
Indianapolis
Columbus
Xenia
Vernon
Vincennes
Cincinnati
Baltimore
MARYLAND
WASHINGTON
Delaware B.
Chesapeake Bay
Flora
St. Louis
Evansville
Ohio R.
Louisville
Lexington
VIRGINIE
Richmond
Norfolk
KENTUCKY
Cairo
Nashville
CAROLINE DU NORD
TENNESSEE
Tennessee R.
Mississippi F.
Memphis
Wilmington
CAROLINE DU SUD
MISSISSIPPI
Atlanta
Augusta
Charleston
ALABAMA
Savannah
Alabama R.
Montgomery
GÉORGIE
Wicksburg
Mobile
OCÉAN ATLANTIQUE

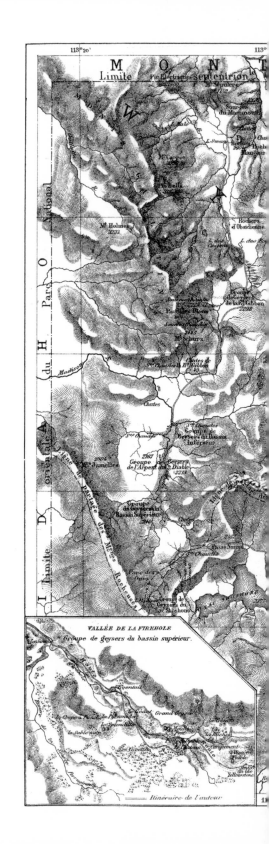

MAP 2. Map of the Yellowstone National Park.

This map was essentially copied and translated into French for Leclercq's book from the map that appeared in Herman Haupt's 1883 guidebook *The Yellowstone National Park*.

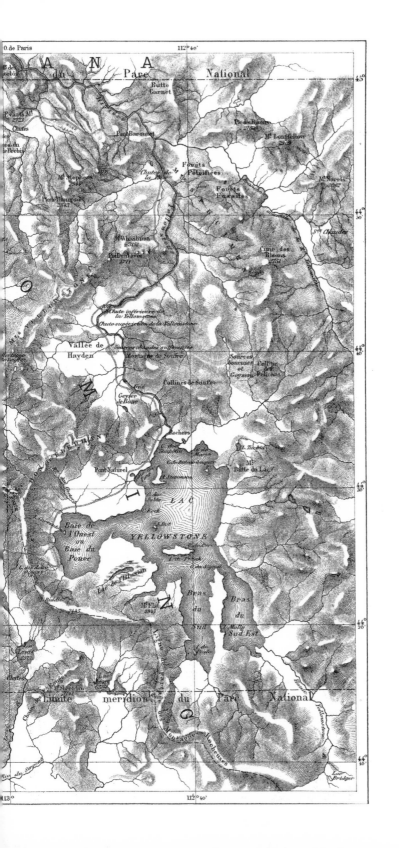

A N A

du   Parc   National

Butte
Garnet

Pics Bisons

M. Longfellow

PontBarouret

Forêts
Pétrifiées

M. Stephens

Forêts
Fossiles

M. Norris

Pics Thompson

M.Whashbun

Cime des
Bisons

S. Chaudes

Pic Dunraven

Chute inférieure de
la Yellowstone

Chute supérieure de la Yellowstone

Vallée de
Hayden

Montagne de Soufre

Sources
fumeuses et
Geysers

Collines de
Pélicans

Collines de Soufre

Geyser
de Boue

Rochers

Pont Naturel

Mt.
Butte du Lac

LAC

Baie de
l'Ouest
ou
Baie du
Pouce

YELLOWSTONE

Lac de

M. Flat

Bras
du

Bras
du

Sud-Est

M. Sheridan

Limite   méridionale   du   Parc   National

Rio du Serpent

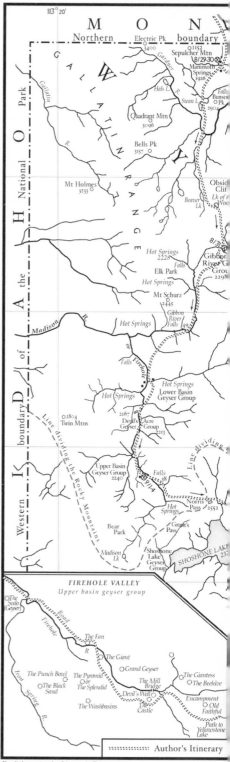

MAP 3. Map of Yellowstone National Park in English created by Linton A. Brown for the translators (2011).

Elevations in meters reflect nineteenth-century measuring methods, and most had been considerably revised by the twenty-first century. The two largest islands in Yellowstone Lake, Stevenson Island and Frank Island, are misrepresented on Leclercq's map. In reality, each is much longer north to south than east to west, and Frank is much larger than Stevenson.

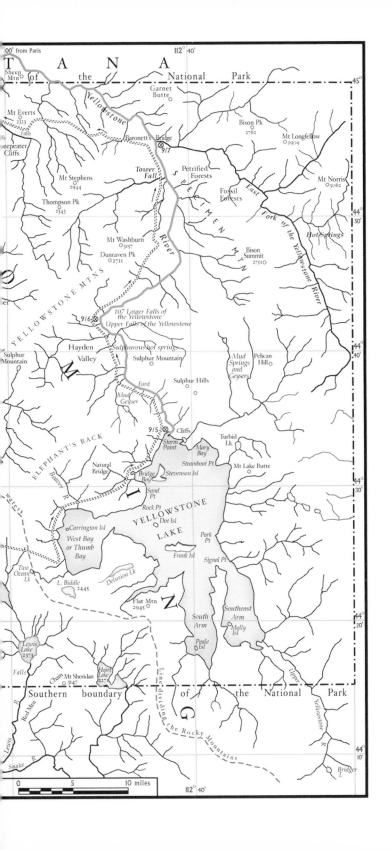

Notes on the Yellowstone National Park map

Early name used by Jules Leclercq (English version)	Present-day approved name and other notes
Beaver River	Arnica Creek. This stream was called Beaver Creek by the Northern Pacific Railroad in an 1883 booklet about the grand opening of their branch line. Whittlesey, *Wonderland Nomenclature*, 30.
Bell's Peak	Antler Peak.
The Black Sand	Black Sand Pool. In the 1880s this pool was called the Black Sand Basin, but the U.S. Board on Geographic Names transferred that name to the entire area in 1927. Whittlesey, *Yellowstone Place Names*, 53.
Devil's Acre Geyser Group	Midway Geyser Basin, also called Hell's or Devil's Half-Acre before 1885.
Devil's Well	Crescent Pool.
East Fork of the Yellowstone River	Lamar River, renamed by Arnold Hague, 1885.
Garnet Butte	Garnet Hill.
Gibbon River Geyser Group	Norris Geyser Basin.
Hals Lake	Now an unnamed lake.
Iron Spring River	Iron Spring Creek.
Lake Biddle	Riddle Lake.
Mt. Lake Butte	Lake Butte.
Mt. Longfellow	Mt. Hornaday.
Mt. Schurz	The mountain where Monument Geyser Basin is located no longer has a name, but there is a Mt. Schurz in the Absaroka Range (southeast Yellowstone).
Mt. Stephens	Prospect Peak.
Mud Springs and Geysers	The Mudkettles and the Mushpots.
Obsidian Cliffs	Obsidian Cliff.
Pelican Hill	Pelican Cone.
Quadrate Mtn.	Quadrant Mountain. Leclercq translated guidebook writer Edwin J. Stanley's "Quadrate Mtn." as "Montagne Carrée." *Quadrate* means square or squared, while a *quadrant* is a quarter of a circle.

Sepulcher Mtn.	Correct elevation is 9,652 ft. (2,942 m).
The Soda Geyser	Sapphire Pool.
Specimen Mtn.	Specimen Ridge.
Sulphur Mtn. (west of Hayden Valley)	May refer to the Highland Hot Springs area, which contains a Sulphur Lake. Whittlesey, *Yellowstone Place Names*, 130. The Sulphur Mountain shown east of the Yellowstone River seems to be misplaced and belongs to the southwest between the upper two tributary streams shown on Leclercq's map. In fact, there are no mountains close to the east side of the Yellowstone River in this area.
Thompson Peak	Cook Peak.
Twin Mtns.	Twin Buttes.
Two Ocean Lake	Lost Lake. Shown as a feature on maps from 1885 to 1961 but never proven to exist. Haines, *Yellowstone Place Names*, 244–45; Whittlesey, *Yellowstone Place Names*, 158–59.
The Washbowls	Terra Cotta Springs.
Yellowstone Mtns. (or Range)	Old name for Absaroka Mountains. Name is transposed to the general area of the Washburn Range on Leclercq's map.

Notes

Translators' Introduction

1. The translators found both factual and qualitative information on Leclercq's life from numerous sources, primarily the following: Rolin, "Notice sur Jules-Joseph Leclercq," 36–60; Académie royale des sciences d'outre-mer, *Biographie coloniale belge*, 593–95; Bertaut, "Notice bio-bibliographique de Jules Leclercq," xlvix–liii; and Leclercq, "La carrière coloniale de Cecil Rhodes."

2. Leclercq, *Voyage au Mexique*, 2.

3. Chittenden, *Yellowstone National Park*, 107n.

4. Cecil Rhodes was an English businessman, financier, and powerful politician in South Africa who founded the modern diamond industry and controlled the politics of Britain's Cape Colony. Part of his great fortune established Oxford's Rhodes Scholarships for students from the United States, Germany, and the British colonies.

5. Rolin, "Notice sur Jules-Joseph Leclercq," 41.

6. Leclercq, *Au pays de Paul et Virginie*, 5.

7. Rolin, "Notice sur Jules-Joseph Leclercq," 48.

Translation and Editorial Method

1. Leclercq refers to Montana as a state several times in the course of his narrative, but in doing so he was ahead of history. As with North and South Dakota, Montana Territory did not achieve statehood until 1889.

2. "Pres. Arthur's Party Arrived at Mammoth Hot Springs Yesterday about Noon . . . ," *Livingston Enterprise*, September 1, 1883; "The Ceremonies Will Begin at 10 a.m. and End at Noon" and "Description of Northern Pacific Railroad President Villard's Train," *Livingston Enterprise*, September 8, 1883; and Whittlesey, "This Modern Saratoga," 131n268.

Original Preface

1. *JL*: "Le Parc National des États-Unis" [The National Park of the United States], *Le Tour du Monde* [Round the World], 1874, 2nd half of year.

2. *JL*: "La Terre des Merveilles: Souvenirs d'une exploration au bassin de la Yellowstone" [Wonderland: Recollections of an exploratory trip in the Yellowstone Basin], by Paul le Hardy. Extract from *La Revue de Belgique*, 1875.

3. *JL*: "Les explorations géologiques à l'ouest des États-Unis" [Geologic explorations in the western United States], by Charles de la Vallée-Poussin, professor in the School of the Sciences of the University of Louvain. Extract from *La Revue Catholique*, 1873.

4. *JL*: "Souvenirs d'un voyage à cheval à travers le désert américain" [Recollections of a horseback trip across the American wilderness], by Henri Gauilleur. *L'exploration*, 1882, 2nd half of year—"Dix jours aux sources du Missouri" [Ten days on the headwaters of the Missouri], by Augustin Seguin. *Le Bulletin de la Société de Géographie de Lyon* [Bulletin of the Lyon Geographical Society], 1881.

5. *JL*: The list of these may be found at the end of this volume.

1. The Land of Wonders

1. In the early nineteenth century countries set their own meridians (zero degrees of longitude). The U.S. meridian ran through Washington DC from 1804 until the International Meridian Conference was held in Washington in 1884. At that time twenty-five countries agreed to adopt the meridian passing through Greenwich, England, as the international standard for zero degrees of longitude. Leclercq's allusion to the "geometric regularity that Americans are fond of" refers to the fact that the boundaries of many western states had been set along degrees of longitude west of the Washington meridian. Leclercq should have said that the Yellowstone boundaries, "approximately from the 110th to the 111th degree of longitude," are west of the (then newly agreed upon) *Greenwich* meridian. Fred Roeder, "The Washington Meridian," April 21, 2009, accessed June 5, 2012, available on the American Surveyor website, http://www.amerisurv.com/content/view/6120/136/.

2. *JL*: Jules Leclercq, *Voyage au Mexique: De New-York à Veracruz par terre* [Trip to Mexico: From New York to Veracruz overland]. Paris, Hachette and Co., publishers [1885].

3. *JL*: *Un été en Amérique: De l'Atlantique aux montagnes rocheuses* [A Summer in America: From the Atlantic to the Rocky Mountains]. E. Plon and Co., Paris, 1877.

4. A league was a unit of length based on the distance a person could walk in an hour, about 4.8 kilometers or 3.0 miles.

2. The First Explorations

1. Meriwether Lewis (1774–1809) and William Clark (1770–1838), spelled "Clarke" by Leclercq, led the first expedition overland across the American continent in 1803–6. On his return journey east Clark came no closer to the

Yellowstone area than the present-day town of Livingston on the Yellowstone River (more than fifty miles from the northern boundary of today's park).

2. John Colter (1775–1813), spelled "Coulter" by Leclercq, visited the Yellowstone area as early as 1807. According to Albert Peale, he "was probably the first white man who ever saw any of the springs or geysers of this wonderful region." "Thermal Springs," 65.

3. Walter Washington DeLacy (1819–92), spelled "de Lacey" by Leclercq, was a civil engineer with an adventurous spirit. Haines, *Yellowstone Story*, 1:64. Leclercq's information about DeLacy comes from Norris, *Fifth Annual Report*, 43–44.

4. John Potts (1776–1810) had been a fellow member of the Lewis and Clark expedition.

5. The story of Colter's run from the Blackfeet appears in an 1819 book mentioned in Bradbury, *Travels*, 25n–29n.

6. Leclercq was apparently unaware of both Joe Meek's 1829 observations (published in 1870 in Victor, *River of the West*, 75) and those of Daniel Potts in an 1826 letter (quoted in Haines, *Yellowstone Story*, 1:41–42).

7. Benjamin Louis Eulalie de Bonneville (1796–1878) was a French-born American who explored extensively in the West in the early 1830s and whose maps and notes Washington Irving used as the basis for his book *The Adventures of Captain Bonneville*, published in 1837.

8. Jim Bridger (1804–81) was a capable guide, fur trapper, and storyteller who probably first entered the Yellowstone area in 1825 and knew it well. See Alter, *Jim Bridger*.

9. Two Ocean Pass is a unique spot where a creek splits in two, one branch leading to the Pacific Ocean and one to the Atlantic. It is theoretically possible for fish to swim over the Continental Divide here when the water is high. Chittenden, *Yellowstone National Park*, 245–46; Michael J. Yochim, National Park Service, personal communication, June 6, 2012.

10. On the naming of the Firehole River, see chapter 8, note 6.

11. Philetus W. Norris (1821–85) served as park superintendent from 1877 to 1882. His annual reports have been invaluable resources for park historical researchers, as has the guidebook section of his book *Calumet of the Coteau*. He earned the title "Colonel" during his four years of service on the Union side in the Civil War. Bowersox, *Standard History of Williams County*, 339.

12. We now use the name Grand Canyon to refer to the canyon of the Colorado River, but in the nineteenth century it meant the canyon of the Yellowstone and was spelled "cañon."

13. In addition to the blockhouse (near the canyon) and marten traps (near Beaver Lake), Colonel Norris discovered evidence of the early presence of white men who had cut trees for breastworks and footbridges. Norris, *Report for 1878*, 989.

14. The initials "J.O.R.," found by Norris on a tree near Yellowstone's Upper Falls (*Fifth Annual Report*, 784–85), have never been explained. Fur trader Alexander Ross may have seen the area by 1819, but those were clearly not his initials, nor was he killed by Blackfeet Indians (as Leclercq states). He died in Manitoba, Canada, of natural causes.

15. Many early writers spread the notion that Native Americans were afraid of Yellowstone's hydrothermal regions, but modern anthropologists have determined this to be quite untrue. In the conclusion to their exhaustive study *Restoring a Presence*, Nabokov and Loendorf write, "We now know that Indian peoples have visited and utilized practically every corner of the park area off and on for almost ten thousand years" (299). And also, "[W]e have argued that geyser activity did not deter them from exploring and exploiting its habitats" (299).

16. The information about the expedition of H. W. Wayant and party (from Silver City, Idaho Territory) and about George Huston's group (next paragraph) comes from Norris, *Fifth Annual Report*, 44–45.

17. David E. Folsom (1839–1918) and Charles W. Cook (1839–1927) led this independent expedition with William Peterson (1834–1919), leaving from Diamond City, Montana Territory, near Helena; the Yellowstone writings of Folsom and Cook have been collected by Haines as *The Valley of the Upper Yellowstone*.

18. Gen. Henry Dana Washburn (1832–71) died from pneumonia exacerbated by his Yellowstone travels soon after leading the expedition described by Leclercq. Haines, foreword to Langford, *Discovery*, ix–x.

19. Gustavus Cheney Doane (1840–92) commanded the military escort that accompanied the Washburn party. He later returned to Yellowstone several times in a similar capacity and tried unsuccessfully to become superintendent of Yellowstone. Leclercq lists Doane's 1870 report as well as *Scribner's Monthly* articles by Truman Everts and N. P. Langford about the 1870 expedition in his "Works to Consult."

20. The correct spelling for the river is "Gardner," but the name of the town at its mouth is spelled "Gardiner." Leclercq erroneously used the latter spelling for the river.

21. Truman Everts (1816–1901) had been Montana's assessor of internal revenue before his Yellowstone adventure. Whittlesey, *Lost in the Yellowstone*, xiv.

22. Leclercq must have read Everts's own account from an 1871 issue of *Scribner's Monthly*. Everts not only recovered from his ordeal but lived to father a son when he was almost seventy-five. Mt. Everts, which was subsequently named for him, was mistakenly thought to be the spot where Everts was found by two mountaineers. Later it was learned that he was actually found on the west slope of Crescent Hill, about ten miles east of the mountain now called Mt. Everts. Whittlesey, *Lost in the Yellowstone*, 59.

23. Ferdinand Vandiveer Hayden (1829–87) earned a medical degree but soon turned his attention to geology. He led geological expeditions of western regions from 1867 to 1878, three of which involved the Yellowstone area. See Foster, *Strange Genius*; and Cassidy, *Ferdinand V. Hayden*.

24. The full name of Hayden's first survey was the Geological and Geographical Survey of the Territories. The voluminous reports produced by survey members formed a basis for work done by Yellowstone researchers for many decades.

25. Hayden was one of a number of men who felt that the Yellowstone area should be preserved by the government and who worked to make it happen. See Schullery and Whittlesey, *Myth and History*.

26. *JL*: Act of March 1, 1872. [Translated into French and quoted by Leclercq; source listed in his "Works to Consult" under United States Department of the Interior. The translators have provided the original English text.]

The tract of land in the Territories of Montana and Wyoming, lying near the headwaters of the Yellowstone River, and described as follows, to wit, commencing at the junction of Gardiner's river with the Yellowstone river, and running east to the meridian passing ten miles to the eastward of the most eastern point of Yellowstone lake; thence south along said meridian to the parallel of latitude passing ten miles south of the most southern point of Yellowstone lake; thence west along said parallel to the meridian passing fifteen miles west of the most western point of Madison lake; thence north along said meridian to the latitude of the junction of Yellowstone and Gardiner's rivers; thence east to the place of beginning.

This territory is hereby reserved and withdrawn from settlement, occupancy, or sale under the laws of the United States, and dedicated and set apart as a public park or pleasuring-ground for the benefit and enjoyment of the people; and all persons who shall locate or settle upon or occupy the same, or any part thereof, except as hereinafter provided, shall be considered trespassers and removed therefrom.

Said public park shall be under the exclusive control of the Secretary of the Interior, whose duty it shall be, as soon as practicable, to make and publish such rules and regulations as he may deem necessary or proper for the care and management of the same. Such regulations shall provide for the preservation, from injury or spoliation, of all timber, mineral deposits, natural curiosities, or wonders within said park, and their retention in their natural condition.

The Secretary may in his discretion, grant leases for building purposes for terms not exceeding ten years, of small parcels of ground, at such places in said park as shall require the erection of buildings for the accommodation of visitors; all of the proceeds of said leases, and all other revenues that may be derived from any source connected with said park, to be expended under his direction in the management of the same, and the construction of roads and bridle-paths therein. He shall provide against the wanton destruction of the fish and game found within said park, and against their capture or destruction for the purposes of merchandise or profit. He shall also cause all persons trespassing upon the same after the passage of this act to be removed therefrom, and generally shall be authorized to take all such measures as shall be necessary or proper to fully carry out the objects and purposes of this act.

27. Hayden's expeditions to the Yellowstone area took place in 1871, 1872, and 1878.

28. Hayden's *Twelfth Annual Report* is referred to here. William H. Holmes (1846–1933) accompanied the Hayden expeditions of 1872 and 1878 as an artist and geologist. Dr. Albert Charles Peale (1849–1914) was a descendant of the Peales who were artists in Philadelphia; like F. V. Hayden, he received an MD degree but shifted his interest to geology. He participated in all three Hayden expeditions as mineralogist. Henry Gannett (1846–1914) was listed as astronomer with the 1872 Hayden expedition and topographer with that of 1878. He later became chief geographer of the U.S. Geological Survey. Haines, *Yellowstone Story*, 1:440–41; Merrill, *Yellowstone and the Great West*, 25.

29. Historian Aubrey L. Haines estimates that there were five thousand visitors in 1885, the same as in 1883 and 1884. Haines, *Yellowstone Story*, 2:478.

3. From the Mississippi to the Yellowstone

1. Throughout this chapter Leclercq uses the name "Livingstone City," which was never the correct spelling. The town of Livingston was named for Johnston Livingston, the Northern Pacific Railroad's "original director," according to historian Aubrey L. Haines. *Yellowstone Place Names*, 258.

2. Atala and Chactas were lovers in the book *Atala* (1801), by François-René de Chateaubriand.

3. Leclercq's experience at Niagara Falls appears in Leclercq, *Un été en Amérique*, 312.

4. Rasmus Bjørn Anderson (1846–1936), a professor at the University of Wisconsin, was appointed U.S. minister to Denmark by President Grover Cleveland in 1885. Leclercq does not say so, but his translation of Anderson's *Scandinavian Mythology* was published in the same year as *La Terre des Merveilles*, 1886.

5. Odin was the chief deity of Norse mythology.

6. James Fenimore Cooper (1789–1851) was a well-known American author of historical novels.

7. Hercules was a Roman mythological hero known for his exceptional strength and large stature.

8. Father Louis Hennepin (1626–ca. 1705) was a French Franciscan priest, missionary, and explorer.

9. Leclercq spelled the name of Father Lucien Galtier (1811–66) "Gaultier."

10. Meschacebé was an alternative name for the Mississippi River, used by the author François-René Chateaubriand (1768–1848) in his work *Les Natchez* (1826).

11. Although both these U.S. fires were catastrophes, Leclercq exaggerated the number of deaths. Twenty-two people died in the Southern Hotel fire in St. Louis on April 11, 1877, and ninety in Milwaukee, where Newhall House burned on January 10, 1883. "Southern Hotel Fire—St. Louis, Missouri," Waymarking.com, accessed May 30, 2012, http://www.waymarking .com/waymarks/WM1RYQ_Southern_Hotel_Fire_St_Louis_Missouri; "Newhall House fire (1883)," Dictionary of Wisconsin History, Wisconsin Historical Society, accessed May 30, 2012, http://www.wisconsinhistory .org/dictionary/.

12. Col. Charles B. Lamborn (1838–1902) was land commissioner of the Northern Pacific Railroad Company.

13. The Northern Pacific's staff photographer, F. Jay Haynes, became the official photographer of Yellowstone National Park the same year as Leclercq's visit, 1883. (Haynes, *Haynes New Guide*, 158).

14. Oliver Dalrymple managed large wheat farms in Minnesota and North Dakota; the North Dakota property of ten thousand acres later known as Bonanza Farms was one of the first and most successful industrialized farms in the United States.

15. Mormons migrated west from Illinois, Missouri, and other Midwestern states in large groups from 1838 through the 1840s.

16. Gen. Alfred Sully (1821–79) was an American military officer during the Civil War and the Indian Wars.

17. The origin of the name "Badlands" (Les mauvaise-terres) is credited to French trappers working in the Dakotas region rather than to local Native Americans. Joan Steiner, "South Dakota Badlands." Badlands National Park Fact Sheet, August 1993, accessed June 5, 2012, http://www3.northern .edu/natsource/HABITATS/Sdbadl1.htm.

18. According to current geologic knowledge, the Badlands were formed by water and wind erosion.

19. The dashing Frenchman Antoine-Amédée-Marie-Vincent Manca de Vallombrosa, Marquis de Morès et de Montemaggiore (1858–96), set himself up in cattle ranching and meat packing and founded Medora, Dakota Territory, in 1883. McCullough, *Brave Companions*, 56–59.

20. "Celestials" was a term used to designate Chinese people and is sometimes considered derogatory.

21. The events Leclercq relates from here to the end of this chapter actually occurred *after* his travels through Yellowstone, but he apparently placed this Livingston experience here for dramatic effect and because it does not fit well into his conclusion.

22. The last-spike ceremony celebrating the joining of the transcontinental Northern Pacific tracks occurred on September 8, 1883, at Gold Creek, near Garrison, Montana Territory, west of Helena. Whittlesey, "This Modern Saratoga," 133n275. Although preliminary newspaper reporting anticipated a "gold spike ceremony," the spike that was actually struck by the dignitaries on September 8 was "a rusty one and somewhat battered, but, as the president announced, was the first spike driven on the Northern Pacific." "The Last Spike," *Livingston Enterprise*, September 10, 1883, 2.

23. Henry Villard, at that time president of the Northern Pacific Railroad, was the organizer of the celebration.

24. The local newspaper gives different numbers for Villard's train—"44 cars divided into 4 sections of 11 each"—but leaves no doubt about the uniqueness of the event. *Livingston Enterprise*, September 8, 1883, 2.

25. In *Voyage au Mexique*, 436, Leclercq explains that President Grant gave him letters of introduction to his friends in Mexico.

4. The Upper Yellowstone

1. According to park historian Whittlesey, the Northern Pacific would have built a standard-gauge railway line south from Livingston in order to accommodate their cars traveling on the transcontinental line. Thus Leclercq must have been mistaken about the "narrow-gauge branch line." Lee Whittlesey, Yellowstone National Park, personal communication, June 11, 2012.

2. According to the *Livingston Enterprise*, the incident of a train derailing occurred on September 5, which would have been four days after President Arthur passed the spot and three days before Leclercq traveled past. A heavy rain had caused a landslide, leaving ten feet of rail unsupported. The engineer and fireman were seriously injured when the locomotive was crushed by the fall of about fifty feet into the Yellowstone River; passengers were shaken but unhurt. "Railroad Wreck: A Passenger Train on the Park Branch Rushes down the Embankment, by a Miracle No One Is Killed," *Livingston Enterprise*, September 6, 1883.

3. Concord stagecoaches, first built in 1827 by the Abbot Downing Company, were so solidly built that they reputedly never broke down but just wore out.

4. Historically called Gate of the Mountains, this narrow passage was also referred to by early explorers as the First Canyon of the Yellowstone River.

5. As Leclercq tells us later, the crystalline boulders (spelled "bowlders" in the nineteenth century) are granite and gneiss brought down by the glaciers from the surrounding mountains.

6. Samuel Davis Sturgis (1822–1899) was a Union general in the American Civil War and later served as a military officer in the Indian Wars. He commanded the Seventh Cavalry just east of Yellowstone Park in a campaign against the Nez Perce tribe in 1877. The French name Nez Percé (pierced nose) was anglicized in the twentieth century by removing the accent over the last *e*.

7. Placer mining—usually for gold or gemstones—removes the valuable product from alluvial sand at the earth's surface.

8. Yankee Jim was a notorious storyteller when drunk. That he was the first miner at Emigrant Gulch is not substantiated; he did not fully build the National Park Toll Road, he only improved it; and historian Richard Bartlett tells us that he "claimed to have spent $25,000 on the road, which was probably $23,500 more than he had ever seen in a calendar year." He was also a meat hunter for the Crow reservation, probably not an Indian tracker under General Sturgis. Whittlesey, personal communication; Whithorn, *Yankee Jim*, 3–7, 13; Bartlett, *Nature's Yellowstone*, 18.

9. *Schnaps* in German can mean dram, brandy, or gin.

10. Geikie, "Geysers of Yellowstone," 220. By the late twentieth century geologists had determined that the so-called Pinedale ice sheet was as much as twenty-four hundred meters (eight thousand feet) deep in the area of Yankee Jim Canyon. Good and Pierce, *Interpreting the Landscapes*, 32, map.

11. The last glacial ice retreated twelve thousand to fourteen thousand years ago.

12. Modern geologists explain that the parallel walls of Devil's Slide are not *dikes* projected into the strata vertically but are instead *sills* that were squeezed in between the older sedimentary layers when they were lying horizontal. Much later, the whole formation was turned to a vertical position by the same forces that created the nearby Beartooth Mountains. Chapple, *Yellowstone Treasures*, 247.

13. The actual distance from Cinnabar Mountain to Mammoth Hot Springs is about nineteen kilometers, or twelve miles.

14. The route up the Gardner River traverses very old sedimentary rocks and recent landslides; here only the mountain to the west of the road is volcanic. Leclercq was probably quoting one of his guidebooks. Fritz and Thomas, *Roadside Geology*, 130–32.

5. Mammoth Springs

1. The terraces at Mammoth are built up of travertine (calcium carbonate), not geyserite (siliceous sinter); Leclercq mistakenly calls the rock "geyserite" several times.

2. Temperature measurements of the waters at Mammoth have never reached the boiling point; the temperature of the Mammoth aquifer has been recorded at 167°F (75°C). Bargar, *Geology and Thermal History*, 11. Rising gas bubbles may make it look like the water is boiling in some springs.

3. The oldest and highest terrace, Terrace Mountain, is about four hundred thousand years old. The average rate of deposit of travertine at Mammoth is 8.5 inches (21 centimeters) per year. Sturchio et al., "Uranium-Series Ages of Travertines," 271; Bargar, *Geology and Thermal History*, 13.

4. Since the early nineteenth century the English word *mammoth* has been used to mean "of very great size," which Leclercq apparently did not know—or perhaps he was being facetious.

5. There are no active or extinct geysers at Mammoth; no one knows as yet just how the Liberty Cap happened to be formed where it is, but its shape has been explained by Keith E. Bargar of the U.S. Geological Survey: Liberty Cap probably formed where water persistently emerged at a single point rather than along a crack in the terrace. The cone ceased growing when the flow of water stopped because of insufficient artesian pressure. Bargar, *Geology and Thermal History*, 7–18.

6. Park superintendent Norris (who served from 1877 to 1882) apparently originated the idea of restoring Liberty Cap. According to park historian Haines, "Coming to the conclusion that Liberty Cap . . . was in danger of toppling, he had it braced with timbers." *Yellowstone Story*, 1:250. Norris himself wrote that he would like to convey water from the higher springs "in order to throw an ornamental column of water to any desired height." *Report for 1880*, 20. By 1882 Norris had erected a pipe to deliver hot spring water to the top of a neighboring formation called Devil's Thumb, but he apparently did not tamper in that way with Liberty Cap.

7. Leclercq's statements are based on only a few years of observation. During many of the park's early decades writers claimed that the hot spring activity at Mammoth and elsewhere was dying out. More recently geologists have determined that, although the activity in the area is constantly changing in strength, temperature, and location, it has not lessened overall in a measurable way since observation began in 1870. Bargar, *Geology and Thermal History*, 31–35, tables 5 and 6.

8. Leclercq's thought that the trees are of considerable age is correct: some of Mammoth's Rocky Mountain junipers (*Juniperus scopulorum*) have recently been proven to be over fifteen hundred years old. John King, Lone Pine Research, personal communication, April 7, 2008.

9. Karl von Münchhausen was an eighteenth-century German baron famous for telling fantastic tales.

10. Jean Anthelme Brillat-Savarin (1755–1826) was a learned French lawyer and statesman, still famous today for his writings on gastronomy and taste.

11. A similar incident a few years earlier (1879) was described in "Through the Yellowstone Park to Fort Custer" by Dr. S. Weir Mitchell, who, with a physician friend, found "gleaming bathtubs full of water . . . so absolutely delicious that we sank for a few moments into motionless, silent enjoyment. Presently my friend uttered words which I may not repeat, and looking up, I

saw that the springs above us had been seized with a fit of prodigality, and had suddenly and liberally overflowed the doctor's dressing-tables. His visage as he got out of the bath with alacrity was something to remember." (694).

6. The Gibbon River

1. Park historian Whittlesey suggests that the guide Jack may have been Jack Bean, a well-known Yellowstone guide of the time, who guided many park visitors, including General Sherman on his July 1883 trip. Whittlesey, personal communication.

2. Since 1928 the official name of this outstanding feature has been Tower Fall, perhaps because of its one, clean drop.

3. Although Leclercq gives few dates in his book, dates of historical events he witnessed indicate that he was in Yellowstone Park from the night of August 29 to September 8 (see the translators' introduction for more details).

4. Lt. Gen. Philip H. Sheridan (1831–88), Union officer in the Civil War and later leader in the Indian Wars, toured Yellowstone at least four times and became a staunch supporter of the park, suggesting the park's enlargement and urging that railroads not be built within its boundaries. Sheridan, "Expedition," 9.

5. Cayuses were native range horses.

6. President Chester A. Arthur (1829–86) was the first American president to visit Yellowstone. He and his party had been in the park for about three weeks at this time, having entered from the South Entrance. They would soon leave by the North Entrance and board the train at the just-established terminus of Cinnabar. Leclercq must have been mistaken about the date, since Arthur arrived at Mammoth on August 31. Whittlesey, "This Modern Saratoga," 131–32nn268–74.

7. The Texas desperadoes story, from the *Wood River Times* of Hailey, Idaho, appears in Hartley, *Saving Yellowstone*, 121.

8. This paragraph is a unique aberration in Leclercq's usually accurate narrative; it seems that Leclercq was following guidebook writer Herman Haupt's confusion here. In a section titled "Lone Star Geyser—'The Orange,'" which begins his section describing the trip from Mammoth Hot Springs to Swan Lake, Haupt writes, "To the left of the road stands the crater of the Lone Star Geyser, a huge mass of geyserite with a globular shape, having on its sides ridges and markings of yellow and buff, resembling an orange; hence the name. It is called the 'Lone Star' from its solitary situation. The times of eruption are uncertain; now it is little more than a spring with an elevated crater." *Yellowstone National Park*, 48. Whittlesey tells us that the future guide but then assistant superintendent George L. Henderson had named this feature Orange Geyser in 1882, at a time when "Henderson and other observers still were unsure of the differences between a geyser and a hot spring." *Yellowstone Place Names*, 195. Its name was changed to the pres-

ent Orange Spring Mound in 1927. Leclercq (or his editors) found a picture of Lone Star Geyser (which is actually southeast of Old Faithful village, and which Leclercq did not see) and inserted it in this book.

9. There are no larch trees (nor their near relatives) anywhere in Yellowstone, but limber pine and Rocky Mountain juniper (in the cedar family) are common near Mammoth.

10. Leclercq must have ridden from Mammoth to Swan Lake Flat up the notoriously steep road between present-day Clagett Butte and Terrace Mountain, through what is now called Snow Pass. In the late summer of 1883, when Leclercq was there, Capt. Dan Kingman of the U.S. Army Corps of Engineers was just beginning the new road through Golden Gate. Haines, *Yellowstone Story*, 2:211.

11. When he built the road north from Mammoth in 1878, Superintendent Norris named the pass Terrace Pass; it is now called Snow Pass.

12. Quadrant Mountain (spelled Quadrate by Leclercq), visible from Swan Lake Flat north of Mammoth, was named in 1878 for the resemblance of its summit to a segment of a sphere. The modern measurement for the height of Quadrant Mountain is 3,113 meters; for Bunsen Peak, 2,610 meters.

13. Leclercq is quoting here from the Haupt 1883 guidebook. Haupt, *Yellowstone National Park*, 50. Castle Rock cannot be seen from today's roads.

14. Dante Alighieri (1265–1321) was an Italian poet, author of the *Divine Comedy*.

15. Paul Gustave Doré (1832–83) was a French artist, engraver, illustrator, and sculptor.

16. Leclercq was misinformed about the nature of obsidian: it is a homogeneous glass, meaning it does not contain crystals. On part of the cliff, columns do appear, but their rock is not basalt (as are those on the British coasts) but rhyolite. He would have seen columnar basalt at Tower Fall near the end of his trip (see figure 44).

17. Obsidian Cliff is now a National Historic Landmark for the very reason that its rock was used by Native Americans in making their hunting weapons for thousands of years and was traded far and wide. Whittlesey, *Yellowstone Place Names*, 191.

18. The name Green Creek was transferred by some observers from Lemonade Creek (which was originally called Green Creek) to Obsidian Creek, the one that was at that time blocked by beavers to create Beaver Lake, just south of Obsidian Cliff. Whittlesey, *Wonderland Nomenclature*, 1305.

19. The usual 1880s tourist route toward Norris (alternately called Gibbon) Geyser Basin turned southeast near Lemonade Creek so as to pass Amphitheater Springs and Lake of the Woods instead of going south past Roaring Mountain. Whittlesey, *Wonderland Nomenclature*, 934.

20. After passing Lake of the Woods, Leclercq encountered a thermal area called Whiterock Springs. Whittlesey, personal communication; U.S.

Geological Survey, Yellowstone National Park, Wyo. — Mont. — Idaho, topographical map, 1961.

7. The First Geysers

1. Gibbon Geyser Basin was an alternate name for Norris Geyser Basin at the time of Leclercq's visit.

2. Hayden and his scientific colleagues wrote voluminous reports after each of their three expeditions, and Hayden also wrote several articles in a more popular style. Leclercq lists most of Hayden's writings in his bibliography, but he does not indicate which of them he is referring to in the text. Hayden's words comparing Upper Geyser Basin to an industrial city appear in his *Preliminary Report*: "Early in the morning of August 30 [1871], the valley was literally filled with columns of steam, ascending from more than a thousand vents. I can compare the view to nothing but that of some manufacturing city like Pittsburgh, as seen from a high point, except that instead of the black coal smoke, there are here the white delicate clouds of steam" (112).

3. Twins, Triplets, and Fountain are geyser names mentioned by several writers contemporary to Leclercq, but they have not yet been traced to any existing features at Norris Geyser Basin. Whittlesey, personal communication. The other geysers Leclercq mentions here have changed or ceased their eruption patterns.

4. Since Leclercq's visit Emerald Spring at Norris Geyser Basin has occasionally been active as a geyser, with extraordinary activity in 1931. Bryan, *Geysers of Yellowstone*, 284.

5. Dr. Albert C. Peale was the geologist with the Hayden expeditions of the 1870s (see chapter 2, note 28). His report on the thermal springs of Yellowstone and the world (Peale, "Thermal Springs") was a very useful reference for Leclercq. His remark about the apparent recent origin of Steamboat Geyser is on both pages 128 and 426.

6. Leclercq's "Steamboat Vent," called simply the new crater by Superintendent Norris and now called Steamboat Geyser, is known to be the tallest active geyser in the world. It has erupted as high as 380 feet but is unpredictable, erupting relatively frequently in the 1960s and 1980s but before and since then frustrating observers with intervals ranging from four days to fifty years. Leclercq paraphrases guidebook writer Winser here (*Yellowstone National Park*, 28), while Norris himself wrote, "The new crater which burst forth in the Norris Geyser Plateau, with such upturning and hurling of rocks and trees, August 11, 1878, and was for the remainder of last year a high crater of hissing gas, steam, and mud, seems this year to have settled down to business as a very powerful flowing geyser, having, in common with many others, a double period of eruption, one some 30 feet high about each half hour, and another of nearly 100 feet and long-continued, each six or seven days, and is doubtless still changing." *Fifth Annual Report*, 16.

8. The Firehole

1. The biblical monarch Nimrod was known to be a "mighty hunter." Hunting was not specifically prohibited in Yellowstone until 1886.

2. Monument Geyser Basin is on the northeastern flank of a now-nameless mountain about eighty-four hundred feet high. At Leclercq's time it had been named for Carl Schurz, secretary of the interior from 1877 to 1881, because he was very supportive of the national park. However, in 1885 (soon after Leclercq's visit) the name was shifted by geologist Arnold Hague to the second-highest mountain in the park (11,163 feet), one of the Absaroka Range peaks east of Yellowstone Lake. Whittlesey, *Yellowstone Place Names*, 174, 181; U.S. Geological Survey, Madison Junction topographic map, 1986.

3. Monument Basin is one area in the park where the early observation that activity was diminishing has held true for the past one hundred years and more. Compare an 1898 description, "geyser cones — some of them steaming and rumbling" (Guptill, *Haynes Guide*, 36–37), with one from 2008, "only one of these is still active" (Bryan, *Geysers of Yellowstone*, 330).

4. The west wall of Gibbon Canyon is not basalt lava but rather consists of pinkish volcanic ash, or tuff, that was thrown out and compressed into stone at the time of the last caldera eruption, while the east wall is rhyolite from subsequent lava flows. For part of its length here the Gibbon River flows along the caldera's boundary. Chapple, *Yellowstone Treasures*, 286; Christiansen, *Geology of Yellowstone National Park*, plate 1.

5. The water ouzel, now usually called the American dipper, is a small bird known for its cheerful song and its fascinating habit of bobbing underwater to feed.

6. Many early visitors believed, quite logically, that the Firehole River was named for the boiling springs within and along it. Rather, the name was transferred before Yellowstone was a park from the Burnt Hole or Fire Hole, a burnt-over section of the Madison River Valley. Whittlesey, *Yellowstone Place Names*, 105.

7. In these two paragraphs pertaining to the area from Gibbon Falls to Nez Perce Creek, Leclercq mentions but probably did not see the confluence of the Gibbon River and the Firehole River (at Madison Junction), since the road bypassed the junction by going southwest and south from Gibbon Falls to come out at the north end of Lower Geyser Basin. Leclercq would have forded the Firehole near its confluence with Nez Perce Creek, about four and one-half miles south of Madison Junction.

8. Leclercq dined at the first Firehole (or Marshall's) Hotel, built on the west bank of the river of the same name in 1880. Norris, *Annual Report for 1880*, 607; Whittlesey, "Marshall's Hotel," 44.

9. *Conferva* in Leclercq's day was a general term for various filamentous green algae that form scum in still or stagnant fresh water. Today scientists are studying such microorganisms intensively.

10. The tent camp where Leclercq's party stayed must have been on the left, or west, bank of the Firehole, since in the next chapter he mentions being across the river from Beehive Geyser.

9. Old Faithful

1. Old Faithful's intervals were never exactly sixty minutes apart, as many people believe, but it was surely the most regular and frequent geyser Leclercq would have seen. Although the eruptions have always been quite dependable, large variations from the average interval have often occurred.

2. Doane wrote that the Firehole valley "contains phenomena of thermal springs unparalleled upon the surface of the globe." Quoted in Bonney and Bonney, *Battle Drums*, 342. On Doane, see chapter 2, note 19.

3. Vulcan was the Roman god of fire. The superheated water below Yellowstone's geyser basins does not exist as an unbroken expanse or "sea of boiling water" but rather occupies the ubiquitous fissures created as the still-hot lava gradually cools and contracts.

4. For Dante, see chapter 6, note 14.

5. Yellowstone has fir trees only at the higher elevations; near the Firehole River Leclercq would have seen lodgepole pines.

6. Old Faithful was seen and named by members of the 1870 Washburn expedition.

7. Leclercq's dimensions for Old Faithful apply to the entire structure, not just the cone. The nineteenth-century engraving reproduced as figure 13 will demonstrate to readers familiar with its present crater the destruction caused by vandals in the early years.

8. Capt. William Ludlow (1843–1901) made a survey of the Yellowstone region in 1875 and wrote an official report. Ludlow, *Report of a Reconnaissance*, 36–37.

9. Lieutenant General Sheridan recommended in 1882 that the park be placed under the control of the U.S. Army. Bartlett, *Yellowstone*, 236, 251n6.

10. A Bengal light was a bright blue flare used in the nineteenth century for signaling and illumination, especially at sea. Today the term is applied to a type of firework.

10. Beehive and Giantess

1. The towers of Notre Dame Cathedral in Paris are 226 feet high. According to Yellowstone researchers E. T. Allen and Arthur Day, in the 1870s Beehive reached a measured height of two hundred feet or more several times. Marler, *Inventory*, 138. Beehive's eruption has a force that could well carry a hat aloft, but present-day visitors are not allowed to approach it closely enough to test that.

2. Arnold Hague of the U.S. Geological Survey and other geologists referred to two types of geysers: cone-type geysers (like Beehive), which emit a

steady column of water from a narrow vent, and fountain-type geysers (like Giantess), which throw out a series of bursts from a broad pool of water. Leclercq might have been aware of one or more of Hague's annual reports, which began in 1883, but he did not list them in his "Works to Consult."

3. Paris houses in the nineteenth century did not exceed twenty meters in height.

4. The Barrière de l'Étoile in Paris consisted of a pair of tollgates where taxes were collected on incoming goods. The Arc de Triomphe was built between them (1806–36). The Barrière buildings were destroyed in 1860, twenty-three years before Leclercq made this comparison. Since people commonly referred to the monuments at this locality in one breath, Leclercq may actually have had in mind the Arc de Triomphe, which stands about fifty-five meters high. For a contemporary illustration of the Barrière de l'Étoile and the Arc de Triomphe, see Imago Mundi: Encyclopédie gratuite en ligne, "Les propylées de Paris," accessed May 23, 2012, http://www.cosmovisions .com/monuParisPropylees.

5. Since Leclercq's time observers have found that at least twelve smaller geysers in the area of Giantess are directly connected to Giantess. Bryan, *Geysers of Yellowstone*, 52.

6. A number of early park observers have written about this halo effect of the sun and steam. It is an optical effect called a Specter of Brocken, which occurs when the sun is in position to project someone's shadow onto thick steam or mist.

7. Hayden, *Preliminary Report*, 123.

8. Giantess erupted on average two or three times per year around the turn of the twenty-first century.

11. Along the Firehole

1. See chapter 9, note 8, about Capt. William Ludlow. He included a map of Upper Geyser Basin in his detailed report about the Yellowstone area, made in 1875. Ludlow, *Report of a Reconnaissance*, 25–29.

2. Numerous early visitors to Yellowstone's geyser basins felt that they were near hell or the devil; some said they were reminded of Hades or of factory cities like Pittsburgh. For example, see Norris, *Fifth Annual Report*, 789; and Ferris, *Life in the Rocky Mountains*, 259.

3. The game of badminton was first played in Europe in the latter part of the nineteenth century, after being brought to England from British India.

4. Guidebooks from the 1880s give Grand Geyser's interval as anywhere from thirteen to thirty-one hours (Marler, *Inventory*, 111), while in the early years of the twenty-first century Grand's intervals mostly fell in the seven- to eleven-hour range and the eruptions were usually predictable within a four-hour window (Geyser Observation and Study Association, "Grand Geyser," accessed May 23, 2012, http://www.geyserstudy.org/geyser.aspx?pGeyserNo=GRAND).

5. Before Leclercq's visit a few writers claimed that Castle Geyser occasionally erupted as high as 250 feet, but Henry Winser's 1883 guide, among others, mentions eruptions "100 feet or more." Winser, *Yellowstone National Park*, 51.

6. Herman Haupt Jr. (1807–1905) published a detailed guidebook following his 1882 visit to Yellowstone. He described his sighting of Castle Geyser's eruption in *Yellowstone National Park*, 99–100.

7. Any disturbance to a superheated pool like Crested Pool will cause it to bubble.

8. On the left bank and downriver from the Castle-to-Sawmill bridge across the Firehole are a few springs where many early tourists washed their clothes and dishes. These springs are now called the Terra Cotta Springs, but one has historically been called Washtub Spring and another, Dishpan Spring. Bryan, *Geysers of Yellowstone*, 63.

9. Grandgousier (Big Gullet), father of Gargantua in the books about Gargantua and Pantagruel by François Rabelais published in the sixteenth century, was known for his voracious appetite. *Uno haustu*: at one draught.

10. Chroniclers of Grotto's eruptions in recent years write of marathon eruptions lasting more than a day and others of one or two hours' duration with from several hours to a day in between eruptions. Marler, *Inventory*, 45–46; Bryan, *Geysers of Yellowstone*, 108–9.

11. Versailles, the seventeenth-century palace built near Paris by King Louis XIV of France, is known for its elaborate fountains that produce sculptures of water, created by the differing shapes of the many spouts, which cause the water to spurt up in bubbles, blades, tongues, or sprays.

12. In recent years, when Fan Geyser erupts, so does its neighbor Mortar. At the time of Leclercq's visit Mortar was not named as a separate geyser.

13. According to Marler, Hayden in 1878 gave the geyser we now call Daisy the name "Comet" and called the one we call Comet "Spray," both of Hayden's names being quite appropriate to their activity. It is not surprising that early observers were confused about the names of geysers in this group: the name Daisy was not used until at least 1884, while Splendid had been named by 1876; today's Comet is a near-perpetual spouter in the Daisy Geyser Complex. Leclercq's illustration labeled "The Comet" (fig. 22) seems to be of a "concerted," or dual, eruption of Splendid and Daisy. Marler, *Inventory*, 87–88; Whittlesey, *Yellowstone Place Names*, 81–82, 235.

14. For the name Firehole, see chapter 8, note 6.

12. Land of Wonders and Land of Ice

1. For Strokkur, see chapter 13, note 14.

2. Hot springs may erupt (as geysers), splash or bubble constantly, or overflow constantly or periodically.

3. Examples of the various incrustations of geyserite around the hot springs can be found throughout the geyser basins — for instance, around

Cauliflower Geyser and Shell Spring at Biscuit Basin. That basin was named primarily for the beautiful formations that used to surround the large Sapphire Pool, but its "biscuits" were destroyed when Sapphire erupted violently as a result of the 1959 Hebgen Lake earthquake. Whittlesey, *Yellowstone Place Names*, 221.

4. Yellowstone Lake's elevation is 7,732 feet.

5. The nineteenth-century German physicist, chemist, and inventor Robert Wilhelm Eberhard von Bunsen (1811–99) studied and theorized about the geysers of Iceland as well as lent his name to the Bunsen burner used in laboratories. His publication on the subject of geyser action (Bunsen, "Physikalische Beobachtungen") is frequently cited.

6. Twentieth-century measurements inside Old Faithful Geyser's vent recorded temperature spikes of 129.5°C (265°F) at a depth of about seventy feet. Hutchinson, Westphal, and Kieffer, "In Situ Observations," 877).

7. *JL*: I included a complete table of the volcanic eruptions in Iceland since 894 in my *La Terre de Glace* [Land of Ice] (p. 247).

8. Ferdinand von Hochstetter (1829–84) was professor of mineralogy and geology at the Polytechnic Institution of Vienna, Austria, and worked in New Zealand. Leclercq quotes here from Hochstetter, *New Zealand*, 434.

9. Leclercq is paraphrasing F. V. Hayden here and in previous paragraphs, from an 1872 article, "Hot Springs and Geysers," 162. Hayden was one of several early writers who spread the myth that Native Americans were afraid of features in the park — usually referring to the geysers and hot springs rather than to earthquakes.

10. In simpler language: the springs' water percolates through the volcanic rock palagonite (similar to basalt) and through tuff (fused volcanic ash — chemically the same type of rock), leaving a solid precipitate behind.

11. From an early twentieth-century U.S. Geological Survey analysis, the chemical composition of travertine at Mammoth proved to be more than 96 percent calcium carbonate, with only a trace of silica. Bargar, *Geology and Thermal History*, 13, table 4.

12. Charles Stuart Forbes (1829–76), commodore of the Royal Navy, traveled to Iceland in 1860. His theory that thermal springs and geysers occur only near lakes, marshes, or rivers is in Forbes, *Iceland*, 246–47.

13. Leclercq and his source, Commodore Forbes, were entirely right: although most geyser water is meteoric — that is, from rain and snow — the best location for geysers is where a large supply of groundwater is available. Bryan, in *Geysers: What They Are and How They Work*, writes, "Geysers require enormous amounts of water. . . . Almost all of this water started out on Earth's surface as rain or snow. In Yellowstone as anywhere else, most snowmelt and rain runs across the land surface, down the rivers, and to the oceans. Perhaps less than 5 percent manages to trickle below the surface and into the geothermal system. Yet that small amount is the water sup-

ply for all of Yellowstone's hot springs. . . . Yellowstone, on the Continental Divide, is a magnet for storms and receives considerable winter snow that seeps into the ground as it melts" (21).

13. Theory of Geysers

1. JL: *Twelfth Annual Report of the United States Geological and Geographical Survey of the Territories, for the Year 1878*. By F. V. Hayden. Section II. "The Thermal Springs of the Yellowstone National Park." By A. C. Peale, M D. Washington, 1883. [In chapter 13 Leclercq paraphrased or translated directly from Peale's report; the translators reproduce the original text wherever appropriate, beginning with the third paragraph of this chapter. Peale, "Thermal Springs," 417–22, 425–26. See chapter 2, note 28, for information about Albert C. Peale.]

2. George S. Mackenzie (1780–1848) wrote *Travels in the Island of Iceland during the Summer of the Year 1810*, an early and very thorough account (for his geyser theory, see 228–31).

3. On Bunsen, see chapter 12, note 5.

4. Karl Gustav Bischof (1792–1870), a German geologist and mineral chemist, was a professor of chemistry at the University of Bonn, Germany. He published on the internal heat of the globe in 1837; Peale quoted from Bischof's *Physical, Chemical, and Geological Researches*, 227–28.

5. Otto Ludwig Krug von Nidda (1810–85) visited Iceland to study its geology in 1833, publishing his work on Iceland soon after his visit. Krug von Nidda, "Geognostische Darstellung."

6. JL: I have given ample details of the formation of geyser tubes in the account of my trip to Iceland. *La Terre de Glace* [Land of Ice], p. 166 and following. Paris, 1883.

7. German physicist J. H. J. Müller (1809–75) wrote about his experiment in the 1850 periodical *Annalen der Physik und Chemie*. Müller, "Über Bunsen's Geysertheorie."

8. Dr. Theodore B. Comstock (1849–1915) was a well-known geologist who wrote about Yellowstone and geysers as well as many other geological subjects. He later became the first director of the Arizona School of Mines.

9. Capt. William A. Jones led an expedition into Yellowstone in 1873 that recorded some scientific measurements. They entered and left the park by passes over the Absaroka Range that were formerly thought to be impassable. Haines, *Yellowstone Story*, 1:201–3.

10. The diagram and quotation were taken by Peale from Comstock's "Geological Report," 255–57, and translated into French by Leclercq.

11. Baring-Gould, *Iceland*, 366–67. Rev. Sabine Baring-Gould (1834–1924) wrote a book about his 1862 trip to Iceland. An eccentric parson from West Devon, England, he is best known for having written the words to the hymn "Onward Christian Soldiers."

12. Campbell, *Frost and Fire*, 417n. This book describes how natural forms are created by glaciers and volcanoes. John Francis Campbell (1821–85) was a Scottish polymath, best known as a collector of Gaelic folklore.

13. Alexander Bryson (1816–66) was a Scottish watchmaker interested in mineralogy and geology. On a visit to Iceland in 1862, he determined that the temperature halfway down the tube of the Great Geyser was 270°F, while at the very bottom it was not more than 240°F. Bryson, *Notes*, 38).

14. Strokkur, whose name means "churn," is now the largest geyser in Iceland and erupts as high as seventy-five feet, according to geyser expert T. Scott Bryan. *Geysers of Yellowstone*, 417–18.

15. Campbell, *Frost and Fire*, 405–7.

16. Niels Horrebow (1712–60), a Danish lawyer, lived in Iceland for two years, studying the animals, plants, weather, and geological features. He published *The Natural History of Iceland* in Danish in 1752. The English translation (1758, by the Right Rev. Erich Pontoppidan), describing a hot spring "well" that "rises up 10 or 12 feet high," states,

> If the water out of the largest well is poured into bottles it will still continue to boil up twice, or thrice, and at the same time with the water in the well. Thus long will the effervescence continue after the water is taken out of the well, but this being over it soon quite subsides and grows cold. If the bottles are corked up the moment they are filled, so soon as the water rises in the well they burst in pieces: this experiment has been proved on many score bottles, to try the effects of the water. . . .
>
> Whatever is cast into the well when the water subsides, it attracts with it down to the bottom, even wood, which on another like fluid would float: but when the water flows again, it throws everything up, which may be found at the side of the bason [*sic*]. This has been often tried with stones as large and as heavy as the stoutest fellows have hardly been able to tumble in. These stones made a violent noise on being plunged to the bottom; but when the water rose again, they were ejaculated with force beyond the edge of the well. A vast many stones lie about that have been used in such experiments. (Horrebow, *Natural History*, 22)

14. Excelsior

1. Midway Geyser Basin is roughly halfway between Upper and Lower Geyser Basins.

2. Only one geyser with eruptions more powerful than Excelsior's has ever been recorded, and those occurred after Leclercq wrote his book; on New Zealand's North Island, Waimangu erupted black mud, water, and rocks up to 450 meters numerous times between 1900 and 1904.

3. Throughout this chapter Leclercq frequently paraphrases Henry J. Winser's guidebook, published the year of Leclercq's visit. In his turn, Winser used information from Hayden, *Preliminary Report* and *Twelfth Annual Report,* including Peale's report in the latter.

4. Philetus W. Norris was superintendent of Yellowstone from April 1877 through February 1882. In his 1881 report to the secretary of the interior he wrote that in late August 1878 he "distinctly heard its [Excelsior's] spoutings when near Old Faithful, 6 miles distant, but arrived too late to witness them." *Fifth Annual Report,* 804. Excelsior was not actually observed to erupt until 1880. To his 1881 report Norris appended a statement and chart by a subordinate, C. H. Wyman, who observed no fewer than sixty-three eruptions of Excelsior between September 27 and October 2, 1880. *Fifth Annual Report,* 798–800.

5. Guidebook writer Edwin J. Stanley tells us that Excelsior was named by Colonel Norris "but has since been named by others the 'Sheridan,' in honor of that distinguished General, who recently visited the Park." *Rambles,* 201. Leclercq learned that General Sheridan witnessed Excelsior from Haupt's guidebook, *Yellowstone National Park,* 81.

6. Haupt's traveling companion was Dr. James Houston Eccleston of Emmanuel Episcopal Church in Baltimore, to whom he dedicated his guidebook. For Herman Haupt, see chapter 11, note 6.

7. No eruptions of Excelsior occurred from 1883 through 1887, but it was seen to erupt in 1888, 1890, 1891, 1901, and 1985. Whittlesey, *Wonderland Nomenclature,* 473–92.

8. Leclercq found this informal post office at Marshall's Hotel, also mentioned in chapter 8, note 8.

9. Young warriors of the Nez Perce tribe did attack, injure, and temporarily capture members of a tourist party near the confluence of present-day Nez Perce Creek and the Firehole River in 1877. Stanley, *Rambles,* 157–68; Haines, *Yellowstone Story,* 1:220–30. The story is told in Leclercq's next chapter. But the "trappers of the Far West" that Leclercq mentions here were almost entirely gone from the area by the 1870s.

15. The Indians in the National Park

1. As mentioned in chapter 2, note 15, the false belief that all Native Americans feared the park was perpetuated for many years by authors who wrote about Yellowstone.

2. The Nez Perces were known as fine horsemen and were relatively friendly to the whites until injustices in the 1870s led them to leave their Idaho reservation and traverse the Yellowstone area in an attempt to join the Crow tribe in Montana. Chief Joseph (1840–1904), whose Native name was In-mut-too-yah-lat-lat (Thunder Traveling over the Mountains), was not a warrior but a strong leader and an important spokesman for his tribe.

He and many of his tribe surrendered to U.S. troops when they reached northern Montana. Joseph, "Indian's View," 415; see also Greene, *Nez Perce Summer*; and Guie and McWhorter, *Adventures in Geyser Land*.

3. Gen. Oliver Otis Howard (1830–1909) was a West Point graduate and Civil War Union general. After the war he helped found Howard University and served as its president for several years. As commander of the army's Department of the Columbia, he led the 1877 campaign against the Nez Perces. "Oliver Otis Howard," *New Perspectives on the West*, PBS, 2001, accessed May 23, 2012, http://www.pbs.org/weta/thewest/people/d_h/howard .htm; Anne Richardson, "Oliver Otis Howard: General in the Civil War, Reconstruction, and Indian Wars," Oregon Cultural Heritage Commission, 2002, accessed May 23, 2012, http://ochcom.org/howard.

4. In this chapter Leclercq paraphrased from Stanley's book, *Rambles*, 158–70. Stanley in turn frequently quoted from Frank Carpenter's account, reproduced in Guie and McWhorter, *Adventures in Wonderland*. The translators use Stanley's original text when appropriate.

5. Radersburg is in west-central Montana, between Helena and Three Forks.

6. A ninth person was in the original caravan, but Leclercq mentions him only in a later paragraph. He was A. J. Arnold of Helena. According to historian Haines, another traveler, William H. Harmon of Colorado, had joined the party by the time of the Nez Perce encounter. Haines, *Yellowstone Story*, 1:220.

7. Chief Looking Glass (ca. 1832–77), whose Nez Perce name was Allalimya Takanin, helped design the military strategies used by the Nez Perces in battling General Howard's forces. He was killed by a Cheyenne scout just after Chief Joseph surrendered at the Battle of the Bears Paw Mountains near Chinook, Montana. "Looking Glass," *New Perspectives on the West*, PBS, 2001, accessed May 23, 2012, http://www.pbs.org/weta/thewest/people/i_r/looking.htm.

8. Chief White Bird (1807–92), whose Nez Perce name was Peo-peo-hix-hiix, helped direct the movement of the tribe from Idaho into northern Montana. Unlike Chief Joseph, who was captured by U.S. troops, he and over one hundred of his band escaped into Canada and lived out their lives there. National Park Service, Nez Perce National Historical Park, Museum Collections, Web site, "People — Peopeotholket," accessed June 12, 2012, http://www.nps.gov/museum/exhibits/nepe/people.html.

9. John Shively was a lone prospector who had lost his horses while passing through the park. Haines, *Yellowstone Story*, 1:220.

10. Here Leclercq omitted Stanley's phrase "and remembering that these Indians were Catholics," which hinted at the important information that some of the Nez Perces had been converted.

11. George Cowan's mishaps were not over after he was found by Howard's troops: the army wagon overturned on a steep hill, spilling him down the slope, and the bedstead in his Bozeman hotel collapsed and rolled him out of bed. Before that an army surgeon had removed the bullet flattened

on his skull, which Cowan later wore proudly as a watch fob. Haines, *Yellowstone Story*, 1:232, 236.

12. The name of Richard Dietrich was misspelled as "Deitrich" by Leclercq as well as by his source, Stanley.

13. Stanley recorded here that before entering the camp Wilkie and Weikert "fired two shots—the signal agreed upon. No response came." *Rambles*, 169.

14. Stanley, *Rambles*, 170–71.

15. James C. McCartney, spelled "Mac Cartney" by Leclercq, had lived in the area since at least 1871. In 1877 he was proprietor of the Mammoth Hot Springs Hotel and bathhouse and served as assistant park superintendent for a brief time. Haines, *Yellowstone Story*, 1:216–17.

16. For Lieutenant Doane, see chapter 2, note 19. At this point of the 1877 Nez Perce War, Doane was camped with a group of Crow scouts, civilians, and cavalrymen at a ranch in Paradise Valley several miles below Mammoth. Haines, *Yellowstone Story*, 1:233.

16. Yellowstone Lake

1. Perhaps Leclercq uses the expression "les fumerolles" (translated here as "steam") metaphorically. *Fumarole* technically means an emission of volcanic gas or, in Yellowstone, any natural opening from which gases escape. A solfatara (mentioned later in the paragraph) is an area that gives off hot gases and sulfuric vapors.

2. Norris Pass no longer has even a maintained trail through it, but at the time of Leclercq's visit it was the route usually taken to travel between Upper Geyser Basin and the West Thumb of Yellowstone Lake.

3. La Brèche de Roland is a deep opening or gap (40 meters across, 100 meters high, at an altitude of 2,804 meters) in the crest of the Pyrenees, leading into the Cirque de Gavarnie. It forms part of the border between France and Spain. See chapter 19, note 4, about the Cirque de Gavarnie.

4. Leclercq's party must have seen only the northern lobe of Shoshone Lake, since the lake is not little: it is about six miles long.

5. Hayden's complete sentences read, "The lake lay before us, a vast sheet of quiet water, of a most delicate ultramarine hue, one of the most beautiful scenes I have ever beheld." And later he adds, "Such a vision is worth a lifetime, and only one of such marvelous beauty will ever greet human eyes." *Preliminary Report*, 96.

6. The three great rivers whose longest tributaries rise near Yellowstone are the Missouri, the Colorado, and the Columbia.

7. The Rigi, a mountain in the Swiss Alps, is 1,797 meters high. Leclercq is comparing the elevation at the level of Yellowstone Lake's water (2,357 meters) to that of the Rigi's summit.

8. Hayden, *Preliminary Report*, 97. Recent soundings place the deepest spot of Yellowstone Lake at 430 feet. Morgan et al., *Floor of Yellowstone Lake*, 96.

9. Hayden relates that members of his 1871 expedition engaged in this activity. *Preliminary Report*, 100. It became a popular sport that early park visitors enjoyed, using Fishing Cone at West Thumb Geyser Basin. Park regulations no longer allow this practice. Often in the early summer this cone is now completely submerged in the lake's waters.

10. This pool at West Thumb must be today's Abyss Pool, one of the park's deepest, but modern instruments have measured its depth at sixteen meters.

11. It was apparently not yet known when Leclercq published this book that, in addition to the conditions listed at the end of his own chapter 13, one or more constrictions must exist below a geyser's pool to initiate true geyser action. Abyss must have developed such constrictions for brief periods of its history, since it erupted as a geyser in the early twentieth century and again between 1987 and 1992. Bryan, *Geysers of Yellowstone*, 306–7.

12. In Greek mythology naiads were nymphs who gave life to bodies of fresh water.

13. Here Leclercq mistakes the siliceous sinter, or geyserite, found in most geyser basins—including West Thumb Geyser Basin—for travertine.

14. Leclercq's trail may have taken him up a one-hundred-meter-high hill near Bluff Point, but the promontory itself is only a few feet above the lake level.

15. It is interesting to note that the *Haynes Guides* from the 1940s to the 1960s describe Carrington Island as "a small rocky bird roost that is submerged when the lake level is high." *Haynes Guide*, 1949: 111; 1964: 112. In the early twenty-first century it had only one tree. Wave action must have changed it drastically over a century's time.

16. Mount Vesuvius is a volcano on the coast of the Bay of Naples, Italy.

17. Natural Bridge, cut from volcanic rock by centuries of water erosion, was seen and described by F. V. Hayden in 1871. Whittlesey, *Yellowstone Place Names*, 186. In one of his reports Superintendent Norris proposed building a carriage road over it, after first plugging the "gaping hole." Norris, *Annual Report for 1880*, 23. The carriage road was never built. Trails lead to the bridge now from the Grand Loop Road and from Bridge Bay Marina.

18. The nine-thousand-foot-high Signal Hills, east of Yellowstone Lake, acquired their name from their use by members of the 1871 Hayden survey for signaling purposes during mapping. Whittlesey, *Yellowstone Place Names*, 227.

19. The only promontory to the west of Yellowstone Lake's outlet is the Elephant Back, which rises about 250 meters above the lake.

20. Lake Lucerne is in central Switzerland.

17. Remarks on Fishing and Hunting
1. This tapeworm genus—still found in Yellowstone Lake trout—is now called *Diphyllobothrium*.

2. Joseph Leidy (1823–91), professor of anatomy at the University of Pennsylvania, was known as the founder of American parasitology. He wrote, "Two species have long been known as parasites of the Salmon and other members of the same genus of fishes in Europe, but the tape-worm of the Yellowstone trout appears to be a different one." Leidy, "Notice of Some Worms," 381.

3. Twentieth-century scientists learned that, in a complicated interaction of species and life forms, this parasitic tapeworm is passed back and forth between the mammals and birds on land and the fish and crustaceans in water. Although unaesthetic, the worms are harmless to humans after the fish is cooked. Varley and Schullery, *Yellowstone Fishes,* 17.

4. Archaeologists have found evidence of indigenous peoples being in the park as long as eleven thousand years ago.

5. Rev. Edwin J. Stanley visited Yellowstone from Deer Lodge, Montana Territory, in 1873 and published his popular guidebook *Rambles in Wonderland* five years later.

6. Norris, *Report for 1879,* 8–9. Leclercq paraphrased or directly translated this grizzly bear story from Norris's annual report; the translators reproduce the original text where appropriate.

7. Leclercq's source for much of the information in the rest of this chapter is Grinnell's "Zoological Report," 63–71. Leclercq very closely translated Grinnell's words from here on, and the translators have used the original English where appropriate.

8. After becoming separated from his expedition and lost, Truman Everts wandered alone for thirty-seven days in the wilderness without food or shelter. Leclercq recounts his adventures in chapter 2.

9. Founder of the Audubon Society, Dr. George Bird Grinnell (1848–1938) was a strong advocate for federal management and control of commercialization in Yellowstone National Park, especially as editor of *Forest and Stream* magazine. His conservation policy became the basis of the American conservation program under President Theodore Roosevelt. While a graduate student at Yale's Sheffield Scientific School, he accompanied the Ludlow expedition of 1875 as its geologist.

10. For Ludlow, see chapter 9, note 8.

11. The subspecies of moose found in parts of the Canadian and American Rockies was named for George Shiras III (1859–1942), a lawyer and short-term congressman from Pennsylvania, who spent much of his life photographing wildlife with his own method of flash photography. See, for example, Shiras, "Wilderness of the Upper Yellowstone."

12. Leclercq uses three different French expressions for moose: *le renne* (*Alce americana*), *le renne d'Amérique,* and *l'élan.* This confusion is not altogether surprising since in French the animal Americans call *moose* is called *élan,* which can mean either moose or elk. Elk have always been more common in Yellowstone National Park than moose.

13. Grinnell was incorrect about pronghorn does; female pronghorns simply have smaller horns than males.

14. See chapter 2, note 26, for the excerpt from the act's text supplied by Leclercq.

15. Ludlow, *Report of a Reconnaissance*, 36.

16. For Herman Haupt Jr., see chapter 11, note 6.

17. JL: One of my compatriots, a mighty hunter before the Lord, traveled through a more southerly part of the Rocky Mountains in the heart of Colorado in 1876. There, too, it is war to the uttermost: hunters told him, and this was repeated to him everywhere, that

> if the game were to be exterminated, they wanted to take the largest amount possible. Therefore, for three or four years, they were killing for the skins. The bighorn sheep were too rare to be hunted for this purpose, but the skin of an "elk" was worth two and a half to four dollars, and to have them, they would spare no thought at losing 300 to 500 pounds of fine meat, which they left to the wolves to devour. It was thus that the buffalo became so rare; "elk" or "wapiti" is becoming rarer every day; and the mule deer and antelope will not be long in diminishing considerably as well. *(Ma vie nomade aux montagnes Rocheuses* [My nomadic life in the Rocky Mountains], by Baron Arnold de Woelmont. Paris, Firmin Dido, 1878)

18. JL: *Report of a Reconnaissance from Carroll, Montana, to Yellowstone National Park.*

18. Sulphur Mountain

1. For Dr. Peale, see chapter 2, note 28.

2. In the twenty-first century the water of Dragon's Mouth Spring is no longer turquoise blue.

3. General Howard conducted a campaign against the Nez Perce tribe, resulting in the surrender of Chief Joseph and most of his tribe in northern Montana. See chapter 15 about the Nez Perces in Yellowstone and chapter 15, note 3, for more about Howard.

4. The Nez Perces may have set up a parapet near the Yellowstone River ford where they camped in 1877 in anticipation of a skirmish with U.S. troops. However, it seems that no other historic source from the late nineteenth century mentions this parapet. Whittlesey, personal communication, December 13, 2010.

5. In Icelandic, the word for glacier is *jökull*.

6. Lake Thingvalla is the largest lake in Iceland, located about nineteen miles east of Reykjavik; Lake Myvatn is a shallow lake in northern Iceland, thirty miles east of Akureyri.

19. The Falls of the Yellowstone

1. Artist Arthur Brown spent two months painting in Yellowstone in 1883 on commission from a British admirer of his work. He returned to the park in 1885 and sold paintings to the Northern Pacific Railroad, which compared his abilities to those of Thomas Moran, but those paintings are now lost. Hassrick, *Drawn to Yellowstone*, 100–101 and nn22–25).

2. Leclercq must not have seen LeHardy's Rapids, about three miles below Yellowstone Lake's outlet and unmistakably an interruption of the "blue-green waters" of the river.

3. *JL*: According to the trigonometric measurements taken by Hayden, the height of the Lower Falls of the Yellowstone is 397 feet (121 meters). At the foot of the falls the depth of the cañon is 675 feet (206 meters). This depth increases as the river descends. At one-half mile below the falls, it is 1,000 feet (305 meters). From the foot of the falls to the entry of Tower Creek, over a course of twenty-two miles, the river descends at the rate of forty feet per mile (seven meters, fifty-eight centimeters per kilometer). [Today's measurements give the height of the Lower Falls as 308 feet and the canyon depth as ranging from 800 to 1,200 feet. Estimated statistics on the canyon and falls have varied widely over 140 years of observation. Leclercq's figures come from Hayden's *Sixth Annual Report*, 131, but different figures can be found in the Gannett essay in Hayden's *Twelfth Annual Report*, 475–78.]

4. A cirque is a bowl-shaped formation in mountains where erosion by glaciers has left steep walls and a rounded valley head. The Cirque of Gavarnie is a famous such spot in the Pyrenees National Park in southwestern France. The Arkansas River in central Colorado has cut a 380-meter-deep canyon, now called the Royal Gorge.

5. For at least the first fifty years of Yellowstone's existence writers echoed each other in declaring the canyon's birds to be eagles, but ospreys (sometimes called fish hawks) —not eagles—have commonly nested there.

6. Nathaniel Pitt Langford (1832–1911) was a member of the 1870 Washburn expedition and the first superintendent of Yellowstone Park; his 1871 articles about the expedition helped convince Congress to set aside the park. Langford, "Wonders of Yellowstone."

7. The information in the next four paragraphs comes largely from Hayden, *Sixth Annual Report*.

8. Modern geologists have concluded that the Grand Canyon of the Yellowstone was cut as a result of flooding from one or more catastrophic breaks in ice dams, in addition to the river's continual down-cutting of canyon rocks weakened by hydrothermal action. Chapple, *Yellowstone Treasures*, 311–12.

9. Nephalism is the total abstinence from alcohol.

20. Mount Washburn

1. Modern measurements give the canyon width as ranging from 450 to 1,200 meters. Chapple, *Yellowstone Treasures*, 178.

2. Leclercq is probably using the word *chaos* to mean "a state of things in which chance is supreme."

3. In the following three paragraphs Leclercq paraphrased or translated directly from Hayden's *Sixth Annual Report*, 50–51.

4. Even Mt. Washburn was deeply buried, not under water but under ice during several glacial ages.

5. Hayden (as quoted by Leclercq in his translation) meant the eastern shore of Yellowstone Lake, where one sees the high peaks of the Absaroka Range. The western shore is within the caldera and has no high mountains.

6. *JL*: Hayden, *Sixth Annual Report*.

7. Andrew Weikert's horse was killed by the Native Americans while he and James McCartney were returning from burying an earlier victim of the Nez Perce raid on park tourists in 1877 (see end of chapter 15), but the incident occurred near Blacktail Ponds, not in the vicinity of Tower Fall. Haines, *Yellowstone Story* 1:233.

8. This remarkable story about an unidentified "old recluse" is taken directly from Haupt, *The Yellowstone National Park*, 157–58. Haupt wrote: "This man—"Billy" [almost certainly tollkeeper Billy Jump]—is a remarkable instance of the pertinacity with which some men cling to life. By the accidental discharge of a blast of Giant Powder in a coal mine in which he was working, numerous particles of rock and a piece of his felt hat were blown through his forehead and into the forepart of his brain . . . yet that man recovered. The complete record of this case may be found in the medical archives of Fort Ellis" (now housed at the National Archives, Harper's Ferry, Virginia).

9. Leclercq probably saw quaking aspen trees (*Populus tremuloides*), related to birch trees; aspen are common in northern Yellowstone.

Conclusion

1. Leclercq evokes the famous refrain "Quoth the raven, 'Nevermore,'" from the poem "The Raven," by Edgar Allan Poe (1809–49), published in 1845.

Translators' Bibliography

This bibliography contains works not listed in Jules Leclercq's original "Works to Consult" but relevant to a modern English translation. While Leclercq's list includes only writings about visits to or research on Yellowstone, this list gives references that he mentions in his text but does not list, references cited in the translators' notes, and selected relevant works that appeared after 1886, the year *La Terre des Merveilles* was published.

Académie royale des sciences d'outre-mer [Royal Academy of Overseas Sciences]. *Biographie coloniale belge* [Belgian Colonial Biography]. Vol. 1. Brussels: Librairie Falk fils, 1948, 594–95.

"An Act to Set Apart a Certain Tract of Land Lying near the Head-Waters of the Yellowstone River as a Public Park." *United States Statutes at Large* 17, chap. 24 (March 1, 1872): 32–33.

Allen, E. T., and Arthur L. Day. *Hot Springs of the Yellowstone National Park*. Washington DC: Carnegie Institution of Washington, 1935.

Alter, Cecil J. *Jim Bridger*. Norman: University of Oklahoma Press, 1962.

Bargar, Keith E. *Geology and Thermal History of Mammoth Hot Springs, Yellowstone National Park, Wyoming*. U.S. Geological Society Bulletin 1444. Washington DC, 1978.

Baring-Gould, Sabine. *Iceland, Its Scenes and Sagas*. London: Smith, Elder, 1863.

Bartlett, Richard A. *Nature's Yellowstone*. Tucson: University of Arizona Press, 1989.

———. *Yellowstone: A Wilderness Besieged*. Tucson: University of Arizona Press, 1985.

Bertaut, René. "Notice bio-bibliographique de Jules Leclercq" [Bio-bibliographical note on Jules Leclercq]. In *Revue bibliographique belge* [Belgian bibliographic review], 13:xlix–lv. Brussels: Société belge de librairie [Belgian Booksellers' Society], 1901.

Bischof, Karl Gustav. *Physical, Chemical, and Geological Researches on the Internal Heat of the Globe.* Translated by A. Mornay. 2 vols. London: Longman, Orme, Brown, Green, and Longmans, 1841. Originally published as *Die Wärmelehre des Inneren unseres Erdkörpers* (Leipzig, Germany: J. A. Barth, 1837).

Bonney, Orrin H., and Lorraine Bonney. *Battle Drums and Geysers.* Part 2, *The Discovery and Exploration of Yellowstone Park; Lt. G. C. Doane's Journal: First Official Report upon the Wonders of the Yellowstone.* Houston: Bonney and Bonney, 1970.

Bowersox, Charles A., ed. *A Standard History of Williams County, Ohio.* Vol. 2, *An Authentic Narrative of the Past, with Particular Attention to the Modern Era in the Commercial, Industrial, Educational, Civic, and Social Development.* Chicago: Lewis, 1920.

Bradbury, John. *Travels in the Interior of America.* London: Sherwood, Neely, and Jones, 1819.

Bryan, T. Scott. *Geysers: What They Are and How They Work.* 2nd ed. Missoula M T: Mountain Press, 2005.

———. *The Geysers of Yellowstone.* 4th ed. Boulder: University Press of Colorado, 2008.

Bryson, Alexander. *Notes on a Trip to Iceland in 1862.* Edinburgh: R. Grant, 1864.

Bunsen, Robert von. "Physikalische Beobachtungen über die hauptsächlichsten Geisir Islands" [Physical observations of the principal geysers of Iceland]. *Poggendorffs Annalen der Physik und Chemie* [Poggendorff's annals of physics and chemistry] (Leipzig, Germany) 72 (1847): 159–70.

Campbell, John Francis. *Frost and Fire.* Vol. 2, *Natural Engines, Tool-Marks and Chips. With Sketches Taken at Home and Abroad by a Traveller.* Edinburgh: Edmonston and Douglas, 1865.

Cassidy, James G. *Ferdinand V. Hayden: Entrepreneur of Science.* Lincoln: University of Nebraska Press, 2000.

Chapple, Janet. *Yellowstone Treasures: The Traveler's Companion to the National Park.* 3rd ed. Menlo Park C A: Granite Peak Publications, 2009.

Chittenden, Hiram Martin. *The Yellowstone National Park Historical and Descriptive.* Cincinnati O H: Robert Clarke, 1885.

Christiansen, R. L. *Geology of Yellowstone National Park — The Quaternary and Pliocene Yellowstone Plateau Volcanic Field of Wyoming, Idaho, and Montana.* U.S. Geological Survey Professional Paper 729-G. Denver, 2001.

Doane, Lt. Gustavus C. *Report of Lieutenant Gustavus C. Doane upon the So-Called Yellowstone Expedition of 1870.* Washington D C: Government Printing Office, 1871.

Ferris, Warren Angus. *Life in the Rocky Mountains, 1830–1835.* Edited by P. C. Phillips. Denver: Old West, 1940.

Forbes, Charles Stuart. *Iceland: Its Volcanoes, Geysers, and Glaciers.* London: J. Murray, 1860.

Foster, Mike. *Strange Genius: The Life of Ferdinand Vandiveer Hayden.* Boulder CO: Roberts Rinehart, 1994.

Fritz, William J., and Robert C. Thomas. *Roadside Geology of Yellowstone Country.* 2nd. ed. Missoula MT: Mountain Press, 2011.

Good, John M., and Kenneth L. Pierce. *Interpreting the Landscapes of Grand Teton and Yellowstone National Parks: Recent and Ongoing Geology.* Moose WY: Grand Teton Natural History Association, 1996.

Greene, Jerome A. *Nez Perce Summer, 1877: The U.S. Army and the Nee-Me-Poo Crisis.* Helena: Montana Historical Society, 2001.

Guie, Heister D., and Lucullus McWhorter, eds. *Adventures in Geyser Land.* Reprinted from *The Wonders of Geyser Land* (1878). Caldwell ID: Caxton Printers, 1935.

Guptill, A. B. *Haynes Guide to Yellowstone Park: A Practical Handbook.* St. Paul MN: F. J. Haynes, 1898.

Haines, Aubrey L., ed. *The Valley of the Upper Yellowstone: An Exploration of the Headwaters of the Yellowstone River in the Year 1869.* Norman: University of Oklahoma Press, 1965.

———. *Yellowstone Place Names: Mirrors of History.* Niwot: University Press of Colorado, 1996.

———. *The Yellowstone Story: A History of Our First National Park.* 2 vols. Boulder: Colorado Associated University Press, 1977.

Hartley, Robert E. *Saving Yellowstone: The President Arthur Expedition of 1883.* Westminster CO: Sniktau Publications, 2007.

Hassrick, Peter H. *Drawn to Yellowstone: Artists in America's First National Park.* Los Angeles: Autry Museum of Western Heritage, 2002.

Haynes, Jack Ellis. *Haynes Guide: Handbook of Yellowstone National Park.* Bozeman MT: Haynes Studios, 1949 and 1964.

———. *Haynes New Guide and Motorists' Complete Road Log of Yellowstone National Park.* St. Paul MN: J. E. Haynes, 1923.

Hochstetter, Ferdinand von. *New Zealand: Its Physical Geography, Geology and Natural History.* Stuttgart, Germany: J. G. Cotta, 1867. Translated by Edward Sauter from *Neu-Seeland* (Stuttgart, Germany: Cotta, 1863).

Horrebow, Neils. *The Natural History of Iceland.* Translated by Erich Pontoppidan. London: A. Linde et al., 1758. Originally published as *Tilforladelige efterretninger om Island*, 1752.

Hutchinson, Roderick A., James A. Westphal, and Susan W. Kieffer. "In Situ Observations of Old Faithful Geyser." *Geology* 25, no. 10 (October 1997): 875–78.

Irving, Washington. *The Adventures of Captain Bonneville, or Scenes beyond the Rocky Mountains of the Far West.* London: Richard Bentley; Philadelphia: Carey, Lea and Blanchard, 1837.

Joseph, Young Chief. "An Indian's View of Indian Affairs." *North American Review* 128, no. 269 (1879): 412–33.

Krug von Nidda, Otto Ludwig. "Geognostische Darstellung der Insel Island" [A geological statement on the island of Iceland]. In *Karstens Archiv für Mineralogie, Geognosie, Bergbau und Hüttenkunde* [Karsten's archive for mineralogy, geology, mining, and metallurgy] (Berlin, Germany) 7 (1834): 421–525.

Langford, Nathaniel Pitt. *The Discovery of Yellowstone Park: Journal of the Washburn Expedition to the Yellowstone and Firehole Rivers in the Year 1870*. Foreword by Aubrey L. Haines. Lincoln: University of Nebraska Press, 1972. First published 1905 by F. J. Haynes, St. Paul MN.

Leclercq, Jules. "La carrière coloniale de Cecil Rhodes" [The colonial career of Cecil Rhodes]. *La Revue Générale* [General review] (Brussels), 75 (1902): 769–82.

———. *Un été en Amérique: De l'Atlantique aux montagnes rocheuses* [A summer in America: From the Atlantic to the Rocky Mountains]. Paris: E. Plon, 1877.

———. *Au pays de Paul et Virginie* [In the country of Paul and Virginia]. Paris: E. Plon, 1895.

———. *La Terre de Glace: Féroë — Islande — les geysers — le mont Hékla*. Paris: E. Plon, 1883.

———. *La Terre des Merveilles: Promenade au Parc National de l'Amérique du Nord* [The Land of Wonders: Promenade in North America's National Park]. Paris: Librairie Hachette, 1886.

———. *Voyage au Mexique: De New-York à Vera-Cruz par terre* [Trip to Mexico: From New York to Veracruz overland]. Paris: Librairie Hachette, 1885.

Mackenzie, George S. *Travels in the Island of Iceland during the Summer of the Year 1810*. 2nd ed. Edinburgh: A. Constable, 1811.

Marler, George D. *Inventory of Thermal Features of the Firehole River Basin and Other Selected Areas of Yellowstone National Park*. U.S. Geological Survey GD 73-018, 1973.

McCullough, David. *Brave Companions: Portraits in History*. New York: Simon & Schuster, 1992.

Merrill, Marlene Deahl. *Yellowstone and the Great West: Journals, Letters, and Images from the 1871 Hayden Expedition*. Lincoln: University of Nebraska Press, 1999.

Morgan, Lisa A., et al. "The Floor of Yellowstone Lake Is Anything but Quiet." *Integrated Geoscience Studies in the Greater Yellowstone Area*, chapter D. U.S. Geological Society Professional Paper 1717. U.S. Dept. of Interior, 2007.

Müller, J. H. J. "Über Bunsen's Geysertheorie" [About Bunsen's theory of geysers]. *Annalen der Physik und Chemie* [Annals of physics and chemistry], ed. J. C. Poggendorff, University of Berlin, 79 (1850): 562–67.

Nabokov, Peter, and Lawrence Loendorf. *Restoring a Presence: American Indians and Yellowstone National Park*. Norman: University of Oklahoma Press, 2004.

Norris, Philetus W. *The Calumet of the Coteau and Other Poetical Legends of the Border.* Philadelphia: J. B. Lippincott, 1883.

Rolin, Henri. "Notice sur Jules-Joseph Leclercq, membre de l'académie" [Remembrance of Jules-Joseph Leclercq, member of the academy]. *Annuaire de l'Académie Royale des Sciences, des Lettres et des Beaux Arts de Belgique* [Yearbook of the Royal Academy of Sciences, Letters, and Fine Arts of Belgium] (1936): 36–60.

Rydell, Kiki Leigh, and Mary Shivers Culpin. *Managing the "Matchless Wonders": A History of Administrative Development in Yellowstone National Park, 1872–1965.* YCR-2006-03. National Park Service, Yellowstone Center for Resources, Yellowstone National Park WY, 2006.

Schullery, Paul, and Lee Whittlesey. *Myth and History in the Creation of Yellowstone National Park.* Lincoln: University of Nebraska Press, 2003.

Shiras, George. "The Wilderness of the Upper Yellowstone." In *Hunting Wild Life with Camera and Flashlight: A Record of Sixty-Five Years' Visits to the Woods and Waters of North America*, 2:315–35. Washington DC: National Geographic Society, 1935.

Société Royale Belge de Géographie. *La fondation de la Société Royale Belge de Géographie et son XXVme anniversaire.* Brussels: Vanderauwera, 1903.

Sturchio, Neil C., Kenneth L. Pierce, Michael T. Murrell, and Michael L. Sorey. "Uranium-Series Ages of Travertines and Timing of the Last Glaciation in the Northern Yellowstone Area, Wyoming-Montana." *Quaternary Research* 41 (1994): 265–77.

Varley, John D., and Paul Schullery. *Yellowstone Fishes: Ecology, History, and Angling in the Park.* Mechanicsburg PA: Stackpole Books, 1998.

Victor, Frances Fuller. *The River of the West: Life and Adventure in the Rocky Mountains and Oregon. . . .* Newark NJ: R. W. Bliss, 1870.

Whithorn, Doris. *Yankee Jim's National Park Toll Road and the Yellowstone Trail.* 1989; reprint, Livingston MT: WAN-I-GAN Press, 2006.

Whittlesey, Lee H., ed. *Lost in the Yellowstone: Truman Everts's "Thirty-Seven Days of Peril."* Salt Lake City: University of Utah Press, 1995.

———. "Marshall's Hotel in the National Park." *Montana, the Magazine of Western History* 30 (Autumn 1980): 42–51.

———. *"This Modern Saratoga of the Wilderness!" A History of Mammoth Hot Springs and the Village of Mammoth in Yellowstone National Park.* National Park Service, unpublished manuscript.

———. *Wonderland Nomenclature: A History of the Names of Yellowstone National Park.* Helena: Montana Historical Society Press, 1988.

———. *Yellowstone Place Names.* 2nd ed. Gardiner MT: Wonderland Publishing, 2006.

Williams, Henry T., ed. *The Pacific Tourist: Williams' Illustrated Trans-Continental Guide.* New York: Henry T. Williams, 1877.

Index

Moran, Thomas, xxiv, xxvi, 239n1
Mormons, 32, 189, 219n15
Mortar Geyser, 229n12
mosquitoes, 23, 67
mountain lions. *See* cougars
mountains, 39, 150–51; elevation of, 8;
    as natural barrier, 13, 38, 163; pure and
    dry air of, 34–35, 71, 180, 181; scenery
    in, 10, 38, 64, 181, 182–83; volcanic ac-
    tivity in, 8–10, 112. *See also* mountains
    of glass; views; volcanic phenomena
mountains of glass, 15, 66. *See also*
    obsidian
Mount Doane, 112, 151
Mount Everts, 216n22
Mount Langford, 112
Mount Schurz, 76, 210, 226n2
Mount Sheridan, 146, 183
Mount Stevenson, 112, 151
Mount Washburn, 240n4; age, 181;
    ascent of, 180–81, 183–84; panorama
    from, 181, 182–83
Mud Caldron (Fountain Paint Pot),
    130, *131*
mud pots, 70, 75–76, 130, *131*, 148, *148*
Mud Volcano, 165–66
Müller, J.H.J., 120, 231n7

National Hotel (at Mammoth), 44
national park designation, 8
National Park Toll Road, 221n8
Native Americans. *See* Indians
Natural Bridge, 150, 236n17
newspapers: of Eau Claire W I, 24–25;
    of Helena M T, 133–34; *Livingston
    Enterprise* (M T), 35, 220n22, 220n24,
    220n2; sensational news in, 62–64
New Zealand, 230n8, 232n2
Nez Perce Creek, 136, 226n7, 233n9
Nez Perces, 221n6, 233n2; attacks on
    tourists by, 134–39, 141, 184; and
    conversion to Catholicism, 234n10;
    on trek through Yellowstone, 133, 166,
    234nn7–8, 238n4
Nez Perce War of 1877, 40, 133, 234n3,
    235n16
Norris, Philetus W.: *Calumet of the*

Coteau, 215n13; career of, 215n11, 233n4;
    discoveries and observations of, 15,
    73, 91, 99, 126, 128, 215n13, 216n14,
    233n4; *Fifth Annual Report* (for 1881),
    126, 216n14, 225n6, 233n4; and the
    grizzly, 155–56; intervening with
    natural features, 66, 222n6, 236n17;
    and naming of features, 107, 224n11,
    225n6, 233n5; *Report for 1880*, 222n6,
    236n17
Norris Geyser Basin, 69–70, 71–73, 210,
    225n1, 225n3
Norris Pass, 144, 235n2
Northern Pacific Railroad, 29, 210,
    218n1, 239n1; branch line of from Liv-
    ingston to Cinnabar, xvii, 37, 220n1;
    and land commissioner, 29, 219n12;
    last-spike ceremony of, 36, 220nn22–
    23; and leaflets offering land, 30; staff
    photographer of, 29, 219n13; stations,
    31, 33. *See also* trains
North Rim (of the Grand Cañon), 179,
    180

obsidian, 43, 144, 150, 224n16; J L's
    theory of formation of, 66
Obsidian Cliff, 66, 210, 224n17
Obsidian Creek, 67, 224n18
Old Faithful Geyser: crater of, *82*, *111*;
    dimensions of, 227n7; discovery of,
    84, 227n6; eruption of, 83–84, *85*;
    interval of, 81, 227ch9n1; temperature
    of, 230n6
optical effects, 95, 228n6
Orange Spring Mound, 64, 223n8
ospreys (called eagles by J L), 175,
    239n5; nests, 172, *176*

paint pots. *See* mud pots
palagonite, 114, 230n10
panoramas. *See* views
Paradise Valley, 39, 235n16
"Le parc national" (Hayden, Doane,
    and Langford), 5
park superintendents: Henderson,
    223n8; Langford, 239n6; McCartney,
    235n15; Norris, 215n11
peace pipe, 138